Central Ideas in the Development of American Journalism:

A Narrative History

COMMUNICATION

A series of volumes edited by
Dolf Zillmann and **Jennings Bryant**

Central Ideas in the Development of American Journalism:

A Narrative History

Marvin Olasky
The University of Texas at Austin

LEA LAWRENCE ERLBAUM ASSOCIATES, PUBLISHERS
1991   Hillsdale, New Jersey   Hove and London

Lawrence Erlbaum Associates, Inc., Publishers
365 Broadway
Hillsdale, New Jersey 07642

Library of Congress Cataloging-in-Publication Data
Olasky, Marvin N.
 Central ideas in the development of American journalism : a narrative
history / Marvin Olasky.
  p. cm.
 Includes index.
 ISBN 0-8058-0893-0
 1. Journalism—United States—History. I. Title.
PN4801.04 1991
071'.3—dc20   90-40153
                                                 CIP

Printed in the United States of Ameica
10 9 8 7 6 5 4 3 2 1

For Peter, David, Daniel, and one to come

Contents

Acknowledgments

This book arose out of 5 years of teaching journalism history at The University of Texas. In lectures I presented both the conventional interpretations and my own, slowly developing contrarian analysis; students who asked hard questions suggested that a wider audience might find my research useful. I thank them for their quiet pressure.

Librarians at The University of Texas, the Library of Congress, and the Newberry Library helped me to find out-of-the-way material, and a grant from the Sarah Scaife Foundation provided additional writing time. The material in Appendix B previously appeared in *American Journalism*. I also thank Jennings Bryant, Robin Marks Weisberg, and others associated with Lawrence Erlbaum; this book shows for a third time their admirable tolerance for decidedly nontrendy ideas.

My children are aspiring journalists who certainly inspired me: Peter (editor of the *Austin Animal-Statesman*), David (editor of an ancient Greek newspaper, *The Ithaca Times*), and Daniel (a crackerjack cub reporter and Civil War general) continued to provide joy and deep satisfaction. My wife Susan is an excellent journalist in her own right; she has a wise head, a gracious heart, and a loveliness that goes beyond narrative. I would not be able to put in a long day of writing if I could not look forward to a family dinner at its close.

Portions of this book appeared as articles in *American Journalism, Antithesis,* and *Academic Questions,* and as columns in the *Houston Post,* the *Rocky Mountain News,* and the *Indianapolis Star.* My thanks to their editors.

Introduction

"Public opinion on any subject," Abraham Lincoln once said, "always has a 'central idea' from which all its minor thoughts radiate."[1] This book applies Lincoln's statement not to American public opinion generally but to journalism specifically (which is often at the base of public opinion). Writers and editors have espoused so many different philosophies over the years that American journalism history might seem to be a crazy-quilt, but the thesis of this book is that a broad look at the whole pattern shows three central ideas achieving dominance, sequentially.

The first of these central ideas in journalism—I call them *macrostories* because they overarch the daily bits and pieces of journalistic coverage—could be called the *official story*. Dominant until the 18th century in most of Europe and America, this macrostory was built on the belief that power knows best, and that editors should merely print whatever the king or governor demands. Published news was what state authorities (and, sometimes, their allies in established churches) wanted people to know.

The press continued to be dominated by the official story until growing numbers of journalists, heavily influenced by the ideas of the Protestant Reformation, began to emphasize the *corruption story*. This macrostory, rather than serving as public relations for the state, emphasized the universality of human failings and the tendency for individuals in positions of power to abuse their authority and then attempt to cover up wrongdoing. Journalists from the 17th through 19th centuries who embraced the corruption story invented much of what

1

we associate with modern journalism at its best: A sense of purpose, a willingness to oppose arrogant rulers, and a stress on accuracy and specific detail.

Mid- and late-19th-century editors such as Horace Greeley and Joseph Pulitzer achieved their prominence and influence on the foundations laid down by corruption story journalists. However, they and others scorned the theology on which that macrostory was based; instead of seeing sinful man and demanding personal change, they believed that man is naturally good but is enslaved by oppressive social systems. In this third of journalism's central ideas, the *oppression story,* problems arise not from personal corruption but from external influences, and the role of journalists is to put a spotlight on those influences. The hope is that if man's environment is changed, man himself changes, and poverty, war, and so on, are no more.

This change affected not only story content but reporters' methods. Corruption story journalists tended to have limited personal agendas because they emphasized personal transformation rather than social revolution. Oppression story journalists, who came to dominate the most influential publications early in the 20th century, believed their own work could be the breakthrough to a better world. As the great ends of oppression story journalism—peace, justice, freedom— began to seem attainable, means began to be negotiable.

This book narrates the history of those macrostories in American journalism from its European beginnings in the 16th and 17th century (my starting point is Martin Luther's editorial on the cathedral door in 1517) up through 1917, when the impact of the Russian Revolution began to open up a new phase in journalistic perceptions. Along the way we take a fresh look at Greeley, Pulitzer, and other legends of journalism history, and we also recall long-forgotten figures such as John Stubbes, an English Puritan who in 1579 wrote a pamphlet criticizing Queen Elizabeth. Stubbes was punished by having his right hand "cut off by the blow of a Butcher's knife."[2] A contemporary account tells of his amazing response: "John Stubbes, so soon as his right hand was off, put off his hat with the left, and cryed aloud, God save the Queene."[3] Such bravery deserves to be remembered, and the motivation for such actions understood.

This book is a narrative history rather than a philosophical tome; a previous book of mine, *Prodigal Press,* examined more systematically questions surrounding objectivity and journalistic ethics. I have retained early spellings whenever the meaning is clear. Four appendices provide additional detail; readers who wish to know more about the macrostory concept itself should not overlook Appendix C.

PART I

RISE OF THE CORRUPTION STORY

Chapter 1

Unnatural Acts

In America, we expect journalists to have some independence from government and other leading power centers. We are not surprised to glance at the morning newspaper or television news show and see exposure of wrongdoing. We assume that the press has a responsibility to print bad news as well as good. And yet, that which seems ordinary to us is unusual in the history of the world, and even in much of the world today.

How did the unnatural act of independent journalism come to seem so natural? To begin answering that question, we need to go back, back beyond the start of American journalism, back even before Gutenberg. *Journalism*—information and analysis concerning recent events, published in multiple copies or disseminated beyond the immediate reach of the speaker's voice — is many centuries old. Journalistic products emerged in many lands and in many varieties, but they most often promoted the *official story* of governmental power and wisdom: "If you obey, we will take care of you." (A more modern way of saying the same might be, "Depend on us to establish the proper environment for your life.") Official, state-allied religion often received protection also. Published news was what authorities wanted people to know.

Throughout the many centuries before printing, *official story* publications came and went. One of the better known early journalistic vehicles was the *Acta Diurna,* a handwritten news sheet posted in the Roman Forum and copied by scribes for transmission throughout the empire. *Acta* emphasized governmental decrees but also gained readership by posting gladiatorial results and news of other popular events. Julius Caesar used the *Acta* to attack some of his opponents in the Roman senate—but there could be no criticism of Caesar. (Had there been independent journalism, he might have faced only character assassination on the Ides of March.) Other handwritten publications also emerged during ancient and medieval times, with the goal of passing on news that state or state–church authorities wished leading citizens to know. This was true in Asia and other continents as well as in Europe. Sometimes, ballads and poems that mocked the official news vehicles were passed on orally from person to person, but the official version, with support from the state church, endured from generation to generation.

In Western Europe, kings with support from the Catholic Church were said to rule by divine right, and the *official story* was the only story allowed. Leaders might acknowledge that a different story prevailed in heaven—there, God was sovereign and biblical principles were practiced—but only those who went away to monasteries or nunneries might be able to see God's will being done on earth as in heaven. This dualistic sense of spiritual and temporal realms removed from each other was evident not only in journalism but in artwork and other cultural realms as well. The Bible itself was removed from daily life and available only to the elite who knew Latin; Pope Innocent IV in 1252 forbade translating the Bible into vernacular languages.

The tiny and fairly barbaric part of the world where English was spoken was no exception to the general rule. In 1275 the statute of Westminister I outlawed "tales whereby discord or occasion of discord or slander may grow between the king and his people or the great men of the realm." Anything that could inspire such discord—including the Bible, which stated laws of God under which every man and woman, whether king or commoner, had to live — was banned. After John Wycliffe disobeyed Papal rulings and translated the Bible into English during the late 14th century, English church authorities cracked down, with the synod of Canterbury in 1408 forbidding the translation of Scripture from one language to another. Wycliffe's books were burned in 1410 and 1412. His bones were dug up and burned in 1428.

A technological revolution began around 1450 with the development of movable type in the Mainz workshop of Johann Gutenberg. But technological changes matter little as long as "world views" — clusters of convictions about what's important in life—remain the same. The demand from monasteries and kings or commercial leaders for big, printed, Latin Bibles was growing. Printed volumes met that demand, but the Bibles were usually for show rather than tell. Printing created potential for change and pressure to change from those who saw opportunities, but as long as reading was discouraged by state and church authorities, and as long as independent printers were jailed or killed, there would be little change.

The limited effect of the technological revolution, *by itself,* was indicated by early post-Gutenberg developments in England. Printing began there in 1476 when William Caxton, given royal encouragement and grant of privileges upon good behavior, set up a press in Westminster. Others followed, but were careful to avoid publishing works that might irritate the king or his ministers. Regulations limited the number of printers and apprentices. Royal patents created printing monopolies. It was illegal to import, print, or distribute threatening books, such as English translations of the Bible. In this policy England remained in line with other state–church countries during the early 1500s—but then came the providential sound of a hammer on a door, and the beginning of a theological onslaught (aided by journalistic means) that changed Europe.

Modern journalism began in 1517 as the German prince Frederick the Wise was putting the finishing touches on his life's work of building up Wittenberg's sacred relic collection. Through purchase and trade he was able to claim a "genuine" thorn from Christ's crown, a tooth of St. Jerome, four hairs from the Virgin Mary, seven pieces from the shroud sprinkled with Christ's blood, a wisp of straw from the place where Jesus was born, one piece of gold brought by the Wise Men, a strand of Jesus' beard, one of the nails driven into Christ's hands, one piece of bread eaten at the Last Supper, one twig of Moses' burning bush, and nearly 20,000 holy bones.

Announcements of relic collection highlights were made regularly through proclamations and assorted announcements, the typical journalistic products of the time. Few people could read—most were discouraged from even trying, for reading could lead to theological and political rebellion—but town criers and local priests passed on *official story* messages promoting the goals of governmental authorities and the official, state-allied religion. In 1517 Wittenberg residents were told that all of Frederick's treasures would be displayed on All Saints Day, and that those who viewed them and made appropriate donations could receive papal indulgences allowing for a substantial decrease of time spent in purgatory, either for the viewer/contributor or someone he would designate. Total time saved could equal 1,902,202 years and 270 days.

Quiet criticism of the indulgence system was coming from Professor Martin Luther, who stated that the Bible gave no basis for belief in indulgences and argued that the practice interfered with true contrition and confession. But, despite Luther's lectures, indulgence–buying continued as champion salesman Tetzel offered altruism at bargain prices:

Listen to the voices of your dear dead relatives and friends, beseeching you and saying, "Pity us, pity us. We are in dire torment from which you can redeem us for a pittance." Do you not wish to? Open your ears. Hear the father saying to his son, the mother to her daughter, "We bore you, nourished you, brought you up, left you our fortunes, and you are so cruel and hard that now you are not willing for so little to set us free. Will you let us lie here in flames? Will you delay our promised glory?" Remember that you are able to release them, for "As soon as the coin in the coffer rings,/ The soul from purgatory springs."[1]

The pitch was strong, but Luther decided to oppose it head-on by making his ideas of protest accessible to all, not just a few. The 95 theses he hammered to the cathedral door in 1517 were not academic sentences but clear, vivid statements. For example, concerning the plan to obtain money to build St. Peter's, Luther wrote:

> The revenues of all Christendom are being sucked into this insatiable basilica. . . . The pope would do better to appoint one good pastor to a church than to confer indulgences upon them all. Why doesn't the pope build the basilica of St. Peter out of his own money? He is richer than Croesus. He would do better to sell St. Peter's and give the money to the poor folk who are being fleeced by the hawkers of indulgences.[2]

Luther then gave printers permission to set the theses in type—and they spread throughout Europe within a month.

The effect of Luther's theses and his subsequent publications is well known—but what often is missed is that Luther's primary impact was not as a producer of treatises, but as a very popular writer of vigorous prose that concerned not only theological issues but their social and political ramifications. Between 1517 and 1530 Luther's 30 publications probably sold well over 300,000 copies, an astounding total at a time when illiteracy was rampant and printing still an infant.[3] Because Luther had such influence through his writing the pressure on him to mute the truth became enormous, but he said "My conscience is captive to the Word of God . . . Here I stand, I can do no other."[4]

Luther's lively style and willingness to risk death for the sake of truth-telling would be enough to make him a model for today's journalists, but it was his stress on literacy that made independent journalism possible at all. Literacy was low throughout Europe until the 16th century—perhaps only about 1 out of 100 persons could read. Reading was looked upon as a servile activity; just as corporate CEOs today have secretaries to do their typing, so the kings of medieval times remained illiterate and had designated readers. Nor were those of low estate encouraged to read by state or church authorities. A 16th century French treatise argued that people should not read on their own, less they become confused; ordinary folk especially should not read the Bible, because they should learn only from priests.[5] As one historian has noted, authorities "held it was safer to have less Scripture reading than more heresy."[6]

Luther and other Reformation leaders, however, emphasized the importance of Bible reading; Christians were to find out for themselves what God was saying. Literacy rates soared everywhere the Reformation took root, and remained low wherever it was fought off. Luther not only praised translation into the vernacular languages but made a masterful one himself. In preparing his German translation Luther so understood the need for specific detail to attract readers that when he wanted to picture the precious stones and coins mentioned in the Bible, he first examined German court jewels and numismatic collections. Similarly, when Luther needed to describe Old Testament sacrifices he visited slaughterhouses and gained information from butchers. He was a vivid reporter as well as a tenacious theologian.

Furthermore, he was a reporter who desired to print not just good news, but bad news also. Luther's Reformed theological understanding led him to write,

> God's favor is so communicated in the form of wrath that it seems farthest when it is at hand. Man must first cry out that there is no health in him. He must be consumed with horror. . . . In this disturbance salvation begins. When a man believes himself to be utterly lost, light breaks. Peace comes in the word of Christ through faith.[7]

Reformation leaders believed that people would seek the good news of mercy only after they became fully aware of the bad news of sin. This was the basis of the *corruption story:* Man needs to be become aware of his own corruption in order to change through God's grace, and writers who help make readers aware of sin are doing them a service.

Luther also made journalism significant by arguing that the path to progress is through change in ideas and beliefs, rather than through forced social revolution or reaction.[8] In Luther's thought the most significant warfare was ideological, not material, so he emphasized dissemination of ideas through publication and opposed attempts to destroy opposing ideas through burning either books or authors. "Heretics," he said, "should be vanquished with books, not with burnings."[9] Luther wanted an exchange of views, not swordthrusts. He described printing as "God's highest and extremest act of grace, whereby the business of the Gospel is driven forward."[10]

Others felt differently about those perceived as heretics. In 1529 Henry VIII of England banned importation of either the writings of Martin Luther or other works, including Bible translations, that supposedly engaged in "reproach, rebuke, or slander of the king."[11] Thomas Hilton was burned in 1530 for selling books by William Tyndale that advocated the supreme authority of Scripture against both state and church. Richard Bayfield, John Teukesbury, and James Bainham were burned in 1531 and 1532, and Tyndale himself was seized in Antwerp in 1536 and killed; his Bible translation was burned in St. Paul's Cathedral. After 1534, as Henry VIII established a national church in England under his headship, those who would not adhere to the latest twist in the *official story* — Sir Thomas More, Bishop Fisher, and others—also suffered execution.[12]

Henry added new antipress legislation almost as often as he added new wives. In 1534 his "Proclamation for Seditious Books" ordered that no one should print any English book without a license from the king's councils or those persons appointed by the king as licensers. His "Proclamation of 1538" left the press with "only one master, the king."[13] The sweeping language of Parliament's regulatory law of 1542–1543 indicates how the official story was to have absolute dominion:

"Nothing shall be taught or maintained contrary to the King's instructions," and nothing shall be published "contrary to the King's instructions or determinations, made or to be made."[14]

Henry VIII's structure of government and society was simple: The state, with its official church, was at the center, giving orders to other social institutions. But in the thought of men such as John Calvin, Scotland's John Knox, and other leaders of the Reformation, the kingdom of God could not be equated with state interests. Instead, the Reformers believed that God reigns everywhere and man can serve God directly in every area of life — government, journalism, education, business, or whatever. Reformed thinkers asserted that there were laws superior to the state or any other institution, and suggested that workers in those various areas did not have to wait for marching orders from the institutional Church, but could instead study the Bible and apply it to their own activities.

The Reformers did not advocate extremist intransigence or easy disobedience of governmental or church authority. John Knox, for instance, appealed for moderation and compromise whenever truly fundamental issues were not at stake. But under such a doctrine, for the first time, journalists could be more than purveyors of public relations. They had their own independent authority and would appeal to biblical principle when officials tried to shackle them.[15] The *corruption story* and the *official story* were heading for the first of their show-downs, and records of Henry's Privy Council, responsible for controlling the press, began to show regular proceedings against writers and speakers for "unfit-ting worddes" and supposedly seditious libel. During the reign of "Bloody Mary" from 1553 to 1558, the confrontation with those who based their lives on "sola scriptura"—the Bible only—began.[16]

One of the first Protestants to die at the stake was John Hooper, publicly burned at Gloucester on February 9, 1555. He was joined by about 75 men and women who were burned as heretics that year, and many more during the following 2 years. Soon, reports of those killings spread illegally throughout England: Ballads and other publications—one was called *Sacke full of Newes*— attacked the queen and praised the heroism of the martyrs. One notable under-ground pamphlet, *The Communication betwene my lord Chauncelor and judge Hales,* depicted the tyranny of the state church.[17]

These journalistic critiques readily went from the theological to the political, because the two were intertwined. Mary's marriage to Philip, heir to the Spanish throne, led many to believe that Spain would soon be ruling England in dictatorial fashion. One pamphlet, *A Warnyng for Englande,* gave an account of

> the horrible practises of the Kyng of Spayne/ in the Kyngdome of Naples/ and the miseries whereunto that noble Realme is brought./ Whereby all Englishe men may understand the plage that shall light upon them/ if the Kyng of Spayn obteyne the Dominion in Englande.[18]

Coverage of the debate and the burnings showed the typical path of 16th century journalism: From theological debate to theological commentary on current news to sensational coverage.[19]

The 16th century journalist who made the greatest impression on several generations of Englishmen and women originally had no desire to report on current events. John Foxe, born in 1516, was an excellent student. He became a fellow at Oxford, but was converted to the Reformed faith and had to give up his stipend. In 1548 he began writing a scholarly history of Christian martyrdom, but it turned journalistic in 1553 when Mary became queen. Facing death in 1554 Foxe left England and began earning a poor living as a proofreader with a Swiss printer, but he continued to collect historical material about past persecutions and testimony about current ones.

Foxe published two volumes in Latin during the 1550s, but switched to English for his journalistic output, with the goal of telling the martyrs' story in a readable manner. He was able to return to England with the ascension of Elizabeth in 1558 and then spend five more years interviewing, collecting materials, and writing, before publishing the sensational account that became known as *Foxe's Book of Martyrs*. To make sure everything was right, he worked 7 years more before putting out in 1570 an expanded, second edition that contained woodcuts portraying burnings and whippings; later, large-scale editions increased the number of illustrations.[20] Foxe showed no interest in ecclesiastical promotion or governmental work. Until his death in 1587 Foxe kept revising the work, inserting corrections or additions that many people sent him, and avoiding the mere substitution of fables of his own for the official stories of old.[21]

Foxe's writing was vivid. For example, he wrote of how John Hooper, tied to a stake, prayed for a short time. Then the fire was lit, but the green wood was slow to burn. Hooper was shown a box and told it contained his pardon if he would give in: "Away with it!" he cried. As the fire reached Hooper's legs a gust of wind blew it out. A second fire then slowly burned up Hooper's legs, but went out with Hooper's upper body still intact. The fire was rekindled, and soon Hooper was heard to say repeatedly, "Lord Jesus, have mercy upon me; Lord Jesus, have mercy upon me; Lord Jesus, receive my spirit!"[22] Hooper's lips continued to move even when his throat was so scorched that no sound could come from it: Even "when he was black in the mouth, and his tongue swollen, that he could not speak, yet his lips went till they were shrunk to the gums." Finally, one of Hooper's arms fell off, and the other, with "fat, water, and blood" dripping out at the ends of the fingers, stuck to what remained of his chest. At that point Hooper bowed his head forward and died.[23]

Foxe also described the deaths of Hugh Latimer and Nicholas Ridley. Ridley, chained over another of those slow-burning fires, was in agony, but Latimer seemed to be dying with amazing ease — Foxe wrote that he appeared to be bathing his hands and face in the fire. Latimer's last words to his suffering friend were, "Be of good comfort, Master Ridley, [so that] we shall this day light such a candle, by God's grace, in England, as I trust shall never be put out."[24]

Foxe's third famous report concerned the death of Thomas Cranmer, Archbishop of Canterbury and leader of the English Protestants. Imprisoned for months without support of friends, Cranmer received daily ideological hammering from theological adversaries; after watching Ridley die, he wrote out a recantation and apology, in return for pardon. When Cranmer was told later that he allegedly had led so many astray that he would have to burn anyway, his courage returned and he resolved to go out boldly. He wrote in one final statement—a press release of a sort—that his recantation was "written with my hand contrary to the truth which is in my heart, and written for fear of death."[25] He offered a pledge: "As my hand hath offended, writing contrary to my heart, therefore my hand shall first be punished; for when I come to the fire, it shall be first burned." Foxe wrote of how Cranmer made good on that promise; sent to the stake, he placed his right hand firmly in the fire and held it steadily there until it appeared like a coal to observers. Soon, Cranmer's entire body was burned.[26]

Foxe's book became very popular not only because of its combination of theological fervor and grisly detail, but through its use of colorful Bible-based imagery. For example, Foxe's report on the impending death of John Hooper described how light overcame darkness as Hooper was led through London to Newgate prison. Officers had ordered all candles along the way be put out; perhaps,

> being burdened with an evil conscience, they thought darkness to be a most fit season for such a business.: But notwithstanding this device, the people having some foreknowledge of his coming, many of them came forth of their doors with lights, and saluted him; praising God for his constancy in the true doctrine which he had taught them. . . .[27]

Significantly, although Foxe was clearly on the side of the martyrs, he was not just a Protestant propagandist, overlooking the sins of his own side. He openly criticized the greed shown by Protestants under Edward VI, and, having written about executions by Catholics, did not favor executions by Protestants. In a long sermon Foxe delivered on Good Friday, 1570, he asked for mercy on many because Christ himself had been crucified by the church–state authorities of his time.

Foxe's stress on accuracy was maintained by Miles Coverdale, who wrote in 1564 that "it doeth us good to read and heare, not the lying legendes . . . triflying toyes & forged fables of corrupted writers: but such true, holy, . . . epistles & letters, as do set forth unto us ye blessed behavior of gods deare servantes."[28] For a time it appeared that a free press, with careful fact-checking, might arise—but, although Queen Elizabeth's version of *glasnost* allowed direct criticism of her predecessor, Mary, it did not allow objections to her reign or to the domination of the established, Anglican religion. A proclamation on July 1, 1570, offered a reward to those who informed against anyone writing or dispersing books in opposition to the queen or any of her nobles. Other ordinances set increasingly harsh penalties for unlicensed printing; on political matters, any challenge to the *official story* was treason.[29]

The secret tribunal known as the Star Chamber did not hesitate to prosecute and persecute. William Carter, a Catholic who printed in 1580 a book critical of the queen, was arrested, tortured, and executed in 1584. More frequently, the victims of state repression were Puritan rebels, including Hugh Singleton, Robert Waldegrave, John Stroud, and John Hodgkins. Puritans as an organized journalistic group first went public in 1572 with *An Admonition to Parliament,* a 60-page attack on state churches. *Admonition* authors John Field and Thomas Wilcocks spent a year in prison, but other pamphlets soon appeared. Puritan John Stubbes in 1579 wrote his critical pamphlet, had his right hand cut off, and then raised his left hand in a salute to the queen.[30]

One of the best-read Puritan products at the end of the 16th century was a series of pamphlets published in 1588 and 1589 and called the Martin Marprelate tracts; these tracts humorously satirized and ridiculed the heavy-handed theological treatises put out by defenders of the established church. The tracts, printed by John Hodgkins on a press that was dismantled repeatedly and moved around by cart, irritated king and court so much that a massive search for its producers began. Hodgkins escaped harm until he was unloading his press one day in the town of Warrington, before curious onlookers. A few small pieces of metal type fell from one of the boxes. A bystander picked up a letter and showed it to an official, who understood the significance of the discovery and summoned constables. Arrested and repeatedly tortured, Hodgkins refused to admit guilt and implicate others.

The bravery of Hodgkins, like that of Martin Luther, John Hooper, John Stubbes, and many others, could not not be ignored; persecution of the Puritans, instead of stamping them out, led to new conversion. When James I became king of England in 1603 and Puritans presented petitions for religious and press freedom, he threatened to "harry them out of the land, or else do worse." James, arguing that he was "above the law by his absolute power," and that "it is presumptuous and high contempt in a subject to dispute what a king can do, or say that a king cannot do this or that," advised subjects to "rest in that which is the king's revealed word in his law."[31] But that is something that Puritan writers, committed as they were to following God's law whatever the costs, would not do.

Royal officials made it clear that proponents of the corruption story would be prosecuted whenever they suggested that all, including the king, were naturally corrupt, in need of God's grace, and obliged to obey Biblical principles. The Star Chamber, in a 1606 case *de Libellis Famosis,* stipulated that truth was no defense against a charge of seditious libel, which was defined as anything that would reduce public respect for the monarch or his officials. The Star Chamber's powers of inquiry were supplemented in 1613 when James I granted to another government body, the High Commission, power over "books, pamphlets and portraitures offensive to the state."[32]

In the long run, however, James himself undermined the idea of royal authoritarianism by setting up a committee of 54 scholars to prepare a new translation of the Bible. When the committee's work was done, the magnificent "King James" translation had made the Bible more popularly accessible than ever. In Ryken's words,

> Beginning with a conviction that the Bible was where a person encountered God most directly, religion became in significant ways a literary experience. The acts of worship emphasized by the Reformers and Puritans were overwhelmingly literary acts: reading the Bible, meditating on its meaning.[33]

According to a contemporary opponent of the Puritans, those who attended one Puritan service had their Bibles open and looked up verses cited by the preachers. They took notes and, after the sermon, "held arguments also, among themselves, about the meaning of various Scripture texts, all of them, men and women, boys and girls, laborers, workmen and simpletons."[34]

The connection of Reformed faith and literacy became evident throughout England as it had in Europe. But that was not the only way the ideas first developed and popularized by Martin Luther had consequences for journalism. The Puritans also set in motion a movement toward a different social structure. The change began with an emphasis on reading and thinking. Edward Reynolds wrote:

> The people are hereby taught, first, to examine the doctrines of men by the rule and standard of the Word; . . . for though the judgment of interpretation belong principally to the ministers of the Word, yet God has given all believers a judgment of discretion, to try the spirits and to search the Scriptures, whether the things which they hear be so or no.[35]

Church authorities were no longer the central arbiters — they also were under the authority of Scripture and could rightfully be criticized by anyone who could point out in the Bible where they had gone wrong. "Capable is the poorest member in Christ's church, being grown to maturity of years, of information in the faith," Reynolds wrote, for "Are we not all a royal priesthood?"[36] Out of this sense of individual competence grew an idea of the formal church organized as a major activity among others, rather than (along with the state) the center of power. Journalists could have independent authority under God, and not merely serve as public relations appendages to state or state–church.

Other innovative journalistic approaches could grow logically out of the Puritan emphasis on individual salvation. Everyday "human interest" stories and not just official doings would for the first time be considered important, for, as Puritan Richard Greenham wrote:

> Surely if men were careful to reform themselves first, and then their own families, they should see God's manifold blessings in our land and upon church and commonwealth. For of particular persons come families; of families, towns; of towns, provinces; of provinces, whole realms.[37]

Furthermore, the Puritans' style of communication reflected a desire to have ordinary individuals receive information that could help them choose rightly. Puritan William Perkins argued that in expressing ideas, "the plainer, the better."[38] Robert Bolton argued that delivery of truth, rather than "self praise and private ends," was the goal of communication, and John Flavel wrote that "words are but servants to matter. An iron key, fitted to the wards of the lock, is more useful than a golden one that will not open the door to the treasures."[39]

All of this, and more, developed in one century from those ideas put down in words hammered onto the door of the Wittenberg cathedral. Material developments were useful, but beliefs and bravery carried the day and led to a new era.

Chapter 2

Perils of the Puritan Press

While James I was asserting his sovereignty in England, new journalistic forms were emerging in the Reformed strongholds of Amsterdam and Augsburg. The first newspapers—printed information sources on a regular (in these cases, weekly) schedule—were published in those cities in 1607 and 1609.[1] By 1620 Amsterdam, known for its Reformed emphasis on literacy and liberty, was the refuge for emigre printers from France, Italy, England, and other countries. In that year the first newspapers ever printed in English and French came out—in Amsterdam. In 1621 another Amsterdam publisher started exporting his English-language newspapers to England, and the king's agents now had to track down bundles of newspapers, not just destroy printing presses.

The British government, under pressure, tried to co-opt the opposition by allowing licensed publication of a domestic newspaper, *Mercurius Britannicus,* and some political pamphlets during the 1620s. Criticism of governmental foreign policy became a sore point, however, and James struck back at his press opponents, issuing edicts decrying "the great liberty of discourse concerning matters of state."[2] Printer Thomas Archer was imprisoned, but Puritan doctrines won increasing acceptance, particularly in English towns. Opposition to James and his successor, Charles I, increased.

When one Puritan critic, Alexander Leighton, wrote and published a pamphlet in 1630 entitled *An Appeal to Parliament,* Charles and his court were outraged. Leighton insisted that Scripture was above everything, including kings, so that subjects could remain loyal while evaluating their rulers against biblical standards; Leighton said his goal was to correct existing problems "for the honour of the king, the quiet of the people, and the peace of the church." The Star Chamber saw the situation differently, terming Leighton's work "seditious and scandalous." On November 16, 1630, Leighton was whipped at Westminster, and had one of his ears cut off, his nose slit, and one side of his face branded. One week later the mutilation was repeated on the other side.

The penalty did not stop other Puritans. John Bastwick, Henry Burton, and William Prynne were hauled into the Star Chamber in 1637 and charged with seditious libel for writing pamphlets that criticized royal actions. Each man was sentenced to "perpetual imprisonment" without access to writing materials, and loss of ears. The royal authorities, believing they had the populace on their side, proclaimed a public holiday highlighted by the public mutilations. But when the three men were allowed to make public statements (according to the custom of the day) as the officials waited with knives, they were cheered. Prynne was actually arrested and maimed twice; when he was released from prison and allowed to return to London, he was greeted by a crowd of 10,000.

Barbarous attempts to control the press prompted even more determined opposition; as a *Boston Gazette* essayist would note over a century later, the English civil war had as its "original, true and real Cause" suppression of the press, and "had not Prynn lost his Ears, K. Charles would have never lost his Head."[3] The verbal battle of Parliament versus crown, Puritans versus Anglicans, official story versus corruption story, led to war during the 1640s. The changed political environment led to a journalistic surge, as Puritan-dominated Parliament, remembering past oppression, abolished in 1641 the torture-prone Star Chamber. The result, according to a parliamentary committee in 1643, was that many printers "have taken upon them to set up sundry private Printing Presses in corners, and to print, vend, publish and disperse Books, pamphlets and papers. . . ."[4]

Some of these publications were regular newspapers with high standards. Samuel Pecke's weekly, *A Perfect Diurnall,* began with these words: "You may henceforth expect from this relator to be informed only of such things as are of credit. . . ."[5] Pecke did not make up things. Although clearly a Puritan partisan, he truthfully reported Royalist military victories, and twice covered wrongful conduct by Parliamentary soldiers. He also gave opponents space to express their views: When Archbishop Laud was executed for murder, Pecke included a transcript of the Archbishop's speech from the scaffold.

Similarly, when John Dillingham began his newspaper *The Parliament Scout* in 1643, he pledged "to tell the truth" and not to "vapour and say such a one was routed, defeated," when there actually had been no battle.[6] Dillingham wrote of plundering by Cromwell's soldiers, the bravery of some captured Royalists, and the need for better medical treatment of the wounded on both sides. Partisanship and fairness could go together, apparently, as editors believed that God could judge them for lying even if their backers cheered.[7]

By 1644 London, a city with a half-million residents, had a dozen weekly newspapers. This was more journalistic variety on a regular basis than had ever before existed.[8] Some Puritan leaders did not like criticism any more than the king's officials did, but most were committed to the idea of biblical rather than personal authority, and of letting individuals read for themselves.[9] One Puritan leader and friend of John Milton, Samuel Hartlib, reflected general hopes when he predicted in 1641 that "the art of Printing will so spread knowledge that the common people, knowing their own rights and liberties, will not be governed by way of oppression."[10]

Parliament in 1643 did pass a law that restricted sales of pamphlets and newsbooks, but it received little enforcement and much criticism. Puritan pamphleteer William Walwyn noted that licensing might restrict some evil publications but would also "stopt the mouthes of good men, who must either not write at all, or no more than is suitable to the judgments or interests of the Licensers."[11] Another Puritan, Henry Robinson, proposed that theological and political combat should "be fought out upon eaven ground, on equal termes, neither side must expect to have greater liberty of speech, writing, Printing, or whatsoever else, than the other."[12]

The most famous response to the new law was penned by Milton himself. Licensing, he wrote, brought back memories of Bloody Mary, she of "the most unchristian council and the most tyrannous inquisition that ever inquired," and was inconsistent with the "mild, free and human government" that the Puritans said they would provide. Milton's most famous words in his *Areopagetica* were,

> Though all the winds of doctrine were let loose to play upon the earth, so truth be
> in the field, we do injuriously by licensing and prohibiting to misdoubt her strength.
> Let her and falsehood grapple; who ever knew truth put to the worse, in a free and
> open encounter.[13]

Milton had faith in God's invisible hand over journalism; he asked, "For who knows not that truth is strong, next to the Almighty? She needs no policies, nor stratagems, nor licensings to make victorious; those are shifts and the defences that error uses against her power."[14]

The greatest journalistic talent of 17th-century England emerged during this mid-1640s period of relative freedom. The story of Marchamont Nedham typifies the 17th-century journalistic attempt to follow the tightrope walk of John Foxe, John Stubbes, and other 16th-century writers who prayed for reformation without revolution.

Nedham was born in 1620 in a small town near Oxford. He studied Greek, Latin, and history as a child, received a bachelor's degree from Oxford University in 1637, and spent the next 6 years as a schoolteacher, law clerk, and dabbler in medicine. During those 6 years, Nedham underwent a theological and political transformation that led him to side with the Puritans. When King Charles established in 1643 his own weekly newspapers, the *Mercurius Aulicus,* Nedham was hired to help out with a competing newspaper from the Parliamentary side,

Mercurius Britanicus. Within a year Nedham was in charge and doing almost all of the writing for a newspaper that was eight pages long and typographically clean enough to make possible headache-less reading of it three centuries later.

Nedham's writing was sensational and colorful; rather than theorizing or preaching, he provided specific detail about the vices of Royalists. Lord Ratcliffe, for example, was "bathing in luxury, and swimming in the fat of the land, and cramming his Hens and Capons with Almonds and Raisins," and Lord Porter was "that Exchequer of Flesh, which hath a whole Subsidie in his small guts and his panch, and hath bestowed the Sessments, and taxes of the State in sawces."[15] Nedham saw himself turning darkness into light by exposing corruption; when Nedham reviewed his first year as editor, he wrote that

I have by an excellent and powerful Providence led the people through the labyrinths of the enemies Plots . . . I have brought the secrets and sins of the Court abroad, from her Majestie to Mistris Crofts her very maid of honour, and from his Majesty to his very Barbour.[16]

Another time, he listed his successes in investigative journalism and exposure:

1. The King could not keepe an evil Councellour, but I must needs speake of him.
2. The Queene could not bring in Popery, but I must needs tell all the world of it. . . .
4. The Common Prayer could not be quiet, but I was still crying out Idolatry, and will-worship.
5. The Bishops, Deans, and Doctors, could not play at Gleeke, and drinke Sacke after evening Prayer, but I gave in their names. . . .
9. I would never let Aulicus tell a lie to the world, but I blew a Trumpet before it, that all might know it.
10. I undisguised the Declarations, and Protestations, and Masqueries of the Court.[17]

Nedham, although thoroughly partisan, was not a propagandist at this time. His leads summarized factually the "new business of King and Parliament."[18] He desired accuracy and criticized the Royalist newspaper editor, John Birkenhead:

Oh! what Prodigious Service hath he done, he could tell of Battailes and victories, when there was not so much as an Alarme or skirmish, he could change Pistolls into Demi-Cannons, and Carbines into Culverings, and Squadrons and Troopes into Regiments and Brigades, he could rally routed Armies and put them into a better condition when they were beaten then before.[19]

Unlike Birkenhead, Nedham commented on his own side's difficulties:

The King is too nimble for us in horse, and his designers ride, while ours go on foot, and we lacquey beside him, and usually fall short of his Army, and we shall scarce be able to encounter him, unless he please to turn back and fight with us.[20]

Furthermore, he made theological points through laying up specific detail, rather than by preaching: "Prince Rupert abides in Westchester . . . the young man is lately grown so devout, that he cannot keep the Lords day without a Bull baiting, or Beare baiting."[21]

Nedham rarely drew attention to himself, but in one issue he explained that "I took up my pen for disabusing his Majesty, and for disbishoping, and dispoping his good subjects."[22] Exposure was his goal: He wanted to take off the "vailes and disguises which the Scribes and Pharisees at Oxford had put upon a treasonable and popish Cause."[23] He enjoyed his effectiveness: "I have served a Parliament and Reformation hitherto in unmaking and unhooding incendiaries of all sorts . . . Everyone can point out the evill Counsellours now."[24] But, in a question-and-answer note (an early version of "Dear Abby") at the end of each issue of *Mercurius Britanicus,* he regularly cautioned against arrogance: When asked, "What are we to do or expect now in this time when our forces are so considerable?" Nedham answered, "Not to trust nor looke too much upon them, but through them to a Diviner power, lest we suffer as we did before."[25]

In short, Nedham saw his calling as one of truth-telling, rather than promoting allegiance to a certain set of leaders. He worked hard to maintain some distance from those Puritan leaders who began to trust in their own power. In June 1645, Nedham made it clear to his readers that Parliament did not tell him what to write—he had independent authority, under God.[26] Two months later, Nedham disobeyed a licenser's request that he delete a hard-hitting passage, and received only a reprimand.[27]

Yet, as some Puritan leaders gained great power and decided they were above criticism, they backed off from their own principles. In May 1646, Nedham published that era's equivalent of the Pentagon Papers; the official charge noted his publication of "divers passages between the two Houses of Parliament and other scandalous particulars not fit to be tolerated."[28] One writer attacked Nedham's "sullen and dogged wit" and suggested that "his hands and feet be as sacrifices cut off, and hung up, to pay for the Treasons of his tongue."[29] Nedham's limbs were spared, but he was jailed for 12 days and released only on condition that he do no more newspaper editing.

Nedham abided by his "no editing" pledge but continued to write. At a time when both Anglicans and Puritan Presbyterians opposed independent churches, Nedham made himself unpopular with both sides by writing a pamphlet that warned those who would not tolerate independent churches, "Take heed therefore lest while ye raile against new lights ye work despight to the Spirit of God. To Quench it in a mans self is a great sin, [but it is worse] to labour to quench it in others."[30] Nedham attacked "compulsive power" in religion—but compulsion increased as tensions between Parliament and Oliver Cromwell's New Model Army grew.

The Army, with hands and guns and support from those members of Parliament who were disposed to use force rather than reason, increasingly seemed determined to brook no opposition. Parliament empowered a Committee on Examinations to investigate pamphlet publishers and to demolish the presses and imprison press owners found to be part of the opposition. On September 27, 1647, the House of Commons provided stiff fines for publication of nonlicensed publications. In 1648 many pamphleteers were arrested. In 1649 Parliament increased penalties, ordered all news-books to be licensed, required every printer to make a bond of 300 pounds not to print anything offensive to the government, and confined printing to London and the universities at Oxford and Cambridge, with limited exception for two other presses.

Some Puritans criticized this tightening. In January 1649, a "Petition of firm and constant friends to the parliament and Commonwealth" urged the granting of liberty to the press, and pointedly told military leaders that if

> you and your army shall be pleased to look back a little upon affairs you will find you have bin very much strengthened all along by unlicensed printing. . . . The liberty [of the press] . . . appears so essential unto Freedom, as that without it, it's impossible to preserve any nation from being liable to the worst of bondage. For what may not be done to that people who may not speak or write, but at the pleasure of Licensers?[31]

John Owen, Cromwell's religious advisor, recognized that it is better to have 500 errors scattered among individuals than to have one error gain power over all.[32] Nevertheless, the tendency to reduce debate continued.

Nedham saw the dictatorship coming. In October 1647, he published a pamphlet anticipating the purge of Parliament that took place the following year, in which the military ousted and excluded from further influence 231 of its Parliamentary opponents. Nedham noted that "Mr. Cromwell hath them [Parliament] in the Mill, grind they must, seeing that they are at his Beck who holds a Whip and a Bell over their guilty Heads." He then presciently argued that when Cromwell "hath used them long enough under the name of Parliament, then (perhaps) they shall be disbanded severall waies, that the Sword-men may stand for ever."[33] Calling Cromwell "King Cromwell" and "The Grand Segnior," Needham saw dictatorship leading to more bloodshed and noted sardonically, "Tis a godly thing States to reforme by Murther."[34] Reflecting on how good intentions can lead to sad results, Nedham exclaimed, "Good God, what a wild thing is Rebellion."[35]

The dramatic result of Nedham's rethinking of rebellion was that he amazed his former allies by joining the Royalists. Presbyterian minister John Hackluyt, a chaplain in the Parliamentary army who shared Nedham's concern about dictatorship, also switched sides, in the hope that a humbled King Charles might consent to a constitutional monarchy. The suggestion of one historian that Nedham joined the king's side because he "liked excitement and power" seems weak: The king's side was a losing side, and in a little over a year Charles would be executed.[36] To become a Royalist late in 1647 showed either great stupidity or uncommon bravery. Nedham was not dumb, and it appears that he was risking all to try to preserve some liberty in England. From September 1647 through January 1649, Nedham edited *Mercurius Pragmaticus,* a newspaper deeply critical of the new dictatorship emerging.

Nedham's reporting, as usual, contained exciting detail and perceptive analysis. He showed how Cromwell and his associates won a Parliamentary majority through intimidation and created public fear through artfully designed troop movements. He exposed other plans and pretensions, including dissension among the army-Parliamentary forces: Cromwell's "face is now more toward an Aristocracie than Zion, which hath raised a deadly feud betwixt him and the Adjutators, who looke upon him as fallen from grace."[37] In 1648 Nedham also produced several satirical pamphlets, including one entitled *Ding Dong or Sr. Pitifull Parliament on his death-bed,* under the pen name Mercurius Melancholicus. In that pamphlet he wrote, "Sir Pitifull Parliament hath taken griefe, which hath so prevailed over his powers, and mastered his faculties, that he is now become a meere Skelleton . . . harke how he groanes."[38]

As the Puritan reforming zeal turned to revolutionary power lust, Nedham week after week in *Mercuricus Pragmaticus* showed the degradation of the movement: "See how Wealth/ Is made their Heaven! They swell/ With Pride! and live by Blood and Stealth,/ As if there were no Hell."[39] Meanwhile, poverty dominated the countryside, and there "the citizens (like silly sheep)/ Must fast, and be content."[40] Civil war, Nedham feared, was bringing out the worst in men: "Faith and Religion bleeding lie,/ And Liberty grows faint:/ No Gospel, but pure Treachery,/ And Treason make the Saint. . . . Away with Justice, Laws and Fear;/ When Men resolve to rise,/ Brave Souls must scorn all Scruples where/ A Kingdom is the Prize."[41] Might apparently was making right, with preaching secondary: "Militia too, they needs must gain,/ Those pretty carnal Tools:/ For Pauls old Weapons they disdain,/ As fit for none but Fools."[42]

In November 1648, two months before King Charles' execution, with the revolutionary party at its height, Nedham published *A Plea for the King and Kingdome.* He decried the movement "to a Military Government" that would lead to "the utter subversion of our Law . . . and the inslaving of the Kingdome." Nedham was not alone in thinking the forces of Cromwell were going too far: Of the 250 men who remained in Parliament following Pride's Purge of December 1648, only about 60 sat regularly as puppets of the army, and fewer than half of those finally approved of the King's execution.

Many Puritans spoke out vigorously against the coup; many were arrested. William Waller, a Puritan general who split from Cromwell, called the takeover tyrannical and labeled it "treason in the highest degree."[43] But the king was executed; in the words of the newspaper *A Perfect Diurnall,* "The executioner at one blow severed his head from his body. Then when the King's head was cut off, the Executioner held it up and showed it to the spectators."[44] This was the first modern revolutionary execution, with millions more to follow.

Soon after Charles' execution, Nedham went into hiding. Other journalists expressed veiled concern about a move toward dictatorship. Dillingham wrote in February 1649, following Charles' execution, "There's Kings gone, them and Lords in two dayes: how easie it is to pull down." He asked readers to turn to II Samuel, where the daughters of Israel are told to weep over Saul. He mocked utopian plans and economic panaceas.[45] Nedham, however, went further than others. For 2 months during the spring of 1649 he put out an underground edition of *Mercurius Pragmaticus* that featured reporting like this:

> Both King and Bishops thus exil'd/ The Saints not yet content:/ Now with fresh flames of Zeal grow wild,/ And cry, No Parliament . . . The State's grown fat with Orphans Tears,/ Whilst Widows pine and moan;/ And tender Conscience in sev'n years,/ Is turn'd t' a heart of stone.[46]

Nedham concluded that "No Powers are safe, Treason's a Tilt,/ And the mad Sainted-Elves/ Boast when Royal Blood is spilt,/ They'll all be Kings themselves."[47]

Nedham, from various hiding places, also sent out several pamphlets that did not endear him to the new masters of England. Immediately after the revolutionary leaders celebrated victory with a parade and feast on June 7, Nedham published *The Great Feast at the Sheep-shearing of the City and Citizens*. The last page gives a sense of the whole:

> At Grocers Hall, they grocely fed,/ With which their paunches out were spread,/ Whilst thousands starve for want of bread,/ Let's thanke the Parliament./ Neere forty Bucks, these Holy ones/ Devour'd, and left the dogs the bones,/ And Musick grac'd with Tunes and Tones,/ This Bacchanalian Feast:/ And after that, a Banquet came . . . Tyrants feast with joy.[48]

With that publication the search for Nedham intensified; a few days later he was captured, sent to Newgate prison, and almost executed. He escaped in August and was free for 2 weeks, but was captured and sent back to prison, where he spent 3 more months.

It turned out that Nedham was not executed, because Oliver Cromwell had other plans for him. Cromwell, in effect the new king, wanted to merge the official story and the corruption story, the latter restricted so as to chastise the corruption of subjects but not the new rulers. He offered Nedham a deal: Write for me, and live. Nedham gave in, signed an oath of allegiance to the new government in November 1649, and was released to begin work on a 100-page pamphlet that presented "The Equity, Utility, and Necessity, of a Submission to the present Government."[49] Nedham argued at length that the Royalist cause was done for, and that wise men, understanding the "improbability of Success in the new Royall enterprize," should submit in recognition of "Necessity, the Custome of all Nations, and the Peace of our own."[50]

One of Nedham's title chapters—"That the Power of the Sword Is, and Ever Hath been, the Foundation of All Titles to Government"—shows how the official story had come to dominate Nedham's thinking or at least his expression, with Cromwell as king. A person disobeying another who had come into power, whether or not the ascent was lawful, and regardless of "allegiances, oaths, and covenants" formerly entered into, was "peevish, and a man obstinate against the reason and custom of the whole world."[51] Nedham used examples from the then recent Thirty Years War to show how allegiances quickly change under pressure:

> One while, you might have seen the same town under the French, the next under the Spaniard. And upon every new alteration, without scruple, paying a new allegiance and submission, and never so much as blamed for it by the divines of their own or any other nation.[52]

Such is life, Nedham argued.

Nedham's writings thoughout the early 1650s showed that mixture of cynical wisdom and broken spirit. Cromwell's government, with its deeply flawed practice but a base in biblical principles, did not prove to be as terrible as Nedham first had feared. The leaders did not engage in the mass murder that characterized revolutions to come. Still, petty dictatorship emerged; as Puritan Denzil Holles complained, in what would also be a preview of future revolutionary outcomes, "The meanest of men, the basest and vilest of the nation, the lowest of the people, have got the power into their hands . . ."[53] It is sad to see Nedham reporting to such individuals and editing the official public relations weekly for the regime, *Mercurius Politicus*.[54]

And yet, Nedham at times was able to work within the system to keep a slight breeze blowing. The Council of State, as publisher, approved of Nedham's plan to have *Politicus* "written in a jocular way" to attract attention.[55] Nedham produced good coverage of local news along with cautionary reports of persons hanged for treason.[56] But Nedham also kept hope alive in his pamphlet *The Excellencie of a Free State*, which he serialized in *Politicus*. Nedham observed that

> The Interest of Freedom is a Virgin that everyone seeks to deflower; and like a Virgin, it must be kept from any other Form, or else (so great is the Lust of mankinde for dominion) there follows a rape upon the first opportunity.[57]

He wondered whether there was political life after rape, or whether government was merely "an artifice . . . occasioned by necessity."[58]

Eventually the petty aspects of Cromwell's rules, not the major thrusts, turned English public opinion massively against what became associated with all of Puritanism, rather than its revolutionary elements that had achieved power. The "rump Parliament" formed after Pride's Purge passed laws forbidding the celebration of Christmas and attacking traditional pastimes such as dancing, playing at cards or dice, and so on. In 1655 Cromwell divided England and Wales into 12 military districts, each ruled by a major-general with authority to "promote godliness and virtue" by enforcing laws against horseracing, cock-fighting, and so on. No recreation was allowed on the Sabbath; in 1659 a French observer wrote that "the religion of England is preaching and sitting still on Sundays."[59] Popular resentment grew.

As the revolution ran down in the late 1650s Nedham saw that a monarchical restoration was likely: "Tis neither dishonour nor scandal," he wrote, that "after all other experiments made in vain, where the ends of government cannot otherwise be conserved, to revert upon the old bottom and foundation."[60] It would have been easy for Nedham, following Oliver Crowell's death in 1658, to join others in beginning to grease the slide on which the dead king's son, Charles II, soon would return. But Nedham did not join the plotters—instead, against his own personal interests, he warned Puritans that hopes of a peaceful, constitutional monarchy were foolish, because Charles II would be vindictive and would once again empower "the Episcopacie."[61] In 1660 Nedham again deliberately stuck with a lost cause, this time suggesting that Charles II should be fought because his promises of mercy were unreliable: "Tush! remember that blessed line of Machiavel; he's an oafe that thinks an oath, or any other tender, can tame a prince beyond his pleasure."[62]

Such jabs killed Nedham's chances to remain in English journalism following the monarchical restoration. They almost killed Nedham. In May 1660, a pamphlet entitled *A Rope for Pol. Or a, a Hue and Cry after Marchamont Nedham,* suggested that he deserved death because of the influence his writing had "upon numbers of unconsidering persons, who have a strange presumption that all must needs be true that is in Print."[63] A broadside, *The Downfall of Mercurius,* argued "now the time is coming which no doube/ Will do him justice, vengeance will find him out./ . . . Thus with the times he turned. next time I hope/ Will up the ladder be and down the rope."[64] In April 1660, Nedham fled to Holland.

He was allowed to return 4 months later, but on the condition that he abstain from any further involvement in political journalism.[65] Nedham stayed out of politics for 15 years and concentrated on medicine. From 1676 to 1678 he wrote four political pamphlets in opposition to the Whig leader Shaftesbury and in opposition to the dictatorship of Louis XIV in France. They did not make much of a mark, nor was Nedham's death in 1678, at age 58, much noted.

The legacy of Nedham—his early fervor, his later suspicion, and his deliberate bad timing—*should* be noted, however. Three times—in 1646, 1649, and 1660— he stuck out his neck for what he believed, and three times he came close to having it chopped off or stretched out. Through that experience he became suspicious of all ideologies that promised earthly salvation; many American journalists would later follow in his footsteps.

His dashed hopes were shared by Puritan journalists generally. In May 1662, the new, Royalist-dominated Parliament passed a bill enacting a new, stringent censorship system. No more, said Parliament, would

> evil disposed persons [sell] heretical, schismatical, blasphemous, seditious and treasonable books, pamphlets and papers. . . indangering the peace of these kingdoms, and raising a disaffection to his most excellent Majesty and his government.[66]

The official story was triumphant, not only in journalism but in legal preaching.[67] English newspapers born during the years of civil strife suffered governmental infanticide. Despite early promises to the contrary, Charles II increasingly tried to rule on the French, divine-right model, and his press clippings reflected that: Palace writers had God always in the background, looking on benevolently, but Charles at the center, master of the realm. A tight censorship eliminated regular news coverage unless it helped to propel the official story.

For proponents of the corruption story, life was even harder than it had been before the revolution. For example, in 1663 John Twyn was convicted of sedition for printing a book arguing that citizens should call to account a king whose decrees violated biblical law. After Twyn refused to provide the name of the book's author, his "privy-members" were cut off before his eyes, and he was then beheaded. Twyn's body was cut into four pieces, and each was nailed to a different gate of the city as a warning to other printers or writers.[68]

Chapter 3

A New Planting of the Corruption Story

After the monarchical restoration in England, British officials across the Atlantic also placed restrictions on press freedoms. Royal governors appeared to believe that the Puritan idea of "read for yourself" simply caused too much trouble. In 1671 Governor William Berkeley of Virginia responded to a query concerning the state of religion in the colony by saying that the drawbacks of emphasizing reading and study would outweigh the benefits:

> There are no free schools nor *printing,* and I hope we shall not have these hundred years; for *learning* has brought disobedience, and heresy, and sects into the world, and *printing* has divulged them, and libels against the best government.[1]

Berkeley's successors in Virginia clamped down hard on any displays of independence. Philip Ludwell was heavily fined in 1678 for calling Governor Herbert Jeffreys a lawbreaker. When printing finally was allowed, it was carefully regulated: Printer John Buckner received a reprimand in 1682 merely for printing the colony's laws without official permission; Buckner was forced to post a bond of 100 pounds that would be forfeited were he ever to print anything again. Governor Francis Lord Howard in 1685 issued a proclamation condemning the "over lycentiousnesse of the People in their discourses" and reminding the public that criticism of the royal government was criminal sedition.[2] Other proclamations and incidents—in 1690, 1693, 1699, 1702, and 1704—also sent a message to those who might wish to oppose the official story.

Attempts at independence often received severe punishment. In 1666, one

Maryland critic of the official story received 39 lashes across his back. Protests concerning such treatment occasionally appeared: In 1689 a Maryland group that called itself the Protestant Association protested the colony's laws,

> especially one that against all Sense, Equity, Reason, and Law Punishes all Speeches, Practices, and Attempts relating to his Lordship and Government, that shall be thought Mutinous and Seditious.[3]

The Protestant Association complained that the government had punished "Words and Actions" it disapproved of by "Whipping, Branding, Boreing through the Tongue, Fine, Imprisonment, Banishment, or Death."[4] But for many years Maryland and other colonies did not have the critical mass of residents committed to the Reformation concept that those in various spheres of society had a right to carry on their activities, under God, regardless of royal approval. Royal governors hoped to avoid all criticism.[5]

Only in New England, the center of Reformation thought in the New World, was publication and education emphasized; the Puritans set up a printing press and college in Cambridge, Massachusetts, in 1636, just 6 years after their arrival in a wilderness where mere survival was not assured.[6] New Englanders tried from the colony's founding to restrict royal authority. John Winthrop had the opportunity to gain special favors for Massachusetts from Puritans then dominating Parliament, but he declined because he did not want to accept the idea that Parliament had jurisdiction over the colony; Winthrop wanted the idea of a self-governing commonwealth to be established. The General Court (Massachusetts' legislature) at one point declared—in a statement that Samuel Adams would pick up a century later—"Our allegiance binds us not to the laws of England any longer than while we live in England."[7]

In the 1660s, however, monarchical restoration in England placed new pressures on New England. Well-connected courtiers in London contested the Massachusetts Bay charter that Charles I had given to Puritan leaders in 1629; the courtiers claimed that they had received previous royal grants to the same land. The General Court, desperate to avoid a royal crackdown, forced evangelist and writer John Eliot in 1661 to retract "such expressions as doe too manifestly scandalize" the government of England." Eliot's book *The Christian Commonwealth,* which advocated election of rulers, was ordered "totally suppressed."[8] In October 1662, the General Court passed the first formal censorship act in Massachusetts, imitating the act passed by Parliament under the urging of Charles II.

Pressure on New England writers did not come only from London. The Puritans allowed wide debate concerning biblical interpretation, but would not allow publication of tracts hostile to the fundamentals or essentials of Reformed Christianity. Quakers, with their reliance on "inner light" rather than the Bible only, and their methods of protest that included walking naked inside churches to protest the "nakedness" of the institutions, were not tolerated. But the Puritans did encourage reporting of bad news that tended to be swept under the rug in most other places.

They were lenient in this way because bad news was seen as a message from God. Boston printer Marmaduke Johnson in 1668 published "God's Terrible Voice in the City of London, wherein you have the Narration of the late dreadful Judgment of Pleague and Fire." In 1674, when Benjamin Goad was hanged in Boston for committing bestiality, Samuel Danforth wrote of crime and punishment and offered a "why":

> God's end in inflicting remarkable judgments upon some, is for caution and warning to all others. . . . Behold now the execution of vengeance upon this lewd and wicked youth, whom God hath hanged up before the Sun, and made a sign and example, and instruction and admonishment, to all New England.[9]

Johnson published a short piece entitled, "Cry of Sodom enquired into, upon occasion of the Arraignment and Condemnation of Benjamin Goad, for his prodigious Villany."[10]

"News sermons," first presented in church and frequently published, became an established form of New England communication. The sermons, Harry S. Stout has pointed out, had a "topical range and social influence" and were "so powerful in shaping cultural values, meanings, and a sense of corporate purpose that even television pales in comparison."[11] In Stout's words:

> Unlike modern mass media, the sermon stood alone in local New England contexts as the regular (at least weekly) medium of public communication. As a channel of information, it combined religious, educational, and journalistic functions.[12]

Sermons on royal births and deaths, military defeats or victories, election results and government decisions, and most of all crimes (preferably with punishments) were common.[13] Printers moved naturally from publication of Bible commentaries to publication of theological treatises and sermons to publication of news sermons and pamphlets on current events.[14]

Puritan theology not only allowed but emphasized the reporting of bad news, for the coming of well-deserved calamities was a sign that God still reigned. It was no accident that the best-known Massachusetts minister of the late 17th century, Increase Mather, also became its leading journalist. Mather argued in 1674 that God was not pleased with the sins of pride and envy that were common in New England, and that "a day of trouble is at hand."[15] The long title of one of his published news sermons in 1675 provided, in order, the "why," "what," "where," "when," "how," and "who" of the news:

The Times of Men Are in the Hands of God. Or a Sermon Occasioned by That Awful Providence Which Happened in Boston in New England, The 4th Day of the 3rd

Month 1675 (When Part of a Vessel Was Blown Up in the Harbor, and Nine Men Hurt, and Three Mortally Wounded).[16]

Mather's forecasts of general disaster hit home in June 1675, when a tribe of Wampanoag Indians burned and looted homes in the town of Swansea and killed nine residents. Indian attacks escalated in August 1675, as Wampanoags led by Chief Metacom ("King Philip") were joined by the Narragansetts and Nipmucks in an attack on towns in western Massachusetts and other outlying areas. A ballad contextualized the news: "O New-England, I understand/ with thee God is offended:/ And therefore He doth humble thee,/ till thou thy ways hast mended."[17] In the summer of 1676 Philip's forces were within 10 miles of Boston, but so many had been killed in battle that a final push was beyond their grasp; when Philip was captured and executed, the war was over. The tribes were left devastated, but 1 in every 16 colonists of fighting age was also dead, many women and children had been killed or carried into captivity, and 12 towns were totally destroyed.

For the Puritans, the war was an exceptionally clear example of judgment for their sins, and many ministers/writers went to work on it. Chief among them was Increase Mather, whose *Brief History of the War with the Indians of New-England* was filled with information about who, what, when, and where:

> March 17. This day the Indians fell upon Warwick, and burnt it down to the ground, all but one house. . . .
>
> May 11. A company of Indians assaulted the Town of Plimouth, burnt eleven Houses and five Barns therein. . . .[18]

Mather then contextualized the news by seeing God's hand not only in the beginning of the war but in its prolongation; reporting on the aftermath of one battle, he wrote, "Had the English immediately pursued the Victory begun, in all likelyhood there had been an end of our troubles: but God saw that neither yet were we fit for deliverance."[19]

Like other Puritan journalists, however, Mather was careful to juxtapose evidence of God's anger with dramatic news of God's mercy. When one house was about to be set on fire by hundreds of Indians who surrounded it, it appeared that

> Men and Women, and Children must have perished, either by unmerciful flames, or more unmerciful hands of wicked Men whose tender Mercies are cruelties, so that all hope that they should be saved was then taken in: but behold in this Jount of Difficulty and Extremity *the Lord is seen.* For in the very nick of opportunity God sent that worthy Major Willard, who with forty and eight men set upon the Indians and caused them to turn their backs . . . however we may be diminished and brought low through Oppression, Affliction, and Sorrow, yet our God will have compassion on us, and this his People shall not utterly perish.[20]

Mather's reportage was a prototype of the cavalry rescues beloved in Western movies, but the emphasis here was on God's grace, not man's heroism. And, Mather reported that when New Englanders recognized their reliance on that grace and pledged covenantal obedience, the war ended.[21]

Emphasizing the importance of accurate reporting, Mather concluded his news account with the words,

> Thus have we in brief, plain, and true story of the war with the Indians in New England, how it began, and how it hath made its progress, and what present hopes there are of a comfortable closure and conclusion of this trouble.[22]

He then appended to the main text of his pamphlet a sermon/editorial on the war, entitled "An Earnest Exhortation to the Inhabitants of New England." In it, Mather explicitly presented the "why" of the war: God's punishment because of sins such as "contention" and "pride."[23] But he also argued that too much guilt, like too much pride, could "run into extreams." Instead of pouring it on, Mather offered hope: God's "design, in bringing the Calamity upon us, is not to destroy us, but to humble us, and reform us, and to do us good in the latter end."[24]

The tradition of news and news analysis followed by hard-hitting but eventually upbeat editorial was beginning. The next step for American journalism came in 1681 when a general meeting of the Massachusetts ministers urged careful coverage of "Illustrious Providences," including

> Divine Judgements, Tempests, Floods, Earth-quakes, Thunders as are unusual, Strange Apparitions, or what ever else shall happen that is Prodigious, Witchcrafts, Diabolical Possessions, Remarkable Judgements upon noted Sinners: eminent Deliverances, and Answers of Prayer.[25]

Here was a definition of news not unlike our own in its emphasis on atypical, "man bites dog" events: "unusual" thunders, "strange" apparitions, and other "prodigious" or "remarkable" happenings—except that the "why" was different, because for the Puritans, all unusual occurrences showed a glimpse of God's usually invisible hand.

The ministers' resolution also provided a method for recording of events that anticipated the relation of correspondents and editors that would follow in later years. First, each minister was to be a correspondent, with the responsibility to "diligently enquire into, and Record such Illustrious Providences as have happened, or from time to time shall happen, in the places whereunto they do belong."[26] Second, to avoid the supplanting of fact by fiction, it would be important to rely on eyewitnesses and make sure "that the Witnesses of such notable Occurrents be likewise set down in Writing."[27] Third, it would be important to find a main writer/editor who "hath Leisure and Ability for the management of Such an undertaking."[28]

That person turned out to be Mather himself—and he proved himself to be right for the job. Mather read widely and well, citing in appropriate places in his *Essay* the work of leading scientists of the day such as Johannes Kepler, Tycho Brahe, and Robert Boyle. He himself wrote reports about comets, magnetism, lightning, thunder, and other natural phenomena, and would not report about an event unless a reliable source made a written, signed statement; after noting one extraordinary occurrence, he noted, "I would not have mentioned this relation, had I not received it from serious, faithfull, and Judicious hands. . . ."[29] Mather and others thought accuracy important because events were their report card signed by God, and they wanted to know where they stood, for better or for worse.[30]

American journalism began, in short, because the Puritans, in historian David Nord's words, were "obsessed with events, with the news. They could see all around them the providence of God. The great movements of celestial and human history were the prime considerations, but little things carried meaning as well."[31] In addition, Puritans set the stage for an honoring of the journalists themselves. The idea that God was acting in the world made journalism significant, for Increase Mather wrote that "it is proper for the Ministers of God to ingage themselves [in recording] the providentiall Dispensations of God."[32] Increase's son Cotton even wrote that

> To *regard* the illustrious displays of that Providence wherewith our Lord Christ governs the world, is a work, than which there is none more needful or useful for a Christian.[33]

By the 1680s, with journalism viewed as significant, and Boston becoming populous and prosperous enough to support a weekly newspaper, only a tense political situation was forestalling the establishment of one. Charles II, pressed by courtiers who wished to get their hands on New England's growing wealth, demanded that Massachusetts "make a *full Submission and entire Resignation* of their Charter to his pleasure." Removal of the charter would mean that freedom of the press and other liberties would not be under local control, but under regulation from London. Boston erupted in protest, and Increase Mather told a Boston town meeting that if Massachusetts acquiesced to royal pressure, "I verily Believe We Shall Sin against the GOD of Heaven." Mather asked the townspeople to say no, be patient, and trust God:

> If we make a *full Submission and entire Resignation* to Pleasure, we shall fall into the *Hands of Men* immediately. But if we do it not, we still keep ourselves in the *Hands of GOD;* we trust ourselves with His Providence: and who knows what GOD may do for us?[34]

For the next 6 years, as Mather's advice was taken in Massachusetts, crown and colony were at loggerheads. In 1684 the Court of Chancery in London vacated the charter, and soon all of New England came under the direct control of a royal governor who hated Puritans, Sir Edmund Andros. In 1687 John Wise and five of his associates received heavy fines for stating that taxes were legitimate only when levied by the Assembly.[35] In 1688 Andros, using power given by Charles' successor James II, ordered Increase Mather's son Cotton arrested for editing and supervising the printing of a pamphlet criticizing the Anglican state church. Cotton escaped imprisonment at that time but remained under threat from royal officials who repeatedly complained that the young writer "and others of his gang" opposed orders that "will not serve their interest (by them called the interest of Jesus Christ.)"[36]

Puritan prospects seemed bleak as Increase Mather headed to London to lobby for restoration of the Massachusetts charter. Even when William and Mary, backed by Parliament, seized power from James and in 1689 removed Andros from control of New England, the issue was still in doubt.[37] Journalistic freedom was under attack as the General Court, trying to show itself "trustworthy," warned in 1689 that those who published materials "tending to the disturbance of peace and subversion of the government" would be treated "with uttermost Severity."[38]

One journalistic friend of the Mathers decided at this difficult time to try publishing a Boston newspaper. Printer and writer Benjamin Harris knew first-hand the dangers of independent journalism. In 1679 he had been jailed for publishing in London an independent newspaper, *Domestick Intelligence;* sentenced to a harsh prison regime, Harris said simply, "I hope God will give me Patience to go through it."[39] After Harris did go through it he continued to print pamphlets that exposed wrong-doing. One of the pamphlets suggested that honest investigators followed in the footsteps of a "God [who] will not be mocked: There's no Dissembling with Heaven, no Masquerading with the All-seeing Eye of divine Vengeance."[40]

We know little about Harris the man; he seemed to stay in the background, content with reporting the good and ill deeds of others.[41] But several of his beliefs seem evident from his pamphlets. He stressed accuracy: One pamphlet reported that, "among the many Examples recited in this book, there are none but what are of approved Verity and well Attested."[42] At the same time, however, he wanted to send a clear message:

> I shall only add my Wishes and Prayers, that past Examples may prove future Warnings; and all that read these signal Instances of God's Judgments, may thereby . . . hold fast the Truth . . . conserve the pure Faith, and walk answerable thereunto in their Conversation, which will bring a Blessing in Life, and Comfort in Death, and Glory to Eternity.[43]

Harris clearly had no desire to be a martyr, and clearly felt that one prison term was enough. When royal officials searched his London printshop in 1686, seized pamphlets considered seditious, and issued a warrant for his arrest, Harris and his family escaped to Boston. There he opened a bookstore-coffeehouse and published *The New England Primer,* a best-selling schoolbook filled with Biblical quotations and moral precepts. But Harris could not stay away from journalism. Hoping that the departure of Andros pointed toward greater freedom, and apparently aided by Cotton Mather, Harris on September 25, 1690, published the first newspaper in America, *Publick Occurrences Both Foreign and Domestick.*[44]

Belief in Providence was evident throughout the four-page newspaper. Harris' expressed purpose for publishing it was in line with his previous writing: "That Memorable Occurrents of Divine Providence may not be neglected or forgotten, as they too often are."[45] Harris' combination of reporting and teaching showed as he reported "a day of Thanksgiving to God" for a good harvest and noted, concerning a tragedy averted, that God "assisted the Endeavours of the People to put out the Fire."[46] When a man committed suicide after his wife died, Harris explained that "The Devil took advantage of the Melancholy which he thereupon fell into."[47]

Such reports were politically safe, but when Harris emphasized God's sovereignty not only over local events but over matters involving international relations as well, controversy followed. Harris' report of mistreatment of prisoners by Mohawk Indians, and his criticism of royal officials for making an alliance with those Indians in order to defeat French forces in Canada, was based on his belief in Providence; Harris wrote,

> If Almighty God will have Canada to be subdu'd without the assistance of those miserable Salvages, in whom we have too much confided, we shall be glad, that there will be no Sacrifice offered up to the Devil, upon this occasion; God alone will have all the glory.[48]

Furthermore, Harris took seriously reports of adultery in the French court. British officials, hoping at that time for peace with France, were refraining from comments that could arouse popular concern about trusting those of low morals; because sexual restraint was not a common court occurrence in Restoration England either, they probably thought such news was a non-story. Harris, however, went ahead and reported that Louis XIV "is in much trouble (and fear) not only with us but also with his Son, who has revolted against him lately, and has great reason if reports be true, that the Father used to lie with the Sons Wife."[49]

Puritans who liked to emphasize God's sovereignty over all human activities were pleased with *Publick Occurrences;* Cotton Mather called it "a very noble, useful and laudable design."[50] The royal governor and his council were not amused, however: 4 days after publication the newspaper was suppressed, and Harris was told that any further issues would give him new prison nightmares. Harris gave in. He stayed in Massachusetts for a time and was given some public printing jobs because of his good behavior, but returned to England in 1695 and was arrested for publishing another short-lived newspaper, *Intelligence Domestick and Foreign*. A changed political climate allowed his release, however, and he was able to publish another newspaper, the *London Post,* from 1699 to 1705.[51]

The squelching of *Publick Occurrences* in 1690, by officials desperate to avoid offending the powers of London, represents a low tide in American journalism. But better news came in 1692, when Increase Mather was able to return from England with a new charter that was almost as good as the old one. The King retained the power to appoint a Governor who could veto legislation, but the people of Massachusetts could elect a legislature that alone had the power of taxation. (This part of the new contract became crucial during the 1760s and 1770s.)

Increase Mather had no time to rest, however, because as he returned to Boston, accusations of witchcraft followed by irregular trial procedures, were dominating the news from Salem. Until 1692 Massachusetts was not known as a center for witch-hunting: Historian Chadwick Hansen has pointed out that, "while Europe hanged and burned literally thousands of witches, executions in New England were few and far between."[52] From 1663 through 1691 trials of witches in New England led to twenty acquittals and only one execution, in large part because witches had to be tried for specific acts seen by two unimpeachable witnesses.[53] But in Salem in 1692, judges who overstepped traditional restraints began accepting what was called *spectral evidence,* and the trouble began.

Spectral evidence was testimony by individuals that they had seen not the accused, but a ghostly likeness or spectre of the accused, engaged in actions such as burning houses, sinking ships, and so on. The leading ministers of Massachusetts, including Increase and Cotton Mather, opposed the acceptance of spectral evidence. They did so not only because proceeding without witnesses of flesh and blood action violated common law practice, but because such action opened the door to abuses and general hysteria. In May 1692, before anyone was executed, Cotton Mather pleaded that the Salem judges not stress spectral evidence, for "It is very certain that the divells have sometimes represented the shapes of persons not only innocent, but also very virtuous."[54]

The Salem magistrates did not listen. Led by or leading local hysteria, they jailed several hundred residents and executed 20 from June through September 1692.[55] Cotton Mather was upset. In 1688 he had taken into his house a child diagnosed as suffering diabolical persecution and had apparently cured her. He offered in 1692 to make his own house a shelter home by taking six or more of those who said they were suffering from witchcraft.[56] But Cotton Mather did not publicly condemn Salem justice. Increase acted differently. He went to work investigating the trials and wrote a pamphlet, *Cases of Conscience,* that exposed the judicial practices of Salem and condemned use of spectral evidence.[57]

The Salem magistrates paid attention to Increase Mather's hard-hitting writing, or at least the public furor it stirred. Increase's insistence that self-incriminating confessions should not be accepted as proof hit home. His stress that only the testimony under oath of two actual witnesses, "as in any other Crime of a Capital nature," was sufficient to convict witches, was accepted.[58] Once Increase's pamphlet appeared, executions in Salem stopped. As Perry Miller concluded, "Increase Mather—and he alone—brought the murders to an end."[59] Cotton Mather's quiet protests had not stopped the hangings, but Increase Mather's bold journalism saved lives.

That was a signal triumph for the preacher-journalist. But the end of the witch trials also brought a signal defeat, one that has provided solid ammunition for centuries to those who hate the Mathers because they hate the Mathers' world view. Massachusetts Governor Phipps, worried about reaction in London to reports of New England justice gone berserk, "commanded" Cotton Mather to prepare a defense of judicial conduct in some of the trials.[60] Cotton Mather complied by rushing out an abysmal quasi-justification, *The Wonders of the Invisible World*. (Weird excerpts of it now find their way into history textbooks as "proof" of Puritan zaniness.)

Cotton Mather apparently realized he was doing a bad job even as he was doing it. He gave his hasty public relations work a clearly reluctant beginning: "I live by Neighbours that force me to produce these undeserved Lines."[61] He added an equally mournful note at the end by reporting that he had completed "the Service imposed upon me." In between, in Cotton Mather's most wildly excessive writing, came a pitiful attempt to semi-legitimize for the public what he had in private termed improper judicial procedure.

Perry Miller has pointed out that, because of Mather's defense of judicial murder, "thousands of Americans are still persuaded that Cotton Mather burned witches at Salem."[62] The truth is far more intriguing: Mather accepted a task he should have refused, completed it while gritting his teeth, and has received three centuries of abuse for that which he grudgingly defended. This is not to defend Mather: He disgraced himself. Had he stayed with what he knew to be true he would have stood alongside his father at this point as a 1690s pioneer of journalistic bravery. Sadly, at age 29, Cotton Mather still aimed to please.

Indirectly, the outcome of the charter and witch trial controversies contributed to two major developments in American journalism.

First, the witch trials showed that local governmental authorities could be deadly wrong. Massachusetts citizens began to show more caution in declaring guilty those arrested under ambiguous circumstances, including writers. In 1695 when Massachusetts charged Quaker pamphleteer Thomas Maule with printing "wicked Lyes and Slanders . . . upon Government" and also impugning the religious establishment, he shrewdly pleaded that a printed book was no more evidence of his guilt than "the spectre evidence is in law sufficient to prove a person accused by such evidence to be a witch."[63] When Maule was acquitted by the jury, press freedom had won its first major trial victory in America.[64] Maule celebrated by publishing in 1697 a pamphlet, *New-England Persecutors Mauled with their own Weapons*.[65]

Second, as a considerable degree of self-rule for Massachusetts was reestablished at the end of the century, leaders could return to Reformation principles and relax the censorship procedures that had stopped Benjamin Harris. Licensing laws remained on the books, but in 1700 Increase Mather published a treatise without a license, as did others. Moreover, even as ministers were complaining of theological laxity, the corruption story was being widely accepted, even by political officials, as the most appropriate narrative framework. That broad acceptance opened the way for publication in 1704 of the *Boston News-Letter,* America's first newspaper to last more than one issue.

The *News-Letter*'s first editor, Boston postmaster John Campbell, had good ties to both the political establishment and to theological leaders. Campbell's writing was duller than that of Benjamin Harris, but he also was ready to print bad news noting that an "awful Providence" was "a Warning to all others to watch against the wiles of our Grand Adversary."[66] Campbell faithfully recorded what Increase Mather had termed "extraordinary judgments," and also reported mercies such as the rapid extinguishing of a fire through "God's good signal Providence."

Like Harris, Campbell hoped through his newspaper to see "a great many Providences now Recorded, that would otherwise be lost."[67] He editorially attacked immorality, profaneness, and counterfeiting.[68] Like many of his predecessors, he stressed accuracy: When Campbell reported a minister's prayer at the hanging of six pirates in Boston in June 1704, he noted that he was quoting the prayer "as near as it could be taken in writing in the great crowd."[69] He made many errors but tried to apologize for even small ones, such as the dropping of a comma in one issue.

The popularity of news ballads and news sermons meant that Campbell could run more short news stories and leave some contextualization to others. For example, Campbell gave large space to a great storm that had created much damage in Europe and to the capture and execution of those six pirates, but did not need to contexualize the events fully; Campbell knew that Cotton Mather's sermon on the pirates, and Increase Mather's on the storm, were being published.[70] (Increase Mather was arguing that "We must be deaf indeed if such loud calls, if such astonishing Providences, do not at all awaken us."[71])

The *News-Letter* went on peacefully for the next decade and a half. It survived financially by mixing *corruption story* coverage with profitable publication of official notices. When a new postmaster, William Brooker, was appointed in 1719, Campbell continued publishing his newspaper and Brooker put out his own weekly, the *Boston Gazette.*[72] Two years later a third newspaper, the *New-England Courant,* edited by James Franklin, joined in. Then came one more aftermath of the witch trials, and the most remembered press dispute in Massachusetts colonial history, one that gave Cotton Mather a chance to make journalistic restitution for his cravenness during the witch trials nearly three decades before.[73]

The new conflict began in 1721 when Dr. Zabdiel Boylston, supported by

Cotton Mather, wanted to fight a smallpox epidemic raging in Boston by making use of the latest scientific innovation, inoculation. Dr. William Douglass, the only Boston physician with university training in medicine, knew for certain from his training that inoculation was dangerous nonsense. He tried to outflank Cotton Mather by appearing holier than him: Douglass charged that Boylston and Mather, instead of relying solely on God to fight disease, were restoring to "the extra groundless *Machinations of Men*."[74]

Cotton Mather thought this argument was theological and scientific nonsense. By then he had matured enough to keep from buckling under, and also had confidence in his understanding of the medical questions involved. (He had become known as one of the leading scientists of his day and was voted a member of the Royal Society in London.) Mather argued that God often uses human agencies and accomplishments to serve godly ends, and maintained that position when anti-inoculation politicians attacked him sharply. At one point a committee of Boston selectmen told Boylston to stop inoculations, but Boylston refused and Mather stuck to his supportive position, despite taking great abuse from the *News-Letter* and *Courant*.[75]

Those editors sided with officialdom and opposed inoculation; in doing so, they brought up Mather's defense of the Salem witch trials, and argued that he was deluded then and deluded again.[76] Mather this time did not give in. Because the *Boston Gazette* favored inoculation, Mather and his associates had a ready vehicle for their ideas. The debate raged for weeks, until it became clear that inoculation worked. Mather had erred once before in a crucial situation, but this time his journalistic effort saved lives.[77]

PART II

MACROSTORIES IN CONFLICT

Chapter 4

The Establishment of American Press Liberty

By 1730 the last British attempt to reassert licensing control over the feisty Puritans had failed, and Massachusetts journalism was generally peaceful. Editors such as Bartholomew Green, who succeeded John Campbell as owner of the *News-Letter* in 1723, emphasized press responsibility to help readers know "how to order their prayers and praises to the Great God."[1] Local news continued to be reported in reverential context, as in this coverage of a storm:

> The Water flowed over our Wharffs and into our streets to a very surprising height. They say the Tide rose 20 Inches higher than ever was known before . . . The loss and damage sustained is very great. . . . Let us fear the GOD of heaven, who made the sea and the dry land, who commandeth & raiseth the stormy wind, which lifteth up the waves; who ruleth the raging of the sea, and when the waves thereof arise, He stilleth them.[2]

As editor during a relatively quiet time, Green had the luxury to be known not primarily as a combative journalist but as a gentle man. When he died in 1733, an obituary described Green as "a very humble and exemplary Christian" known for "keeping close and diligent to the work of his calling."[3] In that same year, however, New York editor John Peter Zenger was thrust into the vortex of a controversy that would determine whether the press liberty developed in reformed New England could spread through the other colonies.

Zenger's *New York Weekly Journal* was not the first newspaper outside of New England. Many had been starting in a generally north-to-south movement:

the *New York Gazette* in 1724, the *Maryland Gazette* in 1727, and the *South Carolina Gazette* in 1732.[4] The first newspaper outside New England, the *American Weekly Mercury* (Philadelphia, 1719) had even shown a willingness to see God's sovereignty in politics, although at a distance. Editor Andrew Bradford wrote that Massachusetts royal officials were "remarkable for Hypocrisy: And it is the general Opinion, that some of their Rulers are rais'd up and continued as a Scourge in the Hands of the Almighty for the Sins of the People."[5] But no one outside of Boston had dared to criticize officials close at hand.

Zenger, however, put into practice the ideas taught in the Dutch Reformed church at which he played the organ each Sabbath — God's sovereignty, the Bible above all. He took on William Cosby, New York's royal governor, who clearly thought he was above the law. When a farmer's cart slowed down Cosby's coach, the governor had his coachman beat the farmer with a horsewhip and nearly kill him. When Cosby desired some land owned by Indians, he stole their deed and burned it. When Cosby granted new lands to those who applied legally, he demanded and received bribes often amounting to one third of the estates. Cosby made enemies who were willing to fund Zenger's newspaper and provide anonymous articles for it, but it was Zenger whose name was on the newspaper, and it was Zenger who would go to jail.

Zenger first sent a message in the *Journal*'s second issue by differentiating an absolute monarchy from one based on Biblical principles of fixed law and limitations on power. In an absolute monarchy, the article argued, the "Will of the Prince" was over all, and "a Liberty of the Press to complain of Grievances" was impossible.[6] In a limited monarchy, however,

> Laws are known, fixed, and established. They are the streight Rule and sure Guide to direct the King, the Ministers, and other his Subjects: And therefore an Offense against the Laws is such an Offense against the Constitution as ought to receive a proper adequate Punishment.[7]

Law (applying biblical principles) was above the king, not under him, just as the Bible itself was over all human royalty.

Such a belief undermined the official story in another way as well. Marchamont Nedham under pressure concluded that might makes right, but an early essay in the *Journal* pointedly asked, "If we reverence men for their power alone, why do we not reverence the Devil, who has so much more power than men?"[8] The article concluded that respect was due "only to virtuous qualities and useful actions," and that it was therefore "as ridiculous and superstitious to adore great mischievous men as it is to worship a false god or Satan in the stead of God."[9] Subjects had the right to evaluate their king. Obedience was not guaranteed.

The *Journal* prominently featured "Cato's Letters," written in England by John Trenchard and Thomas Gordon. They argued that governmental authority must be limited, and that such limitation was possible only if individuals were free to speak the truth to those in power. Everyone was to be restrained by Biblical principles of conduct: "Power without control appertains to God alone, and no man ought to be trusted with what no man is equal to."[10] Zenger also reprinted sermons emphasizing freedom from the official story's faith in kingly wisdom. One, by Jonathan Dickinson, argued that "Every person in the world has an equal right to judge for themselves, in the affairs of conscience and eternal salvation."[11] Dickinson showed that the lessons of not only royal domination but Cromwellian rule had been learned; he commented, "What dreadful work has been made in the world by using methods of force in matters of opinion and conscience."[12]

New York's royal governor, not wanting to admit that the state's domain was limited, brought a charge of "seditious libel" again Zenger and threw him into jail. Journalists at that time had little defense against such accusations. Journalists who proved that their statements were true might be even worse off. (Under English law truth made the libel worse by making it more likely that the statements would decrease public support for the king and his officials; a common legal expression was "the greater the truth, the greater the libel.") Jurors were only to determine whether the accused actually had printed the objectionable publication. If they agreed that he had, judges decided whether the statements in question were critical and deserved punishment.

The story of Zenger's trial on August 4, 1735, has often been told. The situation certainly was dramatic: Judges in their red robes and white wigs were ready to convict Zenger for his criticism of the royal governor, but the jury included "common People" among whom Zenger's newspaper had "gain'd some credit." A packed courtroom sympathetic to Zenger kept the judges from silencing defense attorney Andrew Hamilton when he turned directly to the jurors and suggested that they disobey English law: Hamilton wanted them to declare Zenger innocent even though he admitted to printing the material in question and was thus under the power of the judges. Hamilton argued that Zenger deserved such support because he had been "exposing and opposing arbitrary power by speaking and writing Truth," and the jurors agreed.[13] They delivered a verdict of "not guilty"; royal officials decided not to provoke a riot; Zenger went free.[14]

The story has often been told, but why it turned out as it did has rarely been understood. According to one leading textbook, *The Press and America,* the trial began because of a class uprising by "wealthy merchants and landowners" and ended with popular embrace of a "right to criticize officials."[15] But *The Press and America,* along with the other major 20th-century texts, does not explain what Zenger's defense of "speaking and writing Truth" meant in the context of his era. The trial records show that "Truth" was equated with the Bible, and Zenger was said to be merely following the lead of the Bible, which attacked corrupt leaders as "blind watchmen" and "greedy dogs that can never have enough." Zenger's defense, essentially, was that if God's authors produced such a critique, so could New York's.[16]

The context of Zenger's defense is clarified further by an essay published in his newspaper, the *New York Journal,* in 1733. The article proposed that true freedom required the subjecting of consciences "to divine authority," because only through the Bible would people know how to use liberty without turning it into license.[17] In historical context, then, the Zenger verdict was not what the texts say it was: a "class uprising" that led to a proclamation of freedom *from* any restraint. Instead, the journalistic desire to be governed by "Truth" in this context was a desire to *accept* a system of internal restraints developed from biblical principles.

In short, Hamilton won the case not by proposing a new revelation, but by placing Zenger in the line of Martin Luther, John Foxe, John Stubbes, March-amont Nedham, Increase Mather, and others. Zenger was one more victim of what Hamilton called "the Flame of Prosecutions upon Informations, set on Foot by the Government, to deprive a People of the Right of Remonstrating (and complaining too), of the arbitrary Attempts of Men in Power."[18] Only the spread of Reformation principles concerning literacy, independent journalism, and the rights of citizens to read for themselves, allowed Hamilton to turn to the jurors and ask them to support the truth-teller, regardless of what royal officials desired.[19]

The verdict meant little legally: A runaway jury had disobeyed established English law and gotten away with it. But as the verdict reverberated through the colonies and through England itself, it encouraged corruption story proponents and discouraged the officials from trying printers for seditious libel; no case of that sort was brought anywhere in America after 1735. The year after the Zenger case, Virginia had its first newspaper—the *Virginia Gazette,* published in Williamsburg. Editor William Parks exposed corruption, including the stealing of sheep by a member of Virginia's House of Burgesses. When Parks was threatened with prosecution, he used the Zenger defense of truth-telling and produced court records showing the accusation was accurate; the case against Parks was dropped. By 1750 there were 14 weekly newspapers published in the British colonies, and the first semiweekly and triweekly newspapers had emerged.

Increasingly, the newspapers were independent of governmental control and free to provide, as *Maryland Gazette* editor Jonas Green promised his readers, not just "a Weekly Account of the most remarkable Occurrences, foreign and domestic," but also an examination of "whatever may conduce to the Promotion of Virtue and Learning, the Suppression of Vice and Immorality, and the Instruction as well as Entertainment of our Readers."[20] Newspapers ran lively debates on many subjects, including politics. The idea that fundamental law came from God, not from the state or from any persons, was opening the door to questioning of many traditions, including even monarchical control. Journalist Elisha Williams argued in 1744 that:

The Powers that be in Great Britain are the Government therein according to its own Constitution:—If then the higher Powers for the Administration rule not according to that Constitution, or if any King thereof shall rule so, as to change the Government from legal to arbitrary . . . no Subjection [is] due to it.[21]

Journalists were the ones who would have "Eyes to see" when rulers went "out of the Line of their Power."[22]

At the same time, the lessons of the failed Puritan Revolution — particularly those concerning the lure and potential abuse of power—were well known to the colonists. Recent college graduate Samuel Adams wrote in 1748,

Neither the wisest constitution nor the wisest laws will secure the liberty and happiness of a people whose manners are universally corrupt. He therefore is the truest friend to the liberty of his country who tries most to promote its virtue.[23]

His conclusion was:

The sum of all is, if we would most truly enjoy this gift of Heaven, let us become a virtuous people: then shall we both deserve and enjoy it. While, on the other hand, if we are universally vicious and debauched in our manners, though the form of our Constitution carries the face of the most exalted freedom, we shall in reality be the most abject slaves.[24]

During the Seven Years (French and Indian) War of 1756 to 1763, colonial newspapers were free to bring charges of graft against those supplying American troops; for example, the *New-York Gazette and Weekly Post-Boy* reported that many of the guns purchased were out of date and practically useless, and joked that beef supplied for soldiers' food was more effective than powder because its odor would drive away the enemy. That such charges, when well-founded, could be made without legal repercussion, showed how firmly independent journalism was established in America. The colonists found themselves surprised, then, after the war, when England began to crack down.

Samuel Adams led the protests in Massachusetts. If transported to our present age of television journalism, Adams would be a washout: he had a sunken chest, a sallow complexion and "wishy-washy gray eyes."[25] Adams' lips twitched and trembled, for he suffered from palsy. His clothes were drab and sometimes sloppy. Besides, Adams was a financial misfit who lived in an old, shabby house, and wrote much but earned little. John Adams put the best complexion on the surface prospects of his cousin when he wrote that "in common appearance he was a plain, simple, decent citizen, of middling stature, dress, and manners."[26]

Looking beyond appearances, however, Adams possessed advantages. His good classical education made ancient times as real to him as his own; references to the political ups and downs of ancient Israel, Greece, and Rome came easily to his pen. He had the ability to write under almost any conditions. Adams typically composed his columns after evening prayers; his wife Elizabeth would go to bed but would sometimes wake in the middle of the night and hear only the sound of her husband's quill pen scratching on and on. But when Adams had to, he could write forceful prose amidst a town meeting.

Adams was also in the right place, at what became the right time. He lived in America's largest port city, and the second largest city in all of the colonies, after Philadelphia. The 20,000 residents of Boston in 1770 may not seem like many now, but at that time they were enough to support six weekly newspapers, including, during the decade before revolutionary warfare broke out, the *Boston Gazette*. The *Gazette* was published every Monday afternoon, and a crowd often awaited its issues hot off the press. Adams had a regular column but never signed his own name to it. Instead, he used a pen name—such as "A Puritan"—that connected him with independent journalism's honorable lineage. Other columnists did the same; for example, Josiah Quincy, Jr. signed his columns, "Marchamont Nedham."

Furthermore, Adams was modest. He did not write about himself, and had no problem with being in the background. Many journalists today make themselves the stars of their stories, but Adams believed that "political literature was to be as selfless as politics itself, designed to promote its cause, not its author."[27] Adams' self-effacement has made life harder for some historians: John Adams wrote that his cousin's personality would "never be accurately known to posterity, as it was never sufficiently known to its own age." (A minister wrote on October 3, 1803, the day after Adams' death, that there had been "an impenetrable secrecy" about him.[28]) But Adams' willingness to have others take the credit worked wonders during his time. He chaired town meetings and led the applause for those who needed bucking up; for example, he pulled John Hancock onto the patriot side and promoted Hancock's career.

And, Adams had a strong belief in the God of the Bible. The Great Awakening had made a permanent theological impression on him. That impression is evident in Adams' writings and actions, in his prayers each morning and in his family Bible reading each evening. He frequently emphasized the importance of "Endeavors to promote the spiritual kingdom of Jesus Christ," and in good or bad times wrote of the need "to submit to the Dispensations of Heaven, Whose Ways are ever gracious, ever just.' "[29] During the struggle of the 1760s and 1770s Adams regularly set aside days of fasting and prayer to "seek the Lord." In 1777, when Adams wrote to a friend about the high points of one celebration, he stressed the sermon delivered that day; the friend wrote back, "An epicure would have said something about the clams, but you turn me to the prophet Isaiah."[30]

Adams, in short, worked within the tradition of Foxe, Mather, and others who called for reformation, not social revolution. John Adams called Samuel the Calvin of his day, and "a Calvinist" to the core.[31] (William Tudor in 1823 called Adams "a strict Calvinist . . . no individual of his day had so much the feelings of the ancient puritans." For Tudor, that meant Adams had "too much sternness and pious bigotry."[32]) Yet, Adams did not merely rely on established procedures; he advanced the practice and significance of American journalism in four ways.

First, observing that "mankind are governed more by their feelings than by reason," Adams emphasized appeals to the whole person, not just to a disembodied intellect.[33] Emotions were to be taken seriously, for the "fears and jealousies of the people are not always groundless: And when they become general, it is not to be presum'd that they are; for the people in general seldom complain, without some good reason.[34] Adams assumed democratically that an issue of importance to the populace is not silly.[35] He argued that ordinary citizens could "distinguish between *realities* and *sounds*'; and by a proper use of that reason which Heaven has given them,' they can judge, as well as their betters, when there is danger of *slavery*."[36]

Second, Adams emphasized investigative reporting more vigorously than any American journalist before him had: He did so because "Publick Liberty will not long survive the Loss of publick Virtue."[37] Adams argued that it was vital to track activities of those:

> who are watching every Opportunity to turn the good or ill Fortune of their Country, and they care not which to their own private Advantage. . . . Such Men there always have been & always will be, till human Nature itself shall be substantially meliorated.[38]

He went on to praise exposure of leaders who "having gained the Confidence of their Country, are sacrilegiously employing their Talents to the Ruin of its Affairs, for their own private Emolument."[39] Adams, however, emphasized restraint in such exposure, as he emphasized restraint in all actions: Only those "capable of doing great Mischief' should be held up "to the publick Eye."[40]

Third, Adams defined more thoroughly than his predecessors the limits of protest. His strong sense of lawfulness is indicated by his reactions to two incidents, the Stamp Act demonstrations of August 1765, and the related attacks on private homes such as that of Thomas Hutchinson, the royal governor. Adams favored the former action because legislative methods and petitions already had failed; the House of Commons would not listen, so the demonstration "was the only Method whereby they could make known their Objections to Measures."[41] He opposed the assault on the Hutchinson home, calling it an action of "a truly *mobbish* Nature."[42] When Adams and his colleagues planned the Boston Tea Party, they made it clear that nothing except tea was to be destroyed; when the patriots dressed as "Indians" accidentally broke a padlock, they later replaced it.[43]

So far was Adams from revolution in the way the term is currently understood that he wrote, in the *Boston Gazette* in 1768, that the security of right and property, is the great end of government. Surely, then, such measures as tend to render right and property precarious, tend to destroy both property and government; for these must stand and fall together.[44]

He opposed dictatorship, whether popular or monarchical:

The Utopian schemes of levelling, and a community of goods, are as visionary and impracticable, as those which vest all property in the Crown, are arbitrary, despotic, and in our government unconstitutional. Now what property can the colonists be conceived to have, if their money may be granted away by others, without their consent?[45]

Some of the patriots did not share Adams' emphasis on restraint, and it is not hard to compile a list of patriots' "mobbish" acts. Yet the principles of the revolutionaries, and most of their practice, emphasized defense of property and freedom of political speech.

Fourth, Adams argued that writers should pay careful attention to the connection between attacks on political rights and attempts to restrict religious rights. In a *Boston Gazette* column that he signed, "A Puritan," Adams described how he was pleased with attention paid to politics but

surpriz'd to find, that so little attention is given to the danger we are in, of the utter loss of those *religious Rights,* the enjoyment of which our good forefathers had more especially in their intention, when they explored and settled this new world.[46]

He saw acquiescence in political slavery as preparation for submission to religious slavery:

I could not help fancying that the Stamp-Act itself was contrived with a design only to inure the people to the habit of contemplating themselves as the slaves of men; and the transition from thence to a subjection to Satan, is mighty easy.[47]

It is astounding that some historians have seen Adams solely as a political plotter; for Adams, the religious base came first. One of his arguments against imposed taxes was that the money could go for establishment of a state "Episcopate in America . . . the revenue raised in America, for ought we can tell, may be constitutionally applied towards the support of prelacy. . ."[48]

Adams favored investigative reporting and appropriate emotional appeal because he wanted readers to know about and *care about* attempts to take away their freedom, political and religious. He opposed destructive revolutionary acts because he saw them as eventually reducing freedom, political and religious—with the results of the English civil war as a case in point. From all these strands

Adams was able to weave an understanding of when journalists, and citizens generally, should be willing to fight.

The understanding came out of the Puritan idea of *covenant* and its political–economic corollary, *contract*. In 1765 Adams had written of himself and his neighbors,

> We are the Descendants of Ancestors remarkable for their Zeal for true Religion & Liberty: When they found it was no longer possible for them to bear any Part in the Support of this glorious Cause in their Native Country England, they transplanted themselves at their own very great Expence, into the Wilds of America. . . .[49]

Their ancestors took those risks in order to establish "the Worship of God, according to their best Judgment, upon the Plan of the new Testament; to maintain it among themselves, and transmit it to their Posterity."[50] Crucially, they did so on the basis of a signed contract: "A Charter was granted them by King Charles the first," Adams noted, and "a successor charter" was granted (through the lobbying of Increase Mather) in 1691.[51]

Adams, in column after column, explained the basis of the contract: The colonists "promised the King to enlarge his Dominion, on their own Charge, provided that They & their Posterity might enjoy such & such Privileges."[52] Adams wrote that the colonists "have performed their Part, & for the King to deprive their Posterity of the Privileges, therein granted, would carry the Face of Injustice in it." Colloquially, a deal's a deal, and London's attempt to tax the colonists was one indication that the deal was being broken, because the charter gave the colonists "an exclusive Right to make Laws for our own internal Government & Taxation."[53]

In emphasizing the breaking of the contract, Adams was not developing new political theology. John Calvin had written that "Every commonwealth rests upon laws and agreements," and had then noted "the mutual obligation of head and members." John Cotton, following that line of argument, had concluded that "the rights of him who dissolves the contract are forfeited."[54] Puritans long had insisted that just as God establishes a covenant with man, so kings have a contract with their subjects (and although God would never break His agreement, kings often did). But Adams took that idea and developed from it a theory of when writers should criticize and when they should refrain from criticism. Once a government had been established along biblical principles, criticism of its departure from those principles was proper—but criticism designed to topple the government in order to establish it on new principles was improper.

To put this another way, Adams in the 1770s approved of a conservative revolution designed to restore previously contracted rights, but not a violent social revolution designed to establish new conditions. This made sense not only as a pragmatic way to avoid bloodshed and chaos, but because of Adams' belief (expressed as early as 1748) that societies in any case represent the strengths and weaknesses of their members. The real need in a contract-based society was individual change (which can lead to social change) and not social revolution.

Other New England writers also argued that London had broken its contract with the colonists. John Lathrop declared in 1774 that a person who "makes an alteration in the established constitution, whether he be a subject or a ruler, is guilty of treason." He asserted that colonists "may and ought, to resist, and even make war against those rulers who leap the bounds prescribed them by the constitution, and attempt to oppress and enslave the subjects. . . ."[55] Lathrop, after referring to writings of Luther, Calvin, Melancthon, and Zwingli, concluded that King and Parliament, by attempting to lord it over colonial assemblies, were overthrowing England's constitution.[56]

During the 1770s patriots outside of New England also expressed such ideas. The single book most quoted by Americans during the founding era was the Book of Deuteronomy, with its emphasis on covenant.[57] The *South-Carolina Gazette* expressed concern that British officials were claiming "the power of breaking all our charters."[58] A columnist in the *Pennsylvania Evening Post* declared that "resisting the *just* and *lawful* power of government" was rebellion but resisting "*unjust* and *usurped* power was not."[59] The *Virginia Gazette* saw British authorities moving to apply "the Rod of Despotism" to "every Colony that moves in Defence of Liberty."[60] In Connecticut, the *Norwich Packet* argued that liberty was like an inheritance, "a sacred deposit which it would be treason against Heaven to betray."[61]

The patriotic journalists sometimes used non-political stories to make their points. The *Boston Evening-Post* reported a hanging: "Saturday last was executed Harry Halbert, pursuant to his sentence, for the murder of the son of Jacob Wollman.—He will never pay any of the taxes unjustly laid on these once happy lands."[62] Rather than raging against the British system generally, they pointed to specific violations of the contract. Massachusetts citizens were supposed to be able to control their own government, with the royal governor having a relatively minor role and not a large bureaucracy—but Josiah Quincy, Jr., in the *Boston Gazette,* showed how "pensioners, stipendiaries, and salary-men" were "hourly multiplying on us."[63] In New Hampshire, the Executive Council was supposed to provide the governor with a broad array of colonists' views; the colony's correspondent complained in the *Boston Evening-Post* that relatives of Governor John Wentworth filled all but one Council seat.[64]

Increasingly, the patriot journalists saw such exposure of corruption as part of their calling. Adams wrote in the *Boston Gazette,* "There is nothing so *fretting* and *vexatious,* nothing so justly TERRIBLE to tyrants, and their tools and abettors, as a FREE PRESS."[65] Isaiah Thomas, editor of *The Massachusetts Spy,* wrote that, without a free press, there would be "padlocks on our lips, fetters on our legs, and only our hands left at liberty to slave for our worse than Egyptian task masters. . . ."[66] But again, the emphasis was on officeholders' betrayal of existing laws, not on revolutionary imposition of new ones: The mission of the

Boston Gazette, its editors declared, was to "strip the serpents of their stings, & consign to disgrace, all those guileful betrayers of their country."[67]

Examination of many of the stories leading up to the revolution shows how steeped in the Bible the patriot journalists were. That is not surprising, because in New England alone during 1776, ministers were "delivering over two thousand discourses a week and publishing them at an unprecedented rate that outnumbered secular pamphlets (from all the colonies) by a ratio of more than four to one."[68] That is also not surprising because, right up to the revolutionary war, ballads concerning bad news were still putting their stories in corruption story context; for example, in 1774, a fire story noted that "There's not a Day goes by, but we behold/ A Truth, that Men need often to be told:/ That this vain World with all it's glit'ring Toys,/ Does but deceive the Mind with empty Joys."[69] It was natural for the *Massachusetts Spy* to comment simply but evocatively, when the Intolerable Acts closed the Port of Boston, "Tell it in Gath, publish it in Ashkelon."[70]

Under extreme pressure, Adams' response to the Intolerable Acts, contained in a resolution passed by Suffolk County, continued to emphasize contract, not revolution. The resolution recommended economic sanctions against the British and proposed the formation of an armed patriot militia, but it also attacked any attempt

by unthinking persons to commit outrage upon private property; we would heartily recommend to all persons of this community not to engage in riots, routs, or licentious attacks upon the properties of any person whatsoever, as being subversive of all order and government.[71]

Newspapers portrayed the war, once begun, as a defense of order and legitimate government: "We have taken up arms, it is true," the *Virginia Gazette* noted, "but this we have an undoubted right to do, in defence of the British constitution."[72]

Samuel Adams had his counterparts in other colonies: Cornelius Harnett was called "the Samuel Adams of North Carolina" and Charles Thomson was called "the Samuel Adams of Philadelphia."[73] But Adams himself was the best at taking Bible based theories and heightening them journalistically. His printed response to the adoption of the Declaration of Independence shows Adams at his finest, and shows his sense of God's providence."[74] Adams began,

We have explored the temple of royalty, and found that the idol we have bowed down to has eyes which see not, ears that hear not our prayers, and a heart like the nether millstone. We have this day restored the Sovereign to whom alone men ought to be obedient.[75]

He explained that previous generations:

lopped off, indeed, some of the branches of Popery, but they left the root and stock when they left us under the domination of human systems and decisions, usurping the infallibility which can be attributed to revelation alone. They dethroned one usurper, only to raise up another; they refused allegiance to the Pope, only to place the civil magistrate in the throne of Christ, vested with authority to enact laws and inflict penalties in his kingdom.[76]

Adams followed those statements with his key rhetorical question: "Were the talents and virtues which Heaven has bestowed on men given merely to make them more obedient drudges, to be sacrificed to the follies and ambition of a few. . .?" He responded,

What an affront to the King of the universe to maintain that the happiness of a monster sunk in debauchery . . . is more precious in his sight than that of millions of his suppliant creatures who do justice, love mercy, and walk humbly with their God![77]

He crescendoed with the editorial fervency that moved a generation:

The hand of Heaven appears to have led us on to be, perhaps, humble instruments and means in the great providential dispensation which is completing. We have fled from the political Sodom; let us not look back, lest we perish and become a monument of infamy and derision to the world![78]

Chapter 5

First Surge of the Oppression Story

In the end, the patriots saw their victory as a victory of ideas, disseminated through newspapers. As the editor of the *New York Journal* noted in a letter to Adams, "It was by means of News papers that we receiv'd & spread the Notice of the tyrannical Designs formed against America, and kindled a Spirit that has been sufficient to repel them."[1] British officials had a different perspective: Admiral Howe's secretary Ambrose Serles complained,

> Among other Engines, which have raised the present Commotion next to the indecent Harranges of the Prechers, none has a more extensive or stronger influence than the Newspapers of the respective Colonies.[2]

British leaders were appalled that Samuel Adams' central idea of corruption in leadership had defeated their official story of faith in King.

Yet, had the British better known their own country's history, the shock would have been less. Adams, continuing what John Foxe had begun two centuries ago, was merely showing once again that nations rose and fell primarily because of world views, often communicated through journalistic means. By the 1760s, 250 years had passed since Martin Luther first showed the potential power of journalism. During that time, the uses of sensationalism, investigation, and accurate exposure had become apparent, and principles of reforming but non-revolutionary journalism and contextualized coverage had been established.

Those concepts formed the baseline for journalism in the new republic. Some historians call the last quarter of the 18th century a deistic period, and sentiment of that sort certainly was present and growing among societal elites at Harvard College and elsewhere. Yet, in reporting of both crime and political news, news ballads and newspapers of the 1780s and 1790s continued the corruption story emphasis, with its "good news" conclusion. Coverage of a New Hampshire execution, for example, emphasized the evil that had been done, but concluded "O may that God/ Who gave his only Son,/ Give you his grace, in Heaven a place,/ For Jesus' sake—Amen."[3]

Newspapers, rather than embracing deism, often portrayed it as containing the seeds of its own destruction. In 1782, for example, 6 days after a man had killed his wife and four children and then himself, the *Connecticut Courant* reported the news and then contextualized: The perpetrator had

> rejected all Revelation as imposition, and (as he expresses himself) 'renouncing all the popular Religions of the world, intended to die a proper Deist.' Having discarded all ideas of moral good and evil, he considered himself, and all the human race, as mere machines; and that he had a right to dispose of his own and the lives of his family.[4]

The *Courant* related how the man gave opiates to his family and then went around slaughtering the sleepers with knife and ax—but the incident really began when the man "adopted this new theoretic system which he now put in practice."[5] Ideas had consequences.

The most famous journalistic work of the 1780s was *The Federalist*, a collection of 95 columns published in New York newspapers during 1787 and 1788. The columns, written under the pen name of "Publius" by Alexander Hamilton, James Madison, and John Jay, and designed to convince New York voters to ratify the Constitution, showed a thoroughly biblical view of the effects of sin on political life. Madison argued that "faction"—power-grabbing attempts by groups of citizens "united and actuated by some common impulse of passion, adverse to the rights of other citizens"—was impossible to avoid because it grew out of "the nature of man."[6] Hamilton emphasized the "active and imperious control over human conduct" that "momentary passions and immediate interests" would "invariably" assume.[7]

Other pen-named columnists of the period also argued that the nature of man would lead to attempts at dictatorship, unless careful restraint was maintained. "Brutus" (probably Robert Yates, an Albany lawyer) wrote, "It is a truth confirmed by the unerring experience of ages that every man, and every body of men, invested with power, are ever disposed to increase it"; lust for power was "implanted in human nature."[8] The only way to fight the lust was to divide in order to avoid conquest—to limit and decentralize governmental power and to allow private interests to check each other. As Madison wrote in *Federalist* No. 51,

The policy of supplying, by opposite and rival interests, the defect of better motives, might be traced through the whole system of human affairs, private as well as public. We see it particularly displayed in all the subordinate distributions of power, where the constant aim is to divide and arrange the several offices in such a manner as that each may be a check on the other; that the private interest of every individual may be a sentinel over the public rights. These inventions of prudence cannot be less requisite in the distribution of the supreme power of the state.[9]

The press also had a vital role in this slow but freedom-preserving system of checks and balances. John Adams, after noting that the Constitution stipulated the election of key leaders, asked "How are their characters and conduct to be known to their constituents but by the press? If the press is stopped and the people kept in Ignorance we had much better have the first magistrate and Senators hereditary."[10] In Alexandria, Virginia, the *Gazette* also thought the press was vital in the plan to limit governmental power, for

Here too public men and measures are scrutinized. Should any man or body of men dare to form a system against our interests, by this means it will be unfolded to the great body of the people, and the alarm instantly spread through every part of the continent. In this way only, can we know how far our public servants perform the duties of their respective stations.[11]

Such ideas underlay the First Amendment's insistence that "Congress shall make no law . . . abridging the freedom of speech, or of the press." Cromwellian restrictions on the press following the English Civil War showed how quickly a victorious government might clamp down on those trying to check its power; freedom needed to be maintained. Yet, the freedom was not to be absolute. As John Allen of Connecticut argued,

Because the Constitution guarantees the freedom of the press, am I at liberty to falsely call you a thief, a murderer, an atheist? The freedom of the press was never understood to give the right of publishing falsehoods and slanders, nor of exciting sedition, insurrection, and slaughter with impunity. A man was always answerable for the malicious publication of falsehood.[12]

John Adams put it succinctly: Journalism is to be free "within the bounds of truth."[13] Pennsylvania adopted the Zenger principle of truth as a defense in its libel law, and other states would follow.

The first major test of newly established press freedom in America grew out of the French Revolution. France, after turning aside opportunities for Reformation during the 1500s, never had developed decentralized spheres of authority: king and church together continued to claim all power. France never had developed the mass literacy and movement toward independent journalism that animated English during the 1600s and its American colonies during the 1700s. When the monarchy fell in 1789 and church power also diminished, journalists untrained in self-restraint leaped into the enormous vacuum. As historian James Billington has noted, "In revolutionary France journalism rapidly arrogated to itself the Church's former role as the propagator of values, models, and symbols for society at large."[14]

Those French journalistic values were very different from those of Samuel Adams or the *Federalist* authors. French journalists such as Marat were students of Jean-Jacques Rousseau, who demanded not a restrained state but a total state. Rousseau argued that man was essentially good and would, with a proper education, act virtuously. Education was too important to be trusted to parents or churches, so it would be up to the state to teach all children to become "social men by their natures and citizens by their inclinations—they will be one, they will be good, they will be happy, and their happiness will be that of the Republic."[15]

As Paul Johnson has noted, Rousseau's ideas demanded total submission of all individuals to the state. The ideal constitution Rousseau drafted for Corsica required all citizens to swear, "I join myself, body, goods, will and all my powers, to the Corsican Nation, granting her ownership of me, of myself and all who depend on me." State-controlled citizens would be happy, because all would be trained to like their master and to find their personal significance in its grace: "For being nothing except by [the state], they will be nothing except for it. It will have all they have and will be all they are." State control of communication was thus a complement to state control of education, because "those who control a people's opinions control its actions."

Some of this may sound gruesome, but the goal was to create a new type of person by creating a new environment. Rousseau argued that "Everything is at root dependent on politics," because everything can change if only a new social system is created: "Vices belong less to man, than to man badly governed." Individuals had no rights when they stood against the "General Will." This was completely the opposite of the American pattern of a limited government designed to keep sinful men from gaining any more power than absolutely necessary. It also ran counter to the American concept of a limiting press, one designed not to rule but to report on wrongdoing and confront readers with the workings of Providence.

Ideas had consequences. Cromwell had executed a king and several others; the French revolutionaries executed 20,000 in 2 years, then turned on themselves. For a short time after 1789 all French journalists had some freedom. Then only the few in power did, and opponents risked their lives: In 1793 the French National Council decreed the death penalty for anyone who was convicted of writing anything that promoted dissolution of the National Assembly or restoration of the monarchy. (Two journalists were executed, 56 more were arrested or exiled, 42 journals were suspended, and 11 presses were smashed.) Eventually, no journalists had freedom, as a military dictator, Napoleon Bonaparte, seized power.

French journalists, demanding much, helped to create the conditions under which all could be lost. American journalists had grounded themselves in firmly established legal principles, but the French revolutionaries basked in illegality. The American Revolution was a defense of established rights, but the French revolution was an offensive for new entitlements. The American Revolution had fixed goals, but the French Revolution was a star trek—"let's head out there."

Different goals created different reactions. Because the American Revolution was limited, resistance to it was limited. Because the French revolution was unlimited, resistance to it inevitably would grow. That was fine, believed the revolutionaries, because their goal was to break down everything; the current environment was one of *oppression*. Individual change was insufficient, and those who strove for it were selfish, but through total transformation of the oppressive environment mankind could be transformed. Faith that this could occur through governmental action, if vast power were put in the right hands, underlies what I call the *oppression story*. Journalists saw themselves as the transformers; for example, Nicholas Bonneville, editor of *Le Tribun de Peuple,* saw his journal as a "circle of light" whose writers were to be "simultaneously a centre of light and a body of resistance." They were to be "legislators of the universe," preparing a "vast plan of universal regeneration" based on belief in "the Infallibility of the People."[16] But, because the people were to act according to what journalists told them, for Bonneville that pledge essentially meant, "I believe in my own infallibility."

In the United States, a few writers heavily influenced by Rousseauian thought also took that pledge. The leader of the pack was Benjamin Franklin Bache, who had been educated in France while living there with his grandfather Ben Franklin. Bache demanded direct rule by "the people" who were coursing in the streets, and cursed those advocates of separation of power who pointed out the virtues of representative democracy. Typical of Bache's style was his labeling of George Washington as "the man who is the source of all the misfortune of our country."[17] He went on to charge Washington with having "debauched" and "deceived" Americans, and then left as his successor "bald, blind, crippled, toothless Adams."[18]

Adams during his presidency also was regularly defamed by francophile editors such as James Callender, who falsely called Adams a traitor and charged that he had "proved faithful and serviceable to the British interest."[19] Adams was bald, but he could see, walk, and bite back. He opposed plans of Bache and others that "would lead in practice to a hidden despotism, concealed under the party-colored garment of democracy." He attacked those set on "contaminating the country with the foul abomination of the French revolution."[20] Speaker of the House Jonathan Dayton warned of a French-style revolution in America, with assistance from the French navy and French troops invading from the former French territories of Canada and Louisiana. Lawyer Jonathan Hopkinson warned Americans that Bache and his supporters desire "the overthrow of your government and constitution."[21]

Underlying the danger were the ideas; one congressman attacked philosophers who believed in "the perfectability of mankind" and thus became the "pioneers of revolution."[22] Yale University President Timothy Dwight warned of the danger of "the Bible cast into a bonfire . . . our wives and daughters the victims of legal prostitution . . . our sons become the disciples of Voltaire . . ."[23] Some leading journalists were seen as revolutionary moles; Bache, for example, was depicted as a French agent, a "dull-edged, dull-eyed, hagard-looking hireling of France," and Thomas Paine's radicalism and atheism was much decried.[24]

The controversy led to a lowering of self-restraint on both sides. Supreme Court chief justice McKean in 1798 accurately described conditions when he noted "the envenomed scurrility that has raged in pamphlets and newspapers printed in Philadelphia for several years past, insomuch that libeling has become a national crime." He added:

> the contest has been who could call names in the greatest variety of phrases; who could mangle the greatest number of characters, or who could excel in the magnitude of their lies; hence the honor of families has been stained, the highest posts rendered cheap and vile in the sight of the people, and the greatest services and virtue blasted.[25]

How easy it is to tear down, as editor John Dillingham had noted following the Cromwellian takeover in England.

Critics of the press revived the common mid-century distinction between liberty and license—and there was widespread concern that journalists were not using wisely the freedom they had gained. One of Benjamin Franklin's last statements about journalism was a complaint:

> Now many of our printers make no scruple of gratifying the malice of individuals by false accusations of the fairest characters among themselves, augmenting animosity even to the producing of duels, and are, moreover, so indiscreet as to print scurrilous reflections on the government of neighboring states, and even on the conduct of our best national allies, which may be attended with the most pernicious consequences.[26]

Franklin proposed a combination: freedom of the press plus "liberty of the cudgel." Libel laws should be tougher, Franklin suggested, for government officials "at the same time that they secure the person of a citizen from assaults, they would likewise provide for the security of his reputation."[27]

Charles Lee was confident in 1798 that careful lines could be drawn between liberty and license: "The freedom of the press differs from the licentiousness of the press, and the laws which restrain the latter, will always be found to affirm and preserve the former."[28] The Federalists, then the majority party in Congress, searched for the right formula and in 1798 passed the Sedition Act, which stated that "false, scandalous and malicious writing" aimed at the President and other officials was punishable "by a fine not exceeding two thousand dollars, and by imprisonment not exceeding two years."

The furor created by the Sedition Act was surprising in some ways. As Leonard Levy has noted, the act was

> the very epitome of libertarian thought since the time of Zenger's case. The Sedition Act incorporated everything that the libertarians had demanded: a requirement that criminal intent be shown; the power of the jury to decide whether the accused's statement was libelous as a matter of law as well as of fact; and truth as a defense, an innovation not accepted in England until 1843.[29]

But in those charged times the Act was quickly turned into a political weapon not against disloyal revolutionists but against the loyal opposition, the Jeffersonians. The Sedition Act, on the books from July 14, 1798—appropriately, Bastille Day—to its expiration in 1801, led to 14 indictments, 11 trials, and 10 convictions. Four of the five major Republican papers, including the *Boston Independent-Chronicle,* the *New York Argus,* and the *Richmond Examiner* were penalized.

Once some of the less scrupulous Federalists seized the opportunity to prosecute their opponents, the legal situation rapidly deteriorated. For example, Matthew (Spitting) Lyon, a Congressman-editor from Vermont, was jailed for 4 months and fined $1,000 merely for charging John Adams with "unbounded thirst for ridiculous pomp, foolish adulation, and selfish avarice."[30] Lyon was obnoxious—he gained his nickname for spitting in the face of a Congressional opponent during a debate in which words failed him—but opinions of that sort could be fought with scorn rather than suppression. When Lyon's constituents reelected him to the House of Representatives from jail, he became a hero.[31]

Local Federalist politicians overreached even more when a drunkard named Luther Baldwin was arrested while Adams was passing through Newark, New Jersey, on his way from the capital (then in Philadelphia) to his home in Quincy, Massachusetts. One barfly, noting that Adams had already passed by but the cannons for his 16-gun salute still were firing, commented, "There goes the president and they are firing at his ass." Baldwin, drunk, said, "I don't care if they fire through his ass." Arrested for that statement and jailed for several days, Baldwin also emerged a hero.

We might say that the law itself made sense—indeed, was a great leap forward—but its execution was poor. The trouble, however, is that laws of that type always tend to be passed in situations so heated that the execution is likely to be terrible. Armed with examples of abuses, proponents of absolute freedom for journalists went on the offensive. John Nicolas of Virginia denied that journalistic liberty could be distinguished from "licentiousness," or "truth" from "falsehood."[32] George Hay in Philadelphia published *An Essay on the Liberty of the Press* that argued for total freedom for even "false, scandalous, and malicious" comments; Hay's goal was that "A man may say every thing which his passions suggest . . ."[33] Others argued similarly.

The legal debate ended in a draw that lasted for over a century. The extreme views of Nicolas, Hay, and others were not embraced by the courts. The Sedition Act was allowed to expire in 1801; Congress enacted no other Sedition Act until World War I. Instead of either absolute freedom of federal control, the formula for the nineteenth century became that proclaimed by the Massachusetts supreme court in *Commonwealth v. Clap* (1808). The court observed that critiques of government officials or candidates, if true, "are not a libel. For it would be unreasonable to conclude that the publication of truths, which it is in the interests of the people to know, should be an offense against their laws."[34] The court also added sternly, however, that

> For the same reason, the publication of falsehood and calumny against public officers, or candidates for public offices, is an offense most dangerous to the people, and deserves punishment, because the people may be deceived, and reject the best citizens, to their great injury, and it may be to the loss of their liberties.[35]

Truth was a defense against prosecution for libel, but falsehood was no defense. The Zenger jury's faith was now law, and "license" still was excluded.

The political debate also ended in a compromise. Some political fallout was immediate: The Sedition Act helped the Federalists lose the presidential election of 1800. But by 1800, the sails of American supporters of revolutionary ideas were drooping—in large part because potential supporters had seen the consequences of those ideas played out in France. Some of the leading revolutionary journalists left the country (or were pushed out under the Alien Act). Other left this world; Benjamin Franklin Bache died of yellow fever as the Sedition Law was going into effect. But others, witnessing the brutality of the Revolution and its ending in Napoleon's dictatorship, turned away from revolution and the ideas that brought on revolution. On his deathbed, Thomas Paine retracted all the attacks on Christianity he had made in his last book, *The Age of Reason*. He said, "I would give worlds, if I had them, if *The Age of Reason* had never been published. O Lord, help me! Christ, help me! Stay with me! It is hell to be left alone."[36]

Thus ended the first attempt to bring to American journalism the *oppression story* faith that if man's environment were changed through social revolution, man himself would change. But few Americans at that time, trained as they were in biblical ideas of original sin in human nature, were buying such a concept. Instead, the first three decades of the 19th century showed an increasing number of publications that were explicitly Christian in orientation. The total number of newspapers rose from 359 in 1810 to 851 in 1828 and 1,265 in 1834—and, as one contemporary observer noted, "Of all the issues of the press three-fourths are theological, ethical, and devotional."[37] The *New York Christian Advocate* became the largest circulation weekly in the country, with 25,000 subscribers in 1828 and 30,000 in 1830.[38]

With the centralizing attempts of the revolutionaries defeated, the United States was able to continue its decentralized development. As Alexis de Tocqueville observed of early 19th-century America,

> It is in the township, the center of the ordinary business of life, that the desire for esteem [and] the pursuit of substantial interests . . . are concentrated; these passions, so often troublesome elements in society, take on a different character when exercised so close to home and, in a sense, within the family circle. . . . Daily duties performed or rights exercised keep municipal life constantly alive. There is a continual gentle political activity which keeps society on the move without turmoil.[39]

In many European countries, national newspapers emphasized politics above all else; in America, where the central institutions were family, church, and local organization, local newspapers thrived.

In this quiet period for American journalism hundreds of unsung editors went about their business of reporting both sinfulness and special providences. One typical editor, Nathaniel Willis, had at one time been impressed by the journalism of Benjamin Bache. Born in 1780, Willis from 1802 to 1807 edited a vitriolic Maine newspaper, the *Portland Eastern Argus,* and aspired to revolutionize society. During that period he was happy to "spend Sabbaths in roving about the fields and in reading newspapers"; one Sunday, however, he went to hear what he thought would be a political speech by a minister, and was surprised to hear instead a discussion of biblical basics.[40] Willis, "much interested," eventually came to believe "that the Bible is the Word of God—that Christ is the only Saviour, and that it is by grace we are saved, through faith."[41]

Applying that understanding to his occupation, Willis decided that good journalism required analysis of issues and not just partisan political attacks. Local politicians who had backed his Maine newspaper did not care for his new scruples; Willis resigned, moved to Boston, and with co-editor Sidney Morse began putting out the Boston *Recorder.* Willis and Morse announced that they would show theological truth while putting out a concise weekly *news*paper (including "the earliest information of all such events as mankind usually deem important").[42] The *Recorder* also promised accuracy—"Care will be taken to distinguish between rumor and well-authenticated fact"[43]—and promised, if necessary, a salute to government like that offered by John Stubbes:

> When it be necessary to disapprove of public measures, that respect for Government, which lies at the very foundation of civil society, will be cautiously preserved; and in such cases, a tone of regret and sorrow will best comport with the feelings of the Christian patriot.[44]

Coverage of a major Syrian earthquake in 1822, "EARTHQUAKE AT ALEPPO," shows how the *Recorder* combined news and theological contextualization. Its first-person account by missionary Benjamin Barker told how Barker was racing down the stairs of a crumbling house when another shock sent him flying through the air, his fall broken when he landed on a dead body. He saw:

> men and women clinging to the ruined walls of their houses, holding their children in their trembling arms; mangled bodies lying under my feet, and piercing cries of half buried people assailing my ears; Christians, Jews, and Turks, were imploring the Almighty's mercy in their respective tongues, who a minute before did not perhaps acknowledge him.[45]

An overall report continued the theme of sudden destruction, with "hundreds of decrepit parents half-buried in the ruins, imploring the succor of their sons," and "distracted mothers frantically lifting heavy stones," looking for their children.[46] But the *Recorder,* describing how the earthquake led many to think about God and the brevity of life, then stressed the "triumphs of divine grace over the obduracy of the human heart, and over the prejudices of the unenlightened mind."[47]

Coverage of politics showed an emphasis on individual responsibility rather than grand societal solutions. *Recorder* essays argued that civil government has strictly limited jurisdiction, and should be turned to only for defense or punishment of crime; family, church, and voluntary association were to take leadership in dealing with social problems.[48] Other newspapers also emphasized the moral questions involved in both personal and governmental actions. The *Lexington Western Monitor,* a Kentucky newspaper, was typical in its summary of one major role of the press: "To strengthen the hands of virtue and to rebuke vice."[49] The *New York American* viewed "the Press as the great instrument of Liberty," as long as there was a "FREE and INDEPENDENT PRESS, FREE from all controls but that of religion and morality, INDEPENDENT of any influence but the good of our country and mankind."[50]

Newspapers like the *Recorder* covered international news in line with their theological concerns. Missionary activities received great coverage, with many publications complaining that the British East India Company—agent for the British government in India—was restricting the activities of missionaries for fear that Christian development would "prove fatal to the British government in India."[51] The *Columbian Phoenix* complained that British leaders thought "the Religion of the Most High God must not be suffered to interfere with the arrangements of the British government."[52]

Sensational stories about India's "Juggernaut festival"—in which people prepared for sacrifice to local gods were "crushed to death by the wheels" of a moving tower while onlookers shouted with joy[53]—led into reports that British agents were collecting a "Juggernaut tax." The *New Hampshire Patriot* complained that British leaders

> take a premium from the poor ignorant Asiatic idolater to indulge him in falling
> down and worshipping the moulten image, Juggernaut.—By this piece of religious
> fraud, they raise a handsome revenue to the British government.[54]

Great Britain's peaceful coexistence with human sacrifice, wife burning, and infanticide was attacked by *Niles' Weekly Register,* which reported that two American missionaries were evicted from India because "the revenues of Juggernaut must not be unhinged."[55] A Rhode Island newspaper argued that the British government would sponsor the worship of Beelzebub if the state could make money off of it.[56]

Many editors emphasized scandals in the royal family and argued that British evangelical societies were "mere political engines" organized for "pretendedly pious purposes . . . With England religion is merely a political engine. Of what profession it is, is scarcely thought of, so it pays a tribute in cash or in service or pretences."[57] The *Boston Yankee* called England "this modern Babylon . . . We abhor the deep and abominable depravity of her *state* religion, which is no better than popery."[58] One editor ran this pointed reminder: "What has Britain done for the Protestant cause? Why, she has persecuted a large majority of her own Protestant subjects, dissenting from the dogmas of her national church, with inquisitorial cruelty."[59]

The most articulate journalistic writer on politics and morality during the 1830s was William Leggett of the *New York Evening Post.* Leggett's major political principle was support for "equal rights," by which he meant that law should not discriminate among citizens, benefiting some at the expense of others. He believed it unfair for government to be "offering encouragements and granting privileges" to those with political clout. He set about to expose any governmental redistribution of income, whether through taxes, tariffs, or government aid to individuals, businesses, or labor groups.

Leggett foresaw problems whenever "government assumes the functions which belong alone to an overruling Providence, and affects to become the universal dispenser of good and evil."[60] He did not want government to become:

> the greater regulator of the profits of every species of industry, and reduces men
> from a dependence on their own exertions, to a dependence on the caprices of their
> Government.[61]

Leggett complained that some already were beginning to argue "that because our government has been instituted for the benefit of the people, it must therefore have the power to do whatever may seem to conduce to the public good."[62] Yet "under the sanction of such a principle, a government can do any thing on pretense of acting for the public good," and the effect would be erratic,

> not unlike that of weak and vacillating parents over their children, and with about the same degree of impartiality. One child becomes a favourite because he has made a fortune, and another because he has failed in the pursuit of that object; one because of its beauty, and another because of its deformity.[63]

Presciently, Leggett argued that the growth of "this power of regulating—of increasing or diminishing the profits of labour and the value of property of all kinds and degrees, by direct legislation"—would lead to a growth of governmental power and citizen desire to grab some of that power. As Leggett wrote, government was in danger of becoming

> the mere creature of designing politicians, interested speculators, or crack-brained enthusiasts. It will gradually concentrate to itself all the reserved rights of the people; it will become the great arbiter of individual prosperity; and thus, before we know it, we shall become the victims of a new species of despotism, that of a system of laws made by ourselves. It will then remain to be seen whether our chains will be the lighter from having been forged by our own hands.[64]

Once such a system were established, Leggett pointed out, changing it would be difficult:

> One of the greatest supports of an erroneous system of legislation, is the very evil it produces. When it is proposed to remedy the mischief by adopting a new system, every abuse which has been the result of the old one becomes an obstacle to reformations. Every political change, however salutary, must be injurious to the interests of some, and it will be found that those who profit by abuses are always more clamourous for their continuance than those who are only opposing them from motives of justice of patriotism, are for their abandonment.[65]

Yet, if change did not occur, citizens would be left enslaved:

> A government administered on such a system of policy may be called a Government of Equal Rights, but it is in its nature and essence a disguised despotism. It is the capricious dispenser of good and evil, without any restraint, except its own sovereign will. It holds in its hand the distribution of the goods of this world, and is consequently the uncontrolled master of the people.

Leggett died of yellow fever in 1839, at age 38, but other journalists continued to develop similar ideas over the next decade. A common theme was evident on many editorial pages: The world is filled with tyranny; journalists by embracing power have contributed to that pattern; America remains a land in which state governments and local newspapers are their own masters.[66]

Chapter 6

The Great Debates of Journalism

What journalism textbooks call the "penny press era" — the 1830s and 1840s— is the period for which materialist explanations appear to be the strongest. By the 1830s, the traditional newspapers were vulnerable because they were expensive. The typical price was 6¢ per copy, a sum needed to pay for production and distribution, because advertising revenues were small; 6¢ was not small change when the average daily wage for farm laborers was 85¢. A newspaper that sold for 1¢ rather than 6¢ could (in theory) dramatically increase circulation, perhaps sixfold, which would mean that total income from circulation could remain constant, whereas increased advertising rates could pay for the additional costs involved in printing and distributing many more copies.

The change would be feasible only if improvements in production and distribution also came. The necessary technology became available in the 1830s when steam-driven presses, able to produce copies far more quickly than those hand-operated, came on line. The Hoe cylinder press, for example, could produce 4,000 papers per hour. Distribution was improved when newspaper boys, often youth rendered homeless through the family disruption that came with urbanization, were employed to sell single copies of newspapers on the street. All that was needed was an entrepreneur capable of seeing and grasping the new opportunities.

Several tried, but the first to make a success of a "penny newspaper" was printer Benjamin Day, who in 1833 began selling the *New York Sun* in 1833. Day was wise enough to establish a simple and lively style for his newspaper, but to ground it firmly in the same *corruption story* attitude toward the news that had made newspapers such as the *Boston Recorder* successful.[1] He did so primarily by installing as *Sun* editor George W. Wisner, who had worked on traditional Christian newspapers and understood that it is neither accurate nor stimulating to pretend that all is well in the world.

Wisner, like his Puritan predecessors, emphasized sensation, exposure, clarity, accuracy, and specificity. He understood the Mather emphasis on bad news and wrote of how news stories:

> must generally tell of wars and fighting, of deeds of death, and blood, of wounds and heresies, of broken heads, broken hearts, and broken bones, of accidents by fire or flood, a field of possessions ravaged, property purloined, wrongs inflicted. . . . the abundance of news is generally an evidence of astounding misery, and even the disinterested deeds of benevolence and philanthropy which we occasionally hear of owe their existence to the wants or sorrows or sufferings of some of our fellow beings.[2]

Wisner's practice followed his principles: A drunkard hauled into court acknowledged that he "could not see a hole through a ladder."[3] Wisner ran tales of adultery.[4] He told of how a woman was seduced and abandoned.[5]

Wisner believed that specificity was important both to win readers and to make his product morally useful. He listed names of all criminal offenders and saw such posting as an inhibitor of others inclined to vice:

> Much complaint has been made from a certain quarter, and emanating from a particular class of individuals, against the publication of the names of persons who have been arrested by the watch, [but . . .] such publications have a tendency to deter from disorders and crimes, and to diminish the number of criminals."[6]

A typical story shows how Wisner was not afraid to shame offenders:

> Patrick Ludwick was sent up by his wife, who testified that she had supported him for several years in idleness and drunkenness. Abandoning all hopes of a reformation in her husband, she bought him a suit of clothes a fortnight since and told him to go about his business, for she would not live with him any longer. Last night he came home in a state of intoxication, broke into his wife's bedroom, pulled her out of bed, pulled her hair, and stamped on her. She called a watchman and sent him up. Pat exerted all his powers of eloquence in endeavoring to excite his wife's sympathy, but to no purpose. As every sensible woman ought to do who is cursed with a drunken husband, she refused to have anything to do with him hereafter.[7]

The emphasis was still on personal responsibility. Wisner, following the Reformed view that the heavens display the glory of God and the streets show the sinfulness of man, told stories to make his points, and also displayed a sense of humor. He opposed dueling but once accepted a challenge from a seller of quack medicines whom Wisner had criticized. Wisner, given his choice of weapons, said that they would have to be syringes filled with the doctor's own medicine, at five paces. The duel was called off.[8]

After a few years Wisner moved on to Michigan and died shortly thereafter, but others among the new penny papers followed his pattern: They were snappier in tone than some of their predecessors, but had the same willingness to print bad news and demand that people abide by the consequences of their actions. *New York Herald* editor James Gordon Bennett emphasized man's sinfulness, writing in 1836 that "I have seen human depravity to the core—I proclaim each morning on 15,000 sheets of thought and intellect the deep guilt that is encrusting our society."[9] Theologically, Bennett repeatedly told readers that he considered atheism absurd.[10]

The real threat to journalism's long tradition did not come from material change or from Bennett, who was committed to the idea of an independent press, but from the return of the oppression story in the 1840s.[11] Repulsed during the 1790s, it was not a factor in journalism history for the following four decades — yet during that period, much was changing in America theologically, both within Christianity and outside of it. Increasingly, liberal theologians began to proclaim that man was not inherently sinful, and that if man's environment were changed, man himself could become perfect. A host of panaceas, ranging from diet change (meat was out, graham flour was in) to the abolition of private property, became popular as ways of changing mankind.

Many of the proposals for change involved an opposition to property rights, which journalists—aware of how essential privately owned printing presses are to editorial independence — had strongly favored over the years. Unitarian leader William Ellery Channing clearly named one of the assumed villains: "Avarice was the chief obstacle to human progress . . . The only way to eliminate it was to establish a community of property."[12] Channing later moderated his communistic ideas concerning property, but he typified the liberal New Englander's approach to the problem of evil. Evil was created by the way society was organized, not by anything innately evil in man. Change society and evil could be eliminated.

One of the radical attacks on private property was led by Albert Brisbane, who had journeyed to Europe in 1828, at age 18, and eventually become a disciple of Charles Fourier. Fourier, famous in Marxist history as a "utopian socialist," argued that man's natural goodness could be restored if society was reorganized into small units called *phalanxes,* each with 1,620 members. Each phalanx member would be paid from the common product and would live in a common dwelling called a *phalanstery,* with a common dining hall featuring seven meals a day. Bodies might also be in common, because "free love" would be encouraged. The communes would emphasize agriculture, but each member would be free to work when and where he wanted.

For Fourier and Brisbane, this economic vision came from pantheistic theological roots and was designed, in Brisbane's words, to create "a humanity worthy of that Cosmic Soul of which I instinctively felt it to be a part."[13] But Brisbane, desiring success and believing that material change would lead to spiritual trans- formation, learned to downplay his theology before the public:

> I held that it was not worth while to excite religious antipathies to the idea of an industrial reform. The great point to be gained was the organization of society on a true, practical basis. I saw that when once the material operations and relations of men were properly organized, opinions would modify themselves by the influence of a new life and a higher education.[14]

Brisbane began to develop a following. The going was still slow, however, so he asked one veteran journalist, Park Benjamin, how he could gain a mass audience. Benjamin suggested that Brisbane first work on a talented but somewhat loony editor named Horace Greeley, for Greeley was "just damned fool enough to believe such nonsense."

He was. The collaboration of Brisbane and Greeley gave the *oppression story* its first long lasting presence in American journalism. In 1841, Greeley was a 30-year-old frustrated office seeker just starting up a new penny newspaper, the *New York Tribune*.[15] Greeley was enthralled by the "ennobling tendencies" of Transcendentalism and enamored with the movement's leaders: "Its apostles are mainly among the noblest spirits living."[16] He called himself a mere popularizer of Emerson's transcendentalist teachings, and at the same time a Universalist who believed in salvation for every man and salvation of society by man's efforts.[17] Greeley also wanted people to revere him as a great thinker; as fellow editor E. L. Godkin noted, Greeley castigated office seekers, but he was "as time- serving and ambitious and scheming an old fellow as any of them."[18]

Naturally, Greeley was attracted to Brisbane's proposal of salvation through commune. With a new convert's enthusiasm, Greeley published a magazine edited by Brisbane and entitled *The Future, Devoted to the Cause of Association and a Reorganization of Society*. He then gave Brisbane a front-page column on the *Tribune* that gave the communalist the opportunity to "spread ideas broadcast over the whole country, gaining a great number of adherents."[19] As one Greeley biographer noted, "The *Tribune* threw itself wholeheartedly behind Brisbane, and soon found itself building up news interest, discussion, and circulation at an extraordinary rate as it helped him popularize his cause."[20] And, it is arguable that the penny press began making a worldview difference not because of its existence in and of itself, but because of the ideas of Brisbane and Greeley.

In any event, Greeley threw himself personally into the commune movement, as he attended Fourierist conventions, became president of the American Union of Associationists, and financially backed three phalanxes—the Sylvania Associa- tion in Pennsylvania, the North American Phalanx in New Jersey, and Brook Farm in Massachusetts.[21] Greeley received ample stroking; in 1844, for example,

when he went to a New York City banquet honoring Fourier's birthday, Greeley
was toasted by Brisbane as the man who had

> done for us what we never could have done. He has created the cause on this
> continent. He has done the work of a century. Well, then, I will give a toast: 'One
> Continent, One Man!'[22]

Greeley's political activities helped him attract many young, idealistic writers,
some of whom—Margaret Fuller, George Ripley, and Charles Dana particularly—had great literary skill. The *Tribune* became *the* place to work; as editor
E. L. Godkin would later note, "To get admission to the columns of the Tribune
almost gave the young writer a patent of literary nobility."[23] One *Tribune* reporter
recalled that the furnishings were poor, but

> Ill-furnished and ill-kept as the Tribune office was in those days, it harbored a
> moral and intellectual spirit that I met nowhere else during my thirty-five years of
> journalistic experience. Every member of the force, from reporter to editor, regarded
> it as a great privilege to be on the Tribune and to write for its columns. . . .[24]

Greeley himself had great journalistic instincts. He demanded from his reporters "vigor, terseness, clearness, and simplicity."[25] He emphasized comprehensive
news coverage, and described how an editor should make sure that nothing "of
interest to a dozen families occurs, without having the fact daily, though briefly,
chronicled." He noted that if an editor can "secure a wide-awake, judicious
correspondent in each village and township" and have him send "whatever of
moment occurs in his vicinity," readership is assured.[26]

Greeley also insisted on good typography. One anecdote shows how even
Greeley's fiercest competitors respected the *Tribune's* superiority in this regard.
It seems that Greeley once fired a printer who misread Greeley's notoriously
messy handwriting and thought the editor was calling not for an early morning
milk train to bring the fruits of farm labors to New York City, but a "swill train."
When the editorial was published and an angry delegation of Westchester County
farmers assaulted Greeley, he in rage scribbled a note to the composing room
foreman ordering that the printer be fired. The foreman knew Greeley's writing
and could read the message, but to the average reader only the signature was
clear. The fired printer asked to hold onto Greeley's note as a souvenir. He then
took it to other newspapers and answered questions about previous employment
and reliability by flashing the note. The name of Greeley on it — all else being
illegible—was accepted as all the recommendation needed.

All of these factors allowed Greeley the freedom to make his newspaper a
proponent of social revolution without unduly alienating otherwise delighted
subscribers.[27] And for a while, other leaders of New York journalism gave
Greeley a wide berth. In 1846, however, he was challenged to a series of

newspaper debates by his former assistant editor on the *Tribune*, Henry Raymond. Raymond, 26, had moved from assisting Greeley on the *Tribune* to assisting James Watson Webb on the *New York Courier and Enquirer*, and Greeley still had high regard for him; Greeley later would write that he had never seen "a cleverer, readier, more generally efficient journalist" than Raymond.[28] But the philosophical differences between the two were sharp: in 1854 journalist James Parton would muse, "Horace Greeley and Henry J. Raymond, the one naturally liberal, the other naturally conservative—the one a Universalist, the other a Presbyterian. . ."[29]

The debates took place because neither Greeley nor Raymond tried to hide their views, and because both thought their readerships would be informed by a debate on basic issues of political economy. The arrangement agreed to was straightforward: The *Tribune* would publish an initial Greeley column defending Associationism, and the *Courier* would then print that column along with a response by Raymond; Greeley would then print Raymond's reply and a reply of his own; the *Courier* would print Greeley's new column and a new response by Raymond; and so on. Each party agreed to publish a total of 12 articles from its own side and 12 from the other.

The format of the debates was clear, but the course of argumentation was anything but direct. Greeley opened the debate series on November 20 by trying to establish a natural rights base for his opposition to private property: he asserted presuppositionally that each member of "the whole Human Family" had an equal right to the earth, and that, therefore, every New York resident had "a perfect right . . . to his equal share of the soil, the woods, the waters, and all the natural products thereof." The problem, however, was that "Civilized Society, as it exists in our day, has divested the larger portion of mankind of the unimpeded, unpurchased enjoyment of their natural rights"; the solution would be "Association," by which all property would be communal rather than private.[30]

Raymond in response did not challenge Greeley's presuppositions but concentrated on drawing out four steps that logically would follow acceptance of Greeley's theory: (a) if equal distribution of all land was right, then the current unequal distribution was wrong; (b) if the wrong was to be righted, then none of the current patterns of property ownership should stand; (c) if land could not be owned rightfully, than the product of that land could not be owned rightfully; (d) because all property originated in land ownership, no one could rightfully own anything at all. Raymond then went on to argue from history that although difficulties did arise out of property ownership, "without it they would be increased a thousand fold . . . Without it civilization would be unknown—the face of the Earth would be a desert, and mankind transformed into savage beasts."[31]

Greeley at this point could have stood his ground and attempted to argue that private property's detriments were greater than its benefits, but he did not think he could prove that case historically; instead, in his second essay he retreated to a better defensive position by writing that he wanted to argue about current reality, not history and theory, and so would stress the importance of property being used for the good of all rather than for individual, assumedly selfish, purposes.[32] Raymond in his second essay accepted the move away from theory and demanded that Greeley lay out the specifics of his program, and explain how communes could attract needed capital without expropriation by force.[33] Greeley responded with details of the Associationist program, and tried to prove his peaceful and moderate intentions by stipulating that those who provided needed capital for the communes could be rewarded by receiving shares of the commune's production.[34]

Raymond, in his third essay, took that detail and held it high as proof of Greeley's inconsistency; Raymond argued that Greeley was in one breath calling the distribution of capital unjust, and in the next indicating a willingness to ratify that unfairness and even modify Associationism to extend it.[35] Greeley responded that his goal was not so much to rectify past abuses as to prevent further ones, so he therefore was willing to recognize capital accumulations as long as future profits would go primarily to those who labored, not merely those who invested.[36] Raymond, in his fourth reply, wrote that Greeley's scheme was unrealistic because, apart from a market system, it was not possible to determine exactly the value of labor or product.[37]

Here the debaters were approaching what is still a key question of economics, although the current phenomenon of Marxist economies abandoning command manufacturing and pricing decisions indicates that the argument is virtually over. In the mid-19th century, however, massive experience with administered pricing in industrial economies was still in the future, and Greeley could assert in his fifth essay that it would not be hard to distribute proceeds to "Capital, Labor and Skill as impartial justice shall dictate."[38] Raymond for his part replied that administered distribution was impossible without tyranny: those who wished to choose freely and make their own economic arrangements "must be overruled, *put down* by the strong hand: or they must be consulted and gratified—and that would simply be a return to the existing social state."[39] Raymond contended that Greeley was unwilling to confront some basic issues of man's nature—including, most particularly, the question of "sin" and its effect on social progress.[40]

By the end of the fifth debate some key issues in political theory and economics had been discussed, but the debates still had not achieved the intellectual intensity that could make them profound rather than persnickety. Both debaters, in fact, were becoming exasperated with each other's penchant for floating like a butterfly rather than stinging like a bee: Raymond complained on December 24 of "the difficulty of conducting an argument with an opponent who recognizes none of the common rules of reasoning, and who repudiates his positions as fast as they become unpleasant." Greeley replied that Raymond's counterpunching was "founded only in the grossest ignorance and misconception of what I have presented."[41]

With the sixth editorial page essays, however, the long-term salience of the debates increased because Raymond's jabs drove Greeley to confront the question of how social progress could occur. Greeley acknowledged at the start, "I know well that an Association of knaves and dastards—of indolent or covetous persons—could not endure without a moral transformation of its members." Then came Greeley's key emphasis on structural rather than personal change as the root of progress; he argued that the structure of Association "strongly tends to correct the faults inimical to its existence,"[42] for people placed in a good environment will undergo a moral transformation. Raymond, in his sixth essay, pounced on Greeley's admission, arguing that "this concession is fatal to the whole theory of Association. It certainly implies that Individual Reform must *precede* Social Reform—that the latter must have its root in the former."[43]

Raymond went on to call Greeley's assertion that Associationism would be self-correcting "a gross absurdity," for "Association is thus expected to make its own indispensable conditions. It is to create its own creator—to produce its own cause—to effect that personal reform in which it must originate."[44] Raymond then stated his position: Only the "personal reform of individual men," through Christianity, can lead to social progress. Raymond argued that reformers should "*commence* their labors by making individual men *Christians*: by seeking their personal, moral transformation. When that is accomplished, all needed Social Reform will either have been effected or rendered inevitable."[45]

Greeley, in his seventh statement, had two replies to Raymond. First, Greeley defended the causal relationship Raymond attacked. Greeley argued that personal change among the best and the brightest would lead to societal transformation, which in turn would lead to change among the masses:

> Give but one hundred of the right men and women as the nucleus of a true Social Organism, and hundreds of inferior or indifferent qualities might be rapidly molded into conformity with them.[46]

Greeley could write this because he saw man as a product of his environment: "I believe there are few of the young and plastic who might not be rendered agreeable and useful members of an Association under the genial influences of Affection, Opportunity, Instruction, and Hope."[47] Greeley's emphasis on plasticity would become increasingly common in the second half of the century as environmental explanations for social problems became more common.

Greeley's arguments also pointed toward future ideologies by putting forward what a half century later would become known as the "Social Gospel": He tried to show that Raymond's demand for Christ first was absurd, because "Association *is* the palpable dictate of Christianity—the body whereof True Religion is the soul."[48] In arguing that Associationism was Christianity-in-practice, a material emphasis that transcended the spiritual, Greeley described slum living conditions and asked,

Can any one doubt what Christianity must dictate with regard to such hovels as these? Can any fail to see that to fill them with Bibles and Tracts, while Bread is scanty, wholesome Air a rarity, and Decency impossible, must be unavailing? 'Christianity,' say you! Alas! many a poor Christian mother within a mile of us is now covering her little ones with rags in the absence of fuel . . .[49]

Greeley's statement jarred Raymond to lay out his full position on January 20, 1847. He first noted partial agreement with Greeley as to the need for action:

The existence of misery, and the necessity of relieving it, are not in controversy, for we have never doubted either. It is only upon the *remedy to be applied,* that the Tribune and ourselves are at variance.[50]

But Raymond argued that Greeley was unnecessarily revolutionary when he insisted that:

to benefit a part, the whole must be changed; that to furnish some with good dwellings, all must abandon their houses and dwell together under a common roof; that the whole fabric of existing institutions, with all its habits of action and of thought, must be swept away, and a new Society takes its place, in which all must be subject to common customs, a common education, common labor, and common modes of life, in all respects. This, its fundamental position, we deny. We deny the necessity, the wisdom, and the possibility of removing existing evil, by such a process.[51]

Raymond, rather than linking philanthropy with upheaval, saw individual and church action as efficacious. He praised "individuals in each ward, poor, pious, humble men and women, who never dreamed of setting themselves up as professional philanthropists," but daily visit the sick and help the poor. He also argued that:

Members of any one of our City Churches do more every year for the practical relief of poverty and suffering, than any Phalanx [the Associationist name for communes] that ever existed. There are in our midst hundreds of female 'sewing societies,' each of which clothes more nakedness, and feeds more hunger, than any 'Association' that was ever formed.[52]

Raymond then portrayed Greeley's ideas as abstractly ineffective:

Hundreds of thousands of dollars have been expended by the Associationists, in propagating their *theories* of benevolence, and in making benevolent experiments, yet where is the practical good they have accomplished? . . . The *Tribune* sneers at practical Christianity . . . Does the taunt come with good grace from a system which theorizes over starvation, but does not feed it; which scorns to give bread and clothing to the hungry and naked, except it can first have the privilege of reconstructing Society?

Now the two debaters were focusing on the basics. Raymond had called Greeley superficial for not getting at what Raymond saw as the root, spiritual causes of material poverty, and now Greeley struck back with his assessment that capitalism, not spiritual decay, was the culprit: "Association proposes a way . . . of reaching the *causes* of the calamities, and absolutely *abolishing* Pauperism, Ignorance, and the resulting Vices."[53] Journalists, Greeley went on, should not merely praise those who mitigated "woes and degradations," but should fight oppression: "*Relieving* Social Evils' is very well; we think eradicating and preventing them still better, and equally feasible if those who have power will adopt the right means, and give them a fair trial."[54]

Raymond's response on February 10, however, continued to insist that views of human nature, and not merely issues of relief versus prevention, were the continental divide separating his position from that of Greeley. Raymond, instead of accepting Greeley's assertion that Associationism was true Christianity, argued that it was anti-Christian. For example, Raymond pointed out Associationism's belief

> that the Husband and Wife, instead of being *one,* as the laws of God have decreed, shall be entirely independent of each other in name and in property, and that each shall have perfect liberty of action and *affection.*[55]

Raymond argued that the near absolute liberty the communes were designed to allow would inevitably feed into anarchy, and that their maintenance would be possible only through totalitarian "Social Science," which would be designed to "control all departments of Social Life."[56]

Increasingly the debates hinged on the view of man that divided the two editors. When Greeley argued on February 17 that all man's problems "have their root in that *isolation of efforts* and antagonism of interests on which our present Social Order is based," Raymond replied by emphasizing individual corruption rather than social oppression as the root of most social ills.[57] Although Greeley believed that "the Passions, feelings, free impulses of Man point out to him the path in which he should walk," Raymond argued that evil feeds on those passions and impulses of man's natural inclination, and that channelling those inclinations into paths of work and family was the only alternative to anarchy and barbarism.[58]

The last three debates showed even more clearly the conflict of two faiths. Greeley's Associationist belief was that human desires are:

> good in themselves. Evil flows only from their repression or subversion. Give them full scope, free play, a perfect and complete development, and universal happiness must be the result . . . create a new form of Society in which this shall be possible

. . . then you will have a perfect Society; then will you have 'the Kingdom of Heaven . . .'[59]

Raymond, however, argued that:

this principle is in the most direct and unmistakable hostility to the uniform inculcations of the Gospel. No injunction of the New Testament is more express, or more constant, than that of *self-denial*; of subjecting the passions, the impulses of the heart to the law of conscience.[60]

Greeley responded, on March 12, with his faith that the *education* intrinsic to commune life was the key to developing individuals who would not need God's grace or biblical restraint: "I do not believe that a rightly-trained, truly-developed human being will any more have "a passion for a dozen different women,' etc., than he will have a passion to commit a dozen murders."[61] Associationism also stressed structuring of the social environment:

Excesses and vices are not an essential part of the passions, but on the contrary depend on external circumstances, which may be removed. All that is necessary is to discover a society in which every bad route for the action of the passions will be closed, and in which the path of virtue will be strewn with flowers. . . . How could the passions lead to crime, when every thing should be arranged to *satisfy them* in the most agreeable manner?[62]

But Greeley would not assent to Raymond's assertion that Associationism was anti-Christian; rather, he made backing of communes a Christian necessity, and argued in his 11th essay that it is

the duty of every Christian, every Philanthropist, every one who admits the essential Brotherhood of the Human Family, to labor earnestly and devotedly for a Social Order, which shall *secure* to every human being within its sphere the full and true development of the nature wherewith God has endowed him, Physical, Intellectual, and Moral.[63]

Raymond, in his 11th response, argued that Greeley was socialist in economics, antinomian in ethics, and overall a person who was trying to create a new god in Greeley's own image: Greeley's thought, Raymond charged,

pretends to be religious, and even claims to be the only true Christianity. But . . . it rejects the plainest doctrines of the Bible, nullifies its most imperative commandments, and substitutes for them its own interpretation of the laws of *nature*. Thus the God in whom it professes faith, becomes, in its definition, simply the 'principle of universal unity.'[64]

Raymond accused Greeley of similarly twisting the concept of the Trinity and
the meaning of the words "Kingdom of Heaven."[65] He concluded, concerning
Greeley's belief, that:

> Its whole spirit is in the most direct hostility to the doctrines of the Bible. It
> recognizes no absolute distinction between right and wrong . . . and aims at nothing
> beyond the 'full and true development of the nature of man.' . . . It is the exact
> antagonist of Christianity; it starts from opposite fundamental principles and aims
> at precisely opposite results.[66]

The key question that all reformers and journalists should answer, Raymond
insisted, concerned the locus of evil action among humans: did evil come from
within, or was it generated by social institutions? Raymond stipulated that,

> Before a cure can be applied or devised, the cause of the evil must be ascertained:
> and here at the very outset, the theory of Association comes in direct collision with
> the teachings of Christianity.[67]

The cause, Raymond argued, was "the sinfulness of the heart of Man." The
remedy, he argued,

> must reach that cause, or it must prove inefficient. The heart must be changed. The
> law of Man's nature must cease to be the supreme law of his life. He must learn to
> subject that law to the higher law of righteousness, revealed in his conscience and
> in the Word of God. . . . and that subjugation can only be effected by his own
> personal will, with the supernatural aids furnished in the Christian Scheme.[68]

And thus the lines were clearly drawn. Greeley believed that "the heart of man
is not depraved: that his passions do not prompt to wrong doing, and do not
therefore by their action, produce evil."[69] Greeley, in his 12th and final essay,
reiterated his faith that "social distinctions of master and servant, rich and poor,
landlord and landless," are the cause of social problems. He followed Unitarian
practice in referring to Jesus as a "divinely-sent messenger and guide" but was
unwilling to accept Christ as God's son. He concluded his side of the debate on
April 28 with some exasperation:

> I can not see how a man profoundly impressed with the truth and importance of
> Christ's teaching . . . can fail to realize and aspire to a Social polity radically
> different from that which has hitherto prevailed.[70]

Raymond's final response reiterated the centrality of "Sin, as an active power,
in the human heart," and argued that Associationism at best would deal with
superficial problems, but not "the lust, the covetousness, the self-seeking," out

of which battles arise.[71] Greeley trusted man's wisdom, but Raymond concluded that

> the principles of all true REFORM come down from Heaven. . . . The CHRISTIAN RELIGION, in its spiritual, life-giving, heart-redeeming principles is the only power that can reform Society: and it can accomplish this work only by first reforming the individuals of whom Society is composed. Without GOD, and the plan of redemption which he has revealed, the World is also without HOPE.[72]

As the debates ended, interest in them was so high that Harper's quickly published all 24 of the articles in a pamphlet of 83 closely printed, double-columned pages, which sold out.

It is hard to evaluate the long term effect of the debates on American society and journalism. But if we keep in mind the statement of Lincoln's that began this book—"Public opinion on any subject always has a 'central idea' from which all its minor thoughts radiate"—the significance of the debates is clear. Raymond and Greeley were really arguing about what the "central idea" for Americans, and American journalists, should be.

The battle was not one of change versus the status quo. Raymond agreed with Greeley that social problems were great—"Far from denying their existence, we insist that they are deeper and more fundamental in their origin."[73] But Raymond saw himself as arguing for "a more thorough and radical remedy than the Tribune supposes"—namely, the change of heart that acceptance of Christianity brings.[74] That concept was common in the Christian journalism that dominated the early 19th-century press. It underlay the *corruption story* and its emphasis on the universality of sin and the need for all individuals, including rulers, to repent and change. Raymond in the debates repeatedly stated this doctrine:

> No truth is more distinctly taught in the Word of God than that of the sinfulness of the human earth: the proclivity of Man's nature to act in violation of the rule of right. . . . It is solely because malice, covetousness, envy, lust, and selfishness in general exist, as active principles, in the heart of man, that their fruits exist in Society. It is solely because the foundation is poisoned, that the streams which flow from it are bitter.[75]

But would that belief remain dominant in American journalism?

Not if Horace Greeley had anything to do with it. He embraced part of that methodology but rejected the theology behind it. Instead of seeing sinful man and a society reflecting that sinfulness, he believed that man was naturally good but was enslaved by oppressive social systems. Greeley in the debates was developing the rationale of the *oppression story* emphasis on problems arising not from internal sin but from external influences. That is why the debates were so grinding: Raymond and Greeley were arguing not only about theology and economics, but about the future of American society and the future of journalistic practice. The tectonic plates were shifting as they spoke. Soon the earthquake would come.

PART III

BREAKTHROUGH OF THE OPPRESSION STORY

Chapter 7

The Irrepressible Conflict in the Press

Just as the Greeley–Raymond debates did not have a clear winner, so the social upheaval of the 1840s did not have a clear, short term outcome. Despite good press clippings from the *Tribune* and some of its allies, the commune movement died during the 1850s. Virtually all of the communes failed and disappeared; the idea of a noble human nature, so attractive in the abstract, showed its weakness in practice. Commune members often neglected their work. "Free love" proved not to be so free, as disputes raged.[1]

Brisbane believed the reason for failure in the 1840s and 1850s was not too much forced community but too little:

> Unless associative life is completely organized, so that all the sentiments and faculties of the soul find their normal development and action therein, it cannot stand. In fact, it will be discovered one of these days that, according to a law which governs the spiritual or passional nature of man, there must either be the complex harmony of a perfect organization, with a high order of spiritual activity, or man must remain in his little isolated, individual state.[2]

Socialism in one community was insufficient. Control over much more terrain was necessary, and Brisbane recommended to his adherents that they begin a long march through the institutions of American society—"years of patient, careful propagation"—so that the result, decades later, would be "complex harmony."[3] The goal became one of building a strong central government, so that the entire nation could be socialized.

Greeley began his own long march by placing in *Tribune* editorial positions many of his commune associates—most notably Charles Dana and George Ripley. They in turn hired others on the left, including Karl Marx as a European correspondent. Greeley himself continued to look for the magic bullet by which the misery descending on needy citizens could be stopped: "full of error and suffering as the world yet is," he wrote, "we cannot afford to reject any idea which proposes to improve the Moral, Intellectual, or Social condition of mankind."[4] Paralleling Marx, he argued that "The whole relation of Employer and Laborer is so full of antagonism, inequality and injustice, that we despair of any reform in it but a very thorough and radical one."[5]

Greeley worked with many New York proto-Marxists, but did not remain faithful to any particular faction for long.[6] At one time he became a believer in "anti-rentism," the idea that charging rent for use of property or land was wrong.[7] That movement never took off, and Greeley moved on to other brief but entangling alliances. His inability to learn from failures was more serious than his absent-mindedness, which was so extreme that he detailed an office boy to keep him informed as to whether he had eaten anything that day. (Once fellow journalists at a restaurant distracted Greeley as he was about to eat and substituted an empty plate for the full one that had awaited him; when Greeley's attention returned to his table he looked down at the empty plate, sighed, and rose to leave.)[8]

In his habits of mind if not in his enjoyment of food, Greeley was the prototype of some elite American journalists of recent times. He also created the mold in that he became ever more ardent for social change as his personal life disintegrated. Horace and Mary Greeley believed that children were without sin, so they kept their son Arthur (Pickie), born in 1844, isolated from playmates or other means by which corruption could enter into him. At age 5 Pickie's hair had never been cut, less that constrict his freedom, and he still wore baby clothes, to give him freedom of movement: Pickie was to be a beautiful combination of intellect and nature, equipped with "choice" thoughts and language. But one day the 5-year-old stood up before a commune meeting and starting complaining that his mother was "so particular, particular, particular, particular." When she reminded him that he had been saved from corruption, he began shrieking at her, "Don't you dare shut me up in a room . . . I want fun." The Greeleys did not change Pickie's regime, but he died shortly after, during a cholera epidemic.

Commune decline and family silliness, combined with sadness, showed Greeley that utopia was not around the corner. But during the 1850s, as Greeley was looking around for a new cause, one presented itself. He would involve himself deeply during the 1850s in the battle over slavery, and would prod that battle toward a culmination in civil war. The Civil War and its aftermath, with the expansion of federal power that resulted, would change the American republic and the American press system by turning both toward an embrace of centralization as savior and a belief that means are less important than ends.

The war, of course, was a long time coming. It's instructive to go back to

William Leggett, who in the 1830s made his position on slavery and its potential abolition very clear. Leggett called slavery "a deplorable evil and a curse" and favored "the speedy and utter annihilation of servitude and chains."[9] Yet, carrying on John Milton's faith in the combat of ideas, Leggett also demanded "the strenuous assertion of the right of free discussion." He wanted liberation to come through a change in minds and hearts, and not by military arms or even by assertion of national political power: "We disclaim any constitutional right to legislate on the subject."[10]

Leggett had faith that Americans, both north and south, eventually would answer "no" to a series of rhetorical questions he posed:

> Have their ears become so accustomed to the clank of the poor bondman's fetters that it no longer grates upon them as a discordant sound? . . . Can the husband be torn from his wife, and the child from its parent, and sold like cattle at the shambles, and yet free, intelligent men, whose own rights are founded on the declaration of the unalienable freedom and equality of all mankind, stand up in the face of heaven and their fellow men, and assert without a blush that there is no evil in servitude?[11]

Leggett opposed revolutionary violence, but he praised anti-slavery civil disobedience and noted that, pragmatically, suppression does not work in America for long:

> The first great impulse which the abolition cause received in this city was, we are persuaded, the attempt to suppress it by the means of mobs; . . . and we do hope that, in view of the pernicious consequences which have flowed from violent measures hitherto, a course more consistent with the meekness of Christianity, and with the sacred rights of free discussion, will be pursued henceforth.[12]

Leggett died before his faith that free discussion would lead to an anti-slavery outcome could be severely tried. Some 1,000 miles away, however, another journalist put Leggett's optimism into practice under far more difficult conditions. Elijah Lovejoy, born in Maine in 1802, completed his theological training in 1833 at Princeton Theological Seminary (then a stronghold of Calvinist thought) and moved to St. Louis in 1834. There he was ordained as a minister and began editing a Christian newspaper, the *St. Louis Observer*. When he saw a slave, Francis J. McIntosh, burned at the stake, he became an abolitionist and began encountering massive opposition.

Lovejoy stayed in St. Louis as long as he could, but when a pro-slavery mob wrecked his press in July 1836, Lovejoy moved to the free state of Illinois and established the *Alton Observer*.[13] Freedom from slavery did not guarantee freedom of the press, however. Three times, Lovejoy saw his printing presses smashed and thrown into the Mississippi River by pro-slavery men; he did not fight back. Lovejoy became pastor of a Presbyterian church and moderator of the Alton

Presbytery, but he also ordered a new press. When it arrived at the Godfrey &
Gilman warehouse, Lovejoy and 20 of his armed supporters stood guard over it
until it could be installed at the *Alton Observer*.

A pro-slavery mob formed on the night of November 7, 1837. Its participants,
most of them drunk, began hurling rocks at the warehouse windows. The defenders threw back earthenware pots they had found in the warehouse. Soon, gunshots
began coming from both sides. When the mob put up a ladder at the building and
one of its members began climbing to the roof with a smoking pot of pitch in
order to set fire to the building, Lovejoy and a friend rushed out to overturn the
ladder. One mob gunman fired his double barreled shotgun at Lovejoy. Five
bullets hit him, and he died.

Lovejoy's associates then laid down their weapons and were allowed to leave;
the mob broke the press into pieces and dumped the broken parts into the river.
Lovejoy was buried on November 9—his 35th birthday—and after the Civil War
Alton citizens erected a monument to him. It stands to this day on a hill overlooking the Mississippi, with a plaque introducing Lovejoy as "Minister of the Gospel,
Moderator of Alton Presbytery," and explaining in Lovejoy's own words what
befell him: "If the laws of my country fail to protect me I appeal to God, and
with Him I cheerfully rest my cause—I can die at my post but I cannot desert
it."[14]

A few years later and 300 miles to the east, another editor faced similar
persecution. Cassius Clay of Lexington, Kentucky, saw slavery as a sevenfold
evil: "morally, economically, physically, intellectually, socially, religiously,
politically."[15] But he saw the need for long term change that the south could
embrace, and advocated emancipation over a generation's time. To that end, in
1845 (at age 35) Clay began publishing the *True American*, "a paper devoted to
gradual and constitutional emancipation."[16] With the words "God and Liberty"
as his newspaper's motto, Clay advocated a constitutional convention designed
to state "that every female slave, born after a certain day and year, should be free
at the age of twenty-one". Clay argued that over time this plan "would gradually,
and at last, make our state truly free."[17]

The moderate program began to pick up support, and also furious opposition.
Clay soon had the joy of printing letters to the editor such as this one: "C.M.
Clay: You are meaner than the autocrats of hell . . . The hemp is ready for your
neck. Your life cannot be spared. Plenty thirst for your blood—are determined
to have it . . ."[18] But Clay kept at it, arguing that the elimination of slavery would
help the south to prosper economically, spiritually, and socially. In one article
he commented on a rise of divorce in the south and urged southern women to:

> Put away your slaves . . . If you want to drink, go to the pump or to the spring and
> get it; if to bathe, prepare your own bath, or plunge into the running stream; make
> your own beds, sweep your own rooms, and wash your own clothes; throw away
> corsets and nature herself will form your bustles. Then you will have full chests,

glossy hair, rosy complexions, smooth velvet skins, muscular, rounded limbs, graceful tournures, elasticity of person, eyes of alternate fire and most melting languor; generous hearts, sweet tempers, good husbands, long lives of honeymoons, and—*no divorces.*[19]

Clay, expecting attempts to destroy his press, made a fort out of his three story red brick newspaper office, and with six loyal friends prepared for siege. Familiar with the story of Lovejoy's death, they lined the outside doors and window shutters of the building with sheet iron to prevent burning. Clay purchased two small brass cannons at Cincinnati, loaded them to the muzzle with bullets, slugs, and nails, and placed them breast high on a table at the entrance. His friends stockpiled muskets and Mexican lances. Those measures forestalled the attack for a time, but Clay came down with typhoid fever and eventually had to give up and watch as his press was packed up by slaveholders and shipped out of town.

That was the last time he was helpless. In 1847 Clay resumed his anti-slavery writing and speaking, had to fight numerous duels, and survived. (He had a lifetime record of about 107 wins and no losses, compared to Muhammed Ali's 32 and 4 as a pro.)[20] The original Cassius Clay could also talk a good fight. Once, facing a hostile crowd, Clay held up a Bible and said, "To those who respect God's word, I appeal to this book." Then he held up a copy of the U.S. Constitution and said, "To those who respect our fundamental law, I appeal to this document." Then he took out two pistols and his Bowie knife and said, "To those who recognize only force . . ."

Clay, although ready to defend himself, believed that nothing good would come from aggression. He demanded free speech in the hope of convincing his neighbors but did not want to war on them. He stressed the power of personal transformation through God's grace, which would lead to societal reformation. "We recommend less haughtiness and indifference on the part of the rich towards the poor, and less invidiousness toward the rich on the part of the poor," he wrote. "Let true Christianity prevail, and earth will become the foreshadowing of Heaven."[21] And Clay, unlike Lovejoy, managed to survive many assassination attempts. He was knifed and beaten by clubs; once, gushing blood from a lung wound, he even lost consciousness and dramatically gave as his last words, "I died in the defense of the liberties of the people"—but he did not die. He kept speaking out against slavery in the 1840s and helped to form the Republican Party in the 1850s.[22]

By then, the lines were drawn, and it may have been too late for anti-slavery plans that would not end in violence. Any possibility for a peaceful resolution disappeared when anti-slavery journalism moved from corruption story grounds of sadly dealing with sinful man, to an oppression story vision of eradicating slavery as the first step toward social revolution and class warfare. The role of the press in making the conflict irrepressible should not be overstated—and yet, if we examine the four alternative ways of fighting slavery that existed at one time, and then see which one was seized on by some leading journalists, that press role does loom large.

There will be some oversimplification in summarizing in a few paragraphs the options that have been dissected in thousands of books over a century, but baldly describing the lay of the land in this fashion might show the editorial choices that were open. The first of the anti-slavery approaches that editors could call for would be the personal one. Slaveholders could free their slaves, as did Washington and Jefferson on their deaths. Also on the personal level, opponents of slavery could reason with slaveholders, and ministers could preach against it. Editors, for their part, could cover separation of slave families, brutality against slaves, and so on. If all failed, those opposed to slavery could put money alongside their words by buying slaves and then freeing them.

A second alternative was collective but nongovernmental. The first half of the 19th century, as Alexis de Tocqueville observed, was the golden age of associations in America, and anti-slavery individuals frequently came together in the search for a way out. They formed societies to support colonies for ex-slaves in Africa or in the west. Some joined to purchase and then free slaves. Some set up schools for slaves. Some wanted to boycott southern economic products, and others wanted to fund southern industries that would not employ slaves. Thoreau hoped to convince many that nonviolent action, such as non-payment of taxes, could create pressure for change, but he found few supporters.

A third alternative, once tensions had grown to the point of war, could have been Washington's temporary acceptance of secession, followed by a trade embargo that some thought might kill the rebellion. Unlikely as this seems, Greeley embraced the idea in 1851 and stated that the south should secede; he argued that southerners would realize after a couple of independent years that they needed the north's industry, and would then beg for readmission. At that point, Greeley argued, the north would be in a position to make demands, one of which would be the elimination of slavery.[23] Greeley intensified his calls in 1854 as he argued that the north should laugh at

> the too susceptible nerves of our too excitable Southern brethren. Instead of bolting the door in alarm, and calling for help to guard it, in case the South should hereafter threaten to walk out of the Union, we would hold it politely open and suggest to the departing the policy of minding his eye and buttoning his coat well under his chin preparatory to facing the rough weather outside . . .[24]

But Greeley, even though he saw materialism as dominant, was too savvy a journalist to argue for long that change would come that easily. And so he arrived at the fourth alternative, violence: the north eradicating slavery by using its superior numbers and industrial capacity to eradicate part of the south. Greeley thought that a little blood would go a long way, for he believed that only a few wealthy southerners, along with a handful of politicians along for the ride, were truly pro-slavery. Greeley did not travel in the south until after the war, and he employed correspondents who were better preachers against slavery than reporters of actual sentiment. Even in 1860, Greeley's correspondent in Memphis was writing that "an insignificant clique" favored secession, but "the masses are heart and soul for the union," so the north should not be concerned with "threats, or predictions of disunion."[25]

In the early 1840s Greeley's commune enthusiasm led the *Tribune* into expectation of utopia around the corner; Greeley's hopes for rapid social progress during the late 1850s again led him to provide considerable space for unreliable accounts that supported his dreams. For example, a letter from Alabama argued that people in that state were "divided into two classes—the rich and the poor," and that the poor would readily unite with northern workers to "create a new system of Truth, Equality, Justice."[26] Karl Marx, peering across the Atlantic with a dialectic telescope, helped to convince Greeley's assistant Charles Dana that slavery had weakened the south so much that it would be unable to mount a war effort; the north could push hard without losing much blood.[27]

With social revolution so near and slavery the only large obstacle, Greeley became a proponent of terrorist means to gain anti-slavery objectives. As one historian noted concerning *Tribune* correspondents in Kansas during the mid-1850s, "the crew Greeley assembled went forth with hatred in their hearts. . . ."[28] The *Tribune's* coverage of the battle between northerners and southerners in Kansas was predictably propagandistic, with northerners always depicted as peace loving citizens brought to conflict by southern terror. The *Tribune* wanted fighters and weapons shipped to Kansas immediately, to preserve the peace.[29] Correspondent James Redpath wrote that because there would be no peace as long as slavery existed, he would "fight and kill for the sake of peace."[30]

Greeley's response to the events of May 24, 1856, indicates his hardline position. That night in Kansas, John Brown and seven other men invaded the homes of several farming families—the Doyles, the Wilkinsons, and the Harrises. These families had done no one any harm. They did not own slaves. They were simply from the south. They were also trusting: When William Doyle opened his door in response to a request for directions, John Brown's men grabbed him and took him 200 yards from the cabin. John Brown then placed a revolver against Doyle's forehead and pulled the trigger, killing him instantly. Doyle's 22-year-old son William was then stabbed in the face, slashed over the head, and shot in the side. His 20-year-old son Drury had his fingers and arms cut off and his head cut open; then he was stabbed in the chest. A third son, 14-year-old John, also would have been executed, but the mother, Mahala Doyle, clutched him and screamed, "Not him; Oh God, not him." John Brown let him live.[31]

Brown and his followers—four of them were Brown's sons—then moved on to the Wilkinson home, took the man away from his wife and small children, and cut his throat. They then went to the Harris cabin, occupied that night not only by James Harris and his family but by three other men who had stopped by; one had come to buy a cow. The door was unlocked, because the region until then had been safe. Harris and two of the men turned out to be northerners and were allowed to live; the southerner was murdered by the river with sabers. One blow severed his left hand, raised in self-defense; others split open his skull, and he fell into the river. The murderers washed their swords and walked away as the cold water carried away part of the dead man's brain.

The goal of the massacre was terrorism, pure and simple: Kill those who sided with a hated system, focus attention on what became known as "bleeding Kansas," and raise tensions so high that warfare capable of destroying the hated system would become more likely. Terrorists need press publicity, preferably somewhat sympathetic—and John Brown and associates got it. The *Tribune* called Brown's terrorism a self-defense strike needed to disrupt the southern horde of Kansas settlers.[32] Greeley advocated shipment of more arms to Kansas and dispatched a military expert to advise John Brown.[33]

Greeley used events in Kansas to further Republican candidate John Fremont's hopes in the election of 1856; historian Jeter Isely has concluded that "Reading Greeley's journal at this late date gives the impression that his staff had no concern for accuracy with regard to Kansas of 1856."[34] Reporter W. A. Phillips sent frequent articles, and the *Tribune* itself sponsored mass meetings of protest and the establishment within each northern city of "Kansas committees" to send aid. The *Tribune* publicized books, pamphlets, and plays on Kansas, and even serialized a novel telling of how Kansas southerners were "ruffians, half-tipsy, with hair unkempt and beards like cotton-cards, squirting tobacco-juice in every direction, and interlarding their conversation with oaths and curses" aimed at defenseless folk. One of the poor sufferers was the heroine, gentle Alice, who took to her sickbed in fright and remained sorrowful until she had a vision of Fremont's election and Kansas' freedom, at which "the thin lips of Alice quivered tremulously. It was her last smile on earth."[35]

Greeley went at it again following John Brown's raid on Harper's Ferry. During the month following the raid the *Tribune* ran 26 columns and 15 editorials on Brown.[36] The *Tribune* correspondent was consistently pro-Brown and anti-southern; he generalized about the south, "Everything shows how far this region is behind the age."[37] But he was also sarcastic about particular southerners, such as prosecutor Charles Harding, whose "face is a vindictive as well as a degraded one," and who "has a way of expressing profound contempt by ejecting saliva aloft, and catching it on his chin, which he practices with great success."[38]

Greeley displayed extreme arrogance during this crisis, and knew exactly what he was doing: In a letter to his associate editor, James S. Pike, Greeley wrote that he was in the "position of the rich old fellow, who, having built a church entirely out of his own means, addressed his townsmen thus: 'I've built you a meeting-house,/ And bought you a bell;/ Now go to meeting/ Or go to hell!' "[39] Isely commented, "Greeley believed that John Brown's raid . . . would bring thousands into his church. The *Tribune* featured Brown as a saint sprung from the Book of Revelation to herald the coming of universal freedom."[40]

The *Tribune* had feisty competition. Bennett's *New York Herald* had long made fun of Greeley's support for "all the *isms* and *ultras* of the day," including "Fourierism, atheism, community of property socialism—every species of wild and extravagant thought and doctrine."[41] Abolitionism, Bennett wrote, merely was the latest cause of "the clique of enthusiasts, fanatics, Fourierists, and infidels of all descriptions who are engaged in [the *Tribune's*] activities."[42] Bennett called John Brown "a notorious Kansas shrieker—one whose hands had more than once been dipped in human blood."[43] Bennett also called Greeley a member of "an anti-slavery oligarchy" that was attempting to establish a new "inquisition."[44]

The *Herald,* however, had little influence on those who saw American chattel slavery (correctly, I believe) as a central moral problem, and not just an economic one. More influential among some of those who founded the Republican Party was the newspaper built by Greeley's debating adversary of 1846 and 1847, Henry Raymond. That newspaper, begun in 1851 and known as *The New York Times,* opposed slavery fervently, but not without an eye to the difficulty of altering an imbedded institution. Raymond, unlike Greeley, did not see anti-slavery agitation as a step toward class warfare, and did not sanguinely look to blood as the answer to social problems; therefore, he was not taken in by those who said that the outbreak of civil war would lead to a southern social revolution that could then spread north. *Times* reporting from Kansas and Harper's Ferry bemoaned the provocations and appealed for calm.

The most fascinating New York newspaper in the months directly preceding the civil war was probably the *New York World,* a daily newspaper begun in 1860 in an attempt to revive Christian journalism. After Abraham Lincoln was elected in 1860, the *World* proposed that anti-slavery newspapers

> forbear to indulge in that acerbity of tone which, while it has never done any good, has occasioned much of the unfortunate asperity which exists among our Southern brethren. Let the exultation of approaching victory be tempered with manly generosity, and the whole tone, bearing and language of the party be of a character to confirm [hopes for] a moderate, a conciliatory, a conservative, a truly national and constitutional administration.[45]

There can still be peace, the *World* insisted, "if the press and orators of all parties will drop the vituperative style in which they are wont to indulge, and practice a reasonable courtesy and magnanimity."

World news coverage stressed accuracy at a time when propaganda seemed more and more ascendant. "The news from Kansas is uncertain and contradictory," the *World* noted in November, 1860:

> Nothing illustrates the evils of excessive partisanship more than the impossibility of getting trustworthy accounts of important events occurring far from the great

centers. Here is a matter, of which it is extremely important that all parties should know the truth, yet it is impossible to arrive at the truth. The determination of partisan newspapers, and of their correspondents, to throw all the blame upon the other side, leads to distortion, misrepresentation, and even positive mendacity.[46]

The *World,* for its part, criticized many northerners for attempting to excommunicate the south, and criticized southern slaveholders for engaging in

the separation of families, the taking of the parent from the child and the child from the parent, ignoring the marriage tie, withholding even that amount of education which would enable the colored man to read God's oracles—when the South would defend all this as being within the aegis of the quiet of the gospel, the South are doing wrong to the gospel, and perverting it.[47]

The *World* quoted Matthew 5:9—"Blessed are the peacemakers, for they shall be called the children of God"—and asked Christians of both sides "to humble themselves, and confess before God that they have disparaged our common Lord and Redeemer."[48] It favorably covered proposals for gradual emancipation— children of slaves would be freed—and publicized suggestions to smooth the way by payments from the North: "That would test the northern conscience, and put us right under a reformed constitution."[49]

The tendencies of the *World* found some support in the South. In Texas, Governor Sam Houston published his last hope:

Providence has ever guarded the people of these United States. He sustained the hope of our struggling fathers until they gained the liberty that we now enjoy. He gave them the wisdom and the prudence through which our government was formed. For eighty-four years that Same Providence has shielded us, amid danger from without and dissention from within. He has encircled us with His protecting Arm and has preserved our liberties intact. Let us in the hour of Prayer, implore Him to shield us still in the time of peril, that we may be preserved a United people . . ."[50]

By 1860, however, such fairmindedness had little chance to be accepted, for the tensions were too great; Houston, for example, was denounced as a "Texas Brutus."[51]

Columns in the *World* tended to go deeper. One analysis of the divided nation showed how each leading "journalistic fire-brand" thought his own views superior to "written constitutions" and decided to "erect his own judgment or his own happiness, into a tribunal."[52] With extremism rampant, many northern newspapers "vilif[ied] southern states, institutions, and men," and southerners in turn

reacted to vituperation . . . From studying methods of emancipation, they turned to the consideration of schemes for the perpetuation and extension of the happy patriarchal institution . . . masters, alarmed for the safety of their families, clamored for more stringent laws whereby to circumscribe and oppress the slave.[53]

The Greeleyite revolutionary position had not "ameliorated the condition of the servile masses of the South" and held out no "hope than that of insurrection and bloodshed," the column argued. It ended with a plea that journalists "stay the streams of section reviling."[54]

Greeley was the chief culprit, according to the *World*.[55] Southerners who read his work saw him as representing northern hatred of the south—in the words of the *Raleigh Register*, Greeley was "the vilest, the dirtiest, the most mangy hog in the Abolition pen."[56] Other newspapers moving toward the *oppression story*—including the *New York Post, Chicago Tribune,* and *Hartford Courant*—followed Greeley's lead.[57] And the *Tribune* itself, becoming during the 1850s America's first semi-national newspaper, had no readership in the south, but distributed a weekly edition of 200,000 copies from Maine to Minnesota. That was 10% of free state votes, and often the most articulate 10%; as historian James Ford Rhodes recollected years later, *Tribune* readers "were of the thorough kind . . . questions were discussed in their family circles and with their neighbors, and, as differences arose, the *Tribune,* always at hand, was consulted and re-read."[58]

How great was the *Tribune's* influence? According to one press-watcher, "every man, and woman too, of education, culture, and moral feeling" was praising the *Tribune;* it had a grip on "the affections of all the best people."[59] The *Tribune,* in short, "was more than a metropolitan journal, it was a sectional oracle."[60] The *Tribune* prophesied that America was faced with an either/or decision:

It may be that a new era of religion—of Justice and Brotherhood between man and man—is commencing; or it may be that this is only a fresh spasm, to be followed by a more palpable moral lifelessness. Which shall it be?[61]

The *Tribune* may have pushed hundreds of thousands of northerners to push hard for the new era.

The *Tribune,* of course, was not responsible for the Civil War. Journalism was one compelling force among many, and the *Tribune* was one newspaper among many. But if the *Tribune* and its followers had seen the south as a culture and not as the potential arena for class struggle between slave owners and a combined poor White/Black coalition, it seems likely that a wiser course could have been followed. And if the *Tribune* and other newspapers had not glorified in death a man, John Brown, who represented the deepest fears of the south, many southerners might not have believed that the North would soon be sending other Browns to achieve what he tried to start.[62]

Many southern journalists also were irresponsible. One *World* column, "THE

SOUTHERN FRANKENSTEIN," criticized those who had urged on forces that were now out of control:

> The South has, in plain terms, been dragooned into its present rebellious attitude by the unscrupulous and persistent mendacity of its politicians and journals, abetted by some of those at the North. There are indications that some of the southern 'leaders' would be glad, if it were in their power, to allay the storm which they have aided in raising. They begin to discover that the consummation of their plans promises at the best no better thing that absolute hopeless bankruptcy. . . . The sagacious among these suicidal agitators would, doubtless, be glad to annul the share they have had in bringing about the present deplorable disaster. But it is too late.[63]

By the end of 1860 it *was* too late. Bandwagon headlines rolled through southern front pages: "Georgia Moving!" "Ten Thousand Cheers for Florida!" "Alabama All Right—Convention Called."[64] Those who wished to wait were called traitors. In the rapture of the moment, even those few newspapers that had counted the costs of war realistically jumped on the bandwagon. In January 1860, the *Richmond Dispatch* had stated forcefully,

> It is impossible to exaggerate the horrors and sufferings which for years would follow a dissolution of the Union. . . . It would be war from the start, war to the knife and knife to the hilt. The widely extended border between the North and South would be a line of fire and blood. Every accessible bay and inlet of every river would be entered, and, ever and anon, large masses of men hurled upon the capitols and important points of Southern States. But the horrors of ordinary warfare would be far transcended by the barbarities of this cruel strife.[65]

But in January 1861, the *Dispatch* strongly called for secession, and did not mention the costs.[66]

It was too late. Had the south not replied to fanaticism with rage of its own, another course might have been possible. By 1860, however, the alternative courses were being abandoned, and the *oppression story* was about to claim its first few hundred thousand victims. A Georgia newspaper reported that "The tone of the Northern press . . . should convince all southern men that the hour for dissolution is come. . . ."[67] The *Albany [Georgia] Patriot* cited a Greeley report and argued, "We might as well sing Psalms over the dead carcass of a buzzard, as to appeal to the Union for *rights* and *justice*."[68] One month later, the *Patriot* reported that "Insult upon insult has been heaped upon the South, and we are daily informed that these wrongs and aggressions are to be repeated. . . . For our part we would prefer to strike the blow this very hour than to wait for the morrow."[69]

It was too late. In a letter to Stephen A. Douglas, Mississippi lawyer S. S. Fairfield complained that the state's newspapers were "generally in the hands of

young and inexperienced men."[70] Fairfield described how Mississippi agendas
were set:

> When a scheme is put on foot the [Jackson] *Mississippian* roars and all the little
> county papers yelp, the cross road and bar room politicians take it up and so it goes,
> and if any one opposes them they raise the cry of abolitionist and traitor.[71]

A thoughtful North Carolina editor complained, "Madness seems to rule the hour,
and fearful forebodings cloud the prospect."[72] The *New York Herald* feared a
long war and ran a headline, "Blood! Blood! Blood!—Who Will Be Responsible?"[73] But the *New York Tribune,* confident in February 1861, that the radical
upheaval to come could eliminate oppression, added to its masthead the words,
"NO COMPROMISE!/ NO CONCESSIONS TO TRAITORS!"[74] Soon, the cannons were roaring.

Once war began, the *Tribune* plunged ahead with plans to celebrate a quick
victory, on the materialist theory that the nonindustrialized south could not
possibly fight a war. In theory, the northern army could crush its numerically
inferior opponents, the northern navy could blockade the Confederate coast, and
the "laws of trade" would kill the south.[75] Day after day Greeley ran the same
paragraph on the editorial page: "The Nation's War Cry. Forward to Richmond!
Forward to Richmond! The Rebel Congress must not be allowed to meet there
on the twentieth of July! By that date the place must be held by the National
Army!"[76]

Under pressure, the poorly trained Union army advanced and was routed at
Manassas. The *Herald* said it was Greeley's fault. Greeley was in shock: The
material superiority of the north had not led to early victory. The south fought
on, and many of the radical journalists who had predicted northern victory without
bloodshed were angry with President Abraham Lincoln for his early attempts to
win the war with as little bloodshed as possible. Journalists during the first year
of the war called him a "political coward," "timid and ignorant," "pitiable," "too
slow," and "shattered, dazed, utterly foolish."[77] Southern newspapers called their
opponent a drunkard, but northern newspapers were often more creative in their
labeling of Lincoln as "an awful, woeful ass," the "craftiest and most dishonest
politician that ever disgraced an office in America," a "half-witted usurper," a
"mole-eyed monster with a soul of leather," "unmentionably diseased," and the
"woodenhead at Washington."[78]

Lincoln put up with it as best he could, and even laughed at Greeley's frequent
nastiness: "I do not suppose I have any right to complain," Lincoln said, for
"Uncle Horace . . . is with us at least four days out of seven."[79] In any event,
the war ground on. Occasionally, it was brought home to some northern editors;
in July 1863, a mob advanced on the *Tribune* building yelling "Down with the
Tribune." The mob destroyed the furniture on the first floor and started a fire with
the goal of destroying the building, but 100 policemen arrived with orders to "Hit

their temples, strike hard, take no prisoners." Twenty-two men were killed. Many more were seriously wounded.

Hundreds of thousands more died during the civil war, but eventually material did triumph. By 1865, the southern opposition to centralization was demolished, and the road to rapidly increased governmental power was open. The first step was to do away with the defeated opposition leaders; journalists who already had waded in blood reported that "all the interests of humanity demand that Davis, Lee & Company, shall be tried, found guilty, and hanged by the neck until they are dead."[80] The next step was to reconstruct first the south, and then the entire nation, on an economic plan that expropriated large holdings in land, still the primary basis of wealth. Abraham Lincoln did not favor such radical plans, but his assassination removed the enemy of both maddened southerners and ambitious northern radicals. And Andrew Johnson, at first, did not seem likely to present much of a barrier.

Nevertheless, during the quarter century after the Civil War, progress did not come as quickly as Greeleyite journalists had hoped. First, Andrew Johnson and several other conservative political leaders stood in the way; then, a certain realism concerning the limits of federal power sank in for a time. The next chapter examines the obstacles, beginning with Johnson, who saved southern leaders from hanging trees, and in turn saw much of the journalistic wrath turned on himself.

Chapter 8

Obstacles to Power

In one sense, it is surprising that President Andrew Johnson was treated so poorly in the press; his rise contained the stuff of which memorable human interest stories are made. Orphaned and penniless at the age of 4, Johnson became an unschooled tailor who was taught by his wife to read and write. Hard work and good business sense enabled him to make a success of his small shop. Johnson read and thought about politics and government. He paid a man to read to him throughout the day while he plied his needle. Johnson's opponents would often decry his lack of formal education, but the tailor's desire to study and learn began a lifetime pattern of self-education: After Johnson was elected senator from Tennessee, he was one of the leading visitors to and borrowers of books from the Library of Congress.

Johnson's problem as president, however, was that during those years of sewing and listening he developed a fixed set of political principles, at the center of which was opposition to governmental and economic centralization. He worried about states becoming "mere satellites of an inferior character, revolving around the great central power" of Washington."[1] He opposed "concentration of power in the hands of the few."[2] He opposed government economic activities such as railroad grants, predicting that they would result in "nothing but a series of endless corrupting legislation."[3] Consequently, Johnson was called callow and callous by Horace Greeley and other journalists who saw the federal government as hero in an upcoming saga of forced social restructuring.

Underlying the battle of Greeley versus Johnson during the 3 years following the Civil War were Greeley's hopes for a final victory that would make up for the failed hopes of the 1840s and 1850s. The war won by the north at immense cost must be followed by the winning of the peace, he wrote.[4] That peace, he hoped, could end not just the antagonism of master and slave, but also that of capitalist and worker. The federal government could move from restructuring the south to restructuring the entire country. Socialism in one commune had not worked, but perhaps a shake-up of the entire country would.

Some writers have seen the Radical Republican program of the late 1860s merely as an attempt to punish the south for seceding and to ensure enfranchisement of Blacks. But Senator Thad Stevens, the leading radical politician, argued for federal confiscation of all southern landholdings larger than 200 acres; historian Gregg Singer has observed that,

> The radical element of the [Republican] party was determined to carry out a reconstruction policy in the South as a prelude to the reconstruction they intended to bring about in the nation as a whole. The southern states were to be used as social science laboratories . . . as a kind of pilot study for reconstructing the whole nation. . . .[5]

Andrew Johnson was certainly aware of the danger: From the first, he spoke of his responsibility to defend the Constitution against radical attempts to establish dictatorship. His message to Congress in December 1865, called the federal government "a limited government" that must remain limited if the Constitution is to endure, for "the destruction of the one is the destruction of the other." The gauntlet was hurled down.

In February 1866, the Radical Republicans passed a bill (to widespread journalistic applause) that gave the federal government total power in the southern states, with federal agents to act as judge and jury. Johnson vetoed it. He argued that it represented

> an absorption and assumption of power by the General Government which, if acquiesced in, must sap and destroy our federative system of limited powers, and break down the barriers which preserve the rights of the States. It is another step, or rather stride, to centralization and the concentration of all legislative power in the National Government.[6]

He pointed out that punishments for arrested southerners would not be defined by law but imposed by court martial, and that there would be no appeal from those decisions, not even to the U.S. Supreme Court. Furthermore, he believed that presidential appointment of those august Federal agents gave himself or other presidents too much power, power "as in time of peace certainly ought never to be entrusted to any one man."[7] Leading journalists called Johnson a traitor, weakling, coward, bribed drunkard, and murderer: The *Milwaukee Sentinel* ludicrously charged that "Johnson was privy to Lincoln's assassination."[8]

Johnson also disapproved of the welfare parts of the bill's segment concerning aid to Blacks: "A system for the support of indigent persons . . . was never contemplated by the authors of the Constitution."[9] Johnson was not a person who lacked compassion for the ex-slaves: He told a delegation of Black leaders that he wished their goal of full political, social, and economic equality "could be done in the twinkling of an eye, but it is not in the nature of things, and I do not assume or pretend to be wiser than Providence."[10] Johnson preferred charitable initiatives to federal programs, and personally sent $1,000 to support a school to educate Black children in Charleston. Fundamentally, however, Johnson argued that Black labor power was essential in the south; economic laws of supply and demand would lead to Black economic advancement that would then give ex-slaves the power to demand full political rights.

Following his veto, Johnson warned a crowd assembled on the White House lawn that the Radical Republicans wished "to concentrate all power in the hands of a few."[11] He argued that some radicals hoped to lead the United States toward a repeat of the French Revolution.[12] Johnson dared his opponents to do their worst: They "may talk about beheading," he said, "but when I am beheaded, I want the American people to be the witness."[13] He insisted that Blacks would not be able to gain and maintain voting rights merely through new use of federal bayonets: That would just create a White backlash that could delay *permanent* enfranchisement for decades. Such statements were treated with scorn in much of the press, which provided the radicals in Congress with fresh ammunition every day: Virtually every afternoon the Clerk of the House would read to the assembled members an anti-Johnson newspaper clipping, and the radicals would cheer.[14]

Johnson did not give in. In August 1866, he continued to argue that the radicals had "usurped powers which, if permitted, would result in despotism or monarchy itself."[15] Johnson decided to take his case to the country. Before the speaking tour, Senator Doolittle of Wisconsin warned Johnson not to "allow the excitement of the moment to draw from you any *extemporaneous speeches*. You are followed by the reporters of a hundred presses who do nothing but misrepresent."[16] Doolittle was right, as historian George Milton has related:

> Johnson swayed those who heard him. Time after time he faced a hostile crowd and converted it into a friendly one. But while he was convincing a hundred thousand, the Radical correspondents, in reporting his speeches, so distorted and misrepresented them that they turned three million against him.[17]

Greeley's *New York Tribune*, instead of printing the substance of Johnson's remarks, portrayed Johnson as a moron who was good only for "gritting his teeth, and accompanying his words with violent gesticulation."[18]

Johnson, in his speeches, repeatedly answered the accusations against him and tried to explain the world view underlying his policies. In New York City on

August 29, 1866, in Utica on August 31, and in Buffalo on September 3, he talked about the nature of treason, the wonder of God's mercy, and the threat of dictatorship. Just as journalists who emphasized man's corruption and God's grace had done, he applied the Bible to political events, telling St. Louis residents that "The Saviour of man came on earth and found the human race condemned and sentenced under the law, but when they repented and believed, he said let them live."[19] In Cincinnati he proclaimed, "If I have pardoned traitors I have only obeyed the injunction of scripture—to forgive the repentant. . . . Hang eight millions of people! Who ever heard of such a thing? Yet because I refuse to do this, I am called a traitor."[20] He told the crowds that because God had been merciful to them, they should be merciful to other offenders. He typically concluded with his desire to have 36 states in the Union, and not to end up with 25, due to the exclusion of the South.

Radical partisans ridiculed Johnson's concerns. Journalist David Ross Locke had his humorous persona, "Petroleum V. Nasby," give mocking reports of Johnson's supposedly drunken progress:

> He wuz fightin traitors on all sides. . . . all he wanted now wuz to heal the wounds uv the nashen . . . he mite hev been Dicktater, but woodent; and ended with a poetickal cotashun which I coodent ketch. . . . He asked em, ef he was Judis Iskariot who wuz the Saviour? . . . The crowd hollered 'Grant! Grant!' and the President thanked em for the demonstration. It showed him that the people wuz with him in his efforts to close his eyes on a Union uv 36 States and a flag uv 36 stars onto it.[21]

The *Cleveland Leader* called Johnson's speech in that city "the most disgraceful ever delivered by any president of the United States."[22] Greeley's *Tribune* called Johnson's trip "the stumping tour of an irritated demagogue," and Lowell in the *North American Review* labeled it "an indecent orgy."[23]

Testimony during Johnson's impeachment trial would show that one frequent charge against Johnson—that he was a drunkard—was a vicious untruth; the only drunkard during the trip was General Grant, who accompanied Johnson but in Cleveland was put aboard a boat to Detroit so that his condition would not be revealed.[24] The *New York Tribune* and Joseph Medill's *Chicago Tribune* were particularly biased.[25] *The Independent* gave Johnson "lascivious" eyes, "the face of a demagogue" and "the heart of a traitor."[26] The magazine argued that Johnson was a "trickster . . . touched with insanity, corrupted with lust, stimulated with drink."[27]

Month after month the drumbeat went on: "We have demanded and shall continue to demand that this Aaron Burr, this Benedict Arnold, this Andrew Johnson shall be put out of the way of injuring the government which he first disgraced, then betrayed, and would willingly destroy."[28] The roughness of some of Johnson's extemporaneous sentences allowed other put-downs: Greeley snorted in one editorial that Johnson's "verbs never agree with their nominatives, or their hearers or anything else."[29] George Milton has correctly described press coverage of Johnson's speaking in this way:

> The type of thing that the Radical press had to say about this President of the United States shows to what low estate journalism had fallen. Editorially and in their news columns, such papers as Joseph Medill's *Chicago Tribune* and Horace Greeley's *New York Tribune* gave vent to vituperation which a decent man would be asked to apply to a convict.[30]

Johnson had convicted himself in the eyes of many reporters and editors when he refused to support radical demands for governmental centralization and social revolution in the South. There were some limits on Johnson-bashing: A St. Louis reporter was fired after he filed a largely imaginary account of a Johnson speech.[31] But as long as a journalist provided the minimum of fact and contextualized it in a way that heaped ridicule on the President, he was not only safe but often applauded.

In 1867, the situation of the moderates deteriorated further. Thad Stevens was so confident that he began to proclaim openly his revolutionary intentions: When he pushed forward a bill to divide the south into military districts, with commanders having arbitrary power for an indefinite period of time, he argued baldly that "every government is a despotism," and that his bill was crucial because it "would assure the ascendancy of the Union [Republican] party."[32] The radical willingness to use violence had not stopped with John Brown's terrorism and the resultant war: *The Independent*, which earlier had demanded the execution of southern leaders, screamed in September, 1867, "The People [capital P] are waiting anxiously for the impeachment of the President," and if Johnson tried to stop the process, "let him be tried by a court martial, and shot by twelve soldiers in a hollow square."[33]

Many newspapers, serving as organs of a dominant party and perhaps propelling that party toward greater extremism, had their greatest power ever. Those radical newspapers, of course, did not have monopoly power at that time, because moderate newspapers existed in most cities. But the influence of the radical press was great, and newspaper vituperation certainly contributed to Johnson's impeachment by the House of Representatives on February 24, 1868.

Greeley and Medill were exultant following the impeachment, as the House began presenting its evidence for the Senate trial. Johnson did not give up. One Sunday after church Johnson read a Bible passage to an attendant:

> Behold, here I am: Witness against me before the Lord . . . whose ox have I taken? or whose ass have I taken? or whom have I defrauded? whom have I oppressed' or of whose hand have I received any bribe to blind mine eyes therewith? and I will restore it to you.[34]

But truth was a porous defense against a furious Greeley, who charged that any senator who sided with Johnson was dishonest.[35] Magazines such as *The Nation* and newspapers such as the *Washington Chronicle* and the *Philadelphia Press* also fought their opponents not with open argument, but by wholesaling words such as "corrupt," "scoundrel," "fraudulent," and "dishonorable."[36]

A two thirds vote of the Senate was needed to convict Johnson, and the pressure on Republican senators to fall in line was enormous. In the end, when one more Senate vote was needed to convict Johnson, his future came down to a decision by a Kansas printer-turned-politician, Edmund G. Ross. Ross' background—anti-slavery immigrant to Kansas in 1856 and leader of radical forces there—led Greeley to believe that he would vote to convict. Yet, Ross had replied to demands that he prejudge Johnson by writing, "I have taken an oath to do impartial justice according to the Constitution and laws, and trust that I shall have the courage to vote according to the dictates of my judgment. . . ."[37]

Ross displayed that courage and refused to convict Johnson. A Kansas newspaper editorialized that Ross had

> sold himself, and betrayed his constituents; stultified his own record . . . and to the utmost of his poor ability signed the death warrant of his country's liberty. This act was done deliberately, because the traitor, like Benedict Arnold, loved money better than he did principle, friends, honor and his country, all combined. Poor, pitiful, shriveled wretch, with a soul so small that a little pelf would outweigh all things else that dignify or ennoble mankind.[38]

Greeley attacked Ross with particular viciousness, calling him "the greatest criminal of the age . . . a miserable poltroon and traitor."[39]

After Johnson's close escape, Greeley kept up his attacks. For the 1868 election he backed U.S. Grant, who had joined the radicals. Greeley told *Tribune* readers that a Grant triumph would mean great prosperity, but a victory for Democratic candidate Horatio Seymour would begin "the first phase of the counter-revolution . . . Anarchy and strife, terrorism and assassination, will pervade that section where the fires of Rebellion still smolder."[40] Thomas Nast's cartooning in *Harper's Weekly* was so effective that Grant afterward said he owed his election to "the sword of Sheridan and the pencil of Thomas Nast."[41] Meanwhile, Grant received adulatory coverage from the *New York Tribune* and other newspapers; the *Philadelphia Enquirer* was typical in its depiction of him as "the possessor of those analytical powers which enable men to judge character with close and correct appreciation."[42]

In 1869, with Johnson returning to Tennessee and Grant's analytical powers in the saddle, there was no check on the Washington radical forces and their campaign contributors. One observer, George W. Julian, wrote, "I have never seen such lobbying before as we have had in the last few weeks and such crookedness and complicity among members."[43] Another, James W. Grimes, complained that "the war has corrupted everybody and everything."[44] What Leggett had feared was coming true: The federal government now had such power that citizens were becoming "mere puppets of legislative cobbling and tinkering." Those business leaders who had backed the Radical Republican power grab called in their markers, and the *New York Herald* was able to observe that "All our railroad legislation is procured by corrupt practices and is formed in the interest of jobbery."[45]

The corruption of many Radical Republican state governments in the South during Reconstruction is legendary. With radical newspapers—42 in Georgia alone—supported by government revenues, the press often tried to cover up scandals. Newspapers received contracts for public printing at high rates and then received more money than even those contracts allowed. In South Carolina, for example, the *Charleston Republican* was supposed to receive $24,538 but received $60,982 instead; the *Columbia Daily Record,* after contracting at unusually high rates that would have yielded $17,174, was paid $59,988. Bribes and payoffs were so common that one South Carolina senator, C. P. Leslie, was able to produce a classic line in their defense: "The State has no right to be a State until she can afford to take care of her statesmen."[46] The most famous episode of the day came when the Speaker of the South Carolina House of Representatives lost a $1,000 bet on a horse and, 3 days later was voted a gratuity to cover his loss, in tribute to "the dignity and ability with which he has presided."[47]

Ironically, with all this press concern for the character of President Johnson and certain senators, scandals involving Radical Republican leaders at first were downplayed. When radical leader Schuyler Colfax, accused of receiving a bribe, took 10 days to produce a weak defense—he talked about a $1,000 bill arriving unsolicited in the mail—most radical newspapers rushed to his defense. The *Boston Advertiser* was typical when it called the charge "all fuss and parade."[48] Cartoonist Nast, scourge of Tweed Ring politicians and other nonradical miscreants, was told by a friend, "The whole subject offers a rich theme for your pencil, but I doubt the wisdom of availing yourself of it."[49] Nast did not.

Eventually, however, some editors became cranky about covering up ever more scandals. Leading Republican editors such as Greeley, Horace White (who had assumed editorship of the *Chicago Tribune*), and Samuel Bowles of the *Springfield Republican,* joined with moderates such as Murat Halstead of the *Cincinnati Daily Commercial* and Henry Watterson of the *Louisville Courier-Journal,* in a search for an alternative to Grant. At a confused "Liberal Republican" convention in 1872, Greeley fulfilled part of his lifelong ambition by snatching the nomination from Charles Francis Adams, son and grandson of presidents. However, Greeley missed the great prize as he was smashed by Grant's popularity; given the *Tribune's* earlier boosting of Grant, in one sense the Greeley defeat was a story of Frankenstein's monster turning on Frankenstein.

Greeley, heartbroken, died 3 weeks after his electoral defeat. At the funeral, liberal minister Henry Ward Beecher was upbeat: "Today, between the two oceans, there is hardly an intelligent man or child that does not feel the influence of Horace Greeley."[50] But Greeley had a different summing-up. As he was dying, perhaps speaking wildly, he said, "My life has been a fevered march," and he

> had been tempted by the glittering bait of the Presidency. . . . And now, having done wrong to millions while intending only good to hundreds, I pray God that he may quickly take me from a world where all I have done seems to have turned to evil, and wherein each hour has long been and henceforth must be one of agony, remorse, and shame.[51]

In one of his last statements Greeley wrote:

> I stand naked before my God, the most utterly, hopelessly wretched and undone of all who ever lived. I have done more harm and wrong than any man who ever saw the light of day. And yet I take God to witness that I have never intended to injure or harm anyone. But this is no excuse.[52]

Senator Ross of Kansas, who in Greeley's words deserved "everlasting infamy" for refusing to convict Andrew Johnson, had a happier ending, after much suffering. In the short run Ross *was* infamous: He was burned in effigy many times, and a justice of the Supreme Court of Kansas suggested that he commit suicide. At a mass meeting in Lawrence led by a man named Hugh Cameron, Ross was warned not to return to Kansas; when he did so, a local tough invaded his print shop and beat Ross so thoroughly that the ex-senator never completely recovered his health. Years later, however, Grover Cleveland appointed Ross governor of the Territory of New Mexico, and one day Ross was amazed to see Hugh Cameron. Cameron had walked all the way from Kansas to New Mexico to apologize for his leadership of that mass meeting.

During Grant's second term, public opinion turned against the Radical Republicans. In the 1876 election, Democratic candidate Samuel Tilden gained 250,000 more votes than the Republican candidate, Rutherford Hayes, and piled up safe majorities in all the states he needed to win the Electoral College except for three (Florida, South Carolina, and Louisiana) where he had narrower leads. Only some Electoral College chicanery allowed Hayes to assume office—but on condition that the radical program for the south be abandoned.

Johnson's predictions of a southern White backlash proved accurate, and southern Blacks were left free but still in chains for several generations. Their erstwhile allies in the northern press moved on to other concerns; the *New York Tribune* justified its malign neglect by declaring that "after ample opportunity to develop their own latent capacities" the ex-slaves had proven that "as a race they are idle, ignorant, and vicious."[53] A prediction of *The Nation* proved accurate for several generations: "The negro will disappear from the field of national politics. Henceforth the nation, as a nation, will have nothing more to do with him."[54]

The end of reconstruction in the South also signalled the complete failure of attempts to reconstruct economically the north. With the Christian ideas of the early 19th century largely abandoned, but no ideology yet dominant enough to take its place, some reporters in large cities embraced a total cynicism; others, seeing death and destruction occurring apparently at random, embraced a Social Darwinist faith in natural determinism. The chief spokesman of the latter was Yale professor William Graham Sumner, who believed that blind evolutionary forces had created man, and argued that all life is a struggle against the forces of nature, with some surviving and other proving inadequate.[55] Tooth-and-claw was the way the world worked and the way any society had to work:

> Nothing but might has ever made right. . . . If a thing has been done and is established by force (that is no force can reverse it), it is right in the only sense we can know and rights will follow from it which are not vitiated at all by the forces in it.[56]

Reporters who applied that thinking often became ruthless in their invasion of privacy to get a story. For example, the *New York Tribune,* which maintained its materialism following Greeley's death and shifted easily toward Sumner's views, treated suicide as a helpful self-selection of the unfit and cheered for the stronger side in international conflicts, regardless of justification.[57]

Small town newspapers, however, often showed a less strained quality of mercy. Typical news reports showed crime as affecting not only the criminal and his victims, but family members of all involved; one poignant story told of an old outlaw who resisted arrest and was killed, along with his 10-year-old grandson.[58] Concern for family also was evident in a story of a man unable or unwilling to support his wife and two small children, who were housed temporarily in the city hospital: "Mrs. Dongan is hardly thirty, but her sorrows and heartaches have changed her features so that she appears to be fifty years old. Her children are aged 8 and 4."[59] An article headlined "A WIFE BEATER ARRESTED" told how a man

> had tanked up on mean whiskey and went home and lit into his wife, who was dreaming on her pillow. The woman was badly bruised up, and the husband will get his reward in the county court.[60]

When small-town newspaper editors assembled at press association conventions, they frequently spoke about the obligations they felt in protecting "the sacredness of home and private affairs."[61] These beliefs influenced reporting methodology as well as results. For example, a Dallas reporter was interviewing a woman who had abandoned her husband to run away with another man. The new man proved to be a bum. The woman was thinking of returning to her husband. The husband was coming to talk with her. The story of the interview continued as follows:

> Just at this point of the conversation the door of the room in which Mrs. Finnegan and the reporter were in opened and a clean shaved gentleman, neatly dressed, and who looked to be about 30 years old, entered. He glanced from the reporter to Mrs. Finnegan and stretching out his hand appealingly, said, "Jennie."

> The reporter, recognizing in the gentleman by his actions Mrs. Finnegan's husband and feeling the weight of his presence, retired from the room into another where he thought to wait for an interview with Finnegan, but owing to the fact that the husband and wife in their excitement raised their voices so that almost every word they spoke could be heard by the reporter, he left the house not caring to be a listener to their conversation.[62]

Some regional newspapers during this period showed an impressive willingness to take stands against expansion of centralized government power, and to stick to that policy even when it hurt. For example, in 1886 and 1887 West Texas faced an enormous drought, and Congress passed a bill appropriating $10,000 for the distribution of seeds to farmers in that area. When President Grover Cleveland vetoed the bill, arguing that it was wrong "to indulge a benevolent and charitable sentiment through the appropriation of public funds for that purpose," the *Dallas News* supported the veto, even though the appropriation would have benefited some of its own readers.[63]

The *Dallas News* did not stop there, however. It noted that Cleveland's message "recalled Congress more strictly to constitutional lines of thought" and served an additional purpose: The message "advertised in a special manner to the whole country the deplorable fact of the suffering," and proposed private and church philanthropy.[64] The *News* established a relief fund, and so did some newspapers from other states; for example, the *Louisville Courier-Journal* announced plans for raising and forwarding aid to West Texas, and editorialized that

> We believe Kentucky alone will send $10,000 in seed or in money. She will do it because those men are bone of our bone, and to justify the President's confidence that the people will do what is right."[65]

Reporters emphasized the words of Clara Barton, president of the American Red Cross, after she toured the troubled areas: "The counties which have suffered from drought need help, without doubt, but not help from Congress." Private sources could do the job, she added, and she was right. Contributions arrived from all over Texas; the people of Kentucky and other states responded also. West

Texas eventually received not $10,000 of Federal funding, but over $100,000 in private aid.

The editorial power of other regional leaders, such as the *Kansas City Star,* was also in line with the well-known passage from Edmund Burke:

> To be attached to the subdivision, to love the little platoon we belong to in society, is the first principle (the germ as it were) of public affections. It is the first link in the series by which we proceed toward a love to our country, and to mankind.[66]

Star editor William Rockhill Nelson made a success of the newspaper by emphasizing community news and encouraging self-help. He publicized and praised those who grew better corn or cattle, or baked better cakes. Improvements in local butter-making were not seen as of secondary importance to national political developments.[67]

Nelson, like Horace Greeley a generation earlier, promised readers rapid coverage of local events:

> news will be furnished of fires before the smoke has cleared; murders, before the body of the victim is cold in death; and weddings, before the happy bride can collect her senses or the groom put on his traveling duster. The Evening *Star* proposes in brief to give all the news with lightning-like rapidity and deadly precision.[68]

But Nelson differed from Greeley by emphasizing personal rather than societal change; Nelson, uninterested in the *oppression story,* emphasized examination of the ethical conduct (or corruption) of individuals. At a time when the James gang was praised by some for its vaunted (and exaggerated) policy of income redistribution, the *Star* offered a large reward for the arrest of Jesse James and others, and editorialized that

> Few perhaps realize how much damage Missouri has sustained from the exploits of the James and Younger gang. The failure to bring justice on any of those desperadoes has produced a general impression throughout the country that the majority of Missourians are in sympathy with lawlessness and violence.[69]

The *Star* also fought for restrictions on governmental power and on governmental provision of monopolies to favored groups. Eight Kansas City aldermen in 1882 were under the thumb of the Corrigan street-railway monopoly and its mule-drawn cars; the *Star* termed them the "Shameless Eight" and, in a 2-year battle, stopped the franchise monopoly. Nelson wrote,

> If I owned the Metropolitan Street Railway, I would run it just as I try to run the *Star*. I wouldn't ask for a franchise. I would simply furnish such good service that the people would always be scared to death for fear I would go out of business.[70]

The *Star* constantly emphasized individual initiative, not government action. Nelson urged backyard vegetable gardens, conducted an experiment on a trial acre to show that good profits could be realized from intense cultivation of a small tract of land, and distributed free pamphlets giving the results of the experiment. Seeing alcoholism as destructive of character and not wanting to be compromised in his fight against it, Nelson gave up $50,000 in whiskey advertising. He saw the little platoons of the small town that Kansas City still was a crucial force in avoiding the problems beginning to plague eastern and midwestern urban areas: "The fact that local politics in large cities is generally corrupt is no reason why Kansas City should consider gang rule an essential part of its metropolitan government."[71]

This type of *local* emphasis, and interest in rooting out corruption rather than declaiming about oppression, was a serious obstacle to fulfillment of the old, Greeleyite dreams during the last quarter of the century. This became particularly evident as the debate about income inequality and social reform that had led to the commune movement of the 1840s and 1850s broke out anew during the 1880s and 1890s. Emphasis on limiting governmental power could be found not only on the pages of newspapers in Kansas City and Texas but in the columns of the *New York Times,* edited by the successors of Henry Raymond (who had died in 1869, 3 years before Greeley).

The *Times* became known for publicizing and editorially backing the conclusions of New York's most famous social worker of the 1880s, Josephine Shaw Lowell, when she warned that even temporary governmental relief of the poor "has the tendency to become regular and permanent . . . when it has once been accepted, the barrier is broken down. . . ."[72] She argued that guaranteed income "tends to break down character," and added that "it is the greatest wrong that can be done to him to undermine the character of a poor man."[73] Intrinsic in the writing of both Mrs. Lowell and the *Times* was the belief that man is naturally corrupt, and that changes in material are second in importance to changes in worldview.[74]

That understanding was increasingly opposed during the last two decades of the century by some popular journalists who saw natural goodness ruined by an oppressive environment. Edward Bellamy was only one of hundreds who emerged from newspaper work to write "social problem" novels such as *Dr. Heidenhoff's Process* (1879), which enthusiastically forecast modern 'shock' treatments for neurosis. Bellamy hit it big nearly a decade later with *Looking Backward, 2000–1887.* In that novel, a man through a curious mishap found himself alive, without having aged, 100 years in the future. The world was radically transformed, with peace and abundance for all—and the secret was merely "cooperation." Folks could get all they wanted from cooperative stores. Folks also attained oneness with the universe. Freedom was nonexistent—people were members of an industrial army—but this minor flaw was largely ignored.

Hundreds of newspapers serialized and distributed the writings of Bellamy,

Henry George, and other radicals.[75] The set speeches of *Looking Backward* and its follow-up tract, *Equality,* were learned by a generation of future social reformers:

> How can men be free who must ask the right to labor and to live from their fellow-men and seek their bread from the hands of others? How else can any government guarantee liberty to men save by providing them a means of labor and of life coupled with independence; and how could that be done unless the government conducted the economic system upon which employment and maintenance depend?[76]

Underlying this appealing doctrine was a view of man's nature completely opposite to that imbedded within corruption-story journalism:

> Soon was fully revealed what the divines and philosophers of the old world never would have believed, that human nature in its essential qualities is good, not bad, that men by their natural intention and structure are generous, not selfish, pitiful, not cruel, sympathetic, not arrogant . . .[77]

In short, men were "godlike . . . images of God indeed."[78]

In the early 1890s some newspapers and magazines also began giving favorable publicity to the work of early "Christian socialists" such as Professor Richard Ely. Ely founded the American Economic Association "to strive to find out the underlying principles of industrial society";[79] his goal was to apply principles enunciated by Brisbane and Greeley to all of American society, and he demanded that all unite behind the "coercive philanthropy . . . of governments, either local, state, or national."[80] Journalists fulsomely praised the gospel of salvation-through-government that was promoted by books such as William H. Fremantle's *The World as the Subject of Redemption.*[81] Government alone, Fremantle asserted, "can embrace all the wants of its members and afford them the universal instruction and elevation which they need."[82]

Much of the new doctrine was cloaked within older theological robes. Fremantle, for example, praised the worship of governmental power as a mere furtherance of Christian worship of God: "When we think of it [the Nation] as becoming, as it must do more and more, the object of mental regard, of admiration, of love, even of worship (for in it preeminently God dwells) we shall recognize to the fullest extent its religious character and functions."[83] He saw the Nation as the new Church, and as such obligated to take on the church's traditional functions of charity:

> We find the Nation alone fully organized, sovereign, independent, universal, capable of giving full expression to the Christian principle. We ought, therefore, to regard the Nation as the Church, its rulers as ministers of Christ, its whole body as a Christian brotherhood, its public assemblies as amongst the highest modes of

universal Christian fellowship, its dealing with material interests as Sacraments, its progressive development, especially in raising the weak, as the fullest service rendered on earth to God, the nearest thing as yet within our reach to the kingdom of heaven.[84]

It is hard to know how much of this many journalists absorbed and *believed*—but, as the next chapter shows, the notions of Bellamy, Ely, Fremantle, and others began to receive wide press support in the late 1890s and early 1900s. It was easier to attribute problems to social maladjustment than to innate sinfulness; if personality was a social product, individuals were not responsible for their vices. Crime reporting began to change as journalists began to attribute "antisocial action" to the stress of social factors beyond an individual's control. Editorial pages began calling for new governmental action as that action was seen not merely as a way of dividing up spoils but as a means to achieve a cooperative commonwealth, in which men and women could become godlike. Not just at populist meetings and granger halls, but in newspaper offices as well,

thoughts and theories sprouted like weeds after a May shower. . . . They discussed income tax and single tax; they talked of government ownership and the abolition of private property; fiat money, and the unity of labor, . . . and a thousand conflicting theories.[85]

To summarize: During the 30 years after the civil war the *oppression* story, although not apparent on most newspaper front pages, was putting down deep roots. Greeleyite ideas were slowly triumphing over those of Raymond; Greeleyite beliefs in man's natural goodness, and their typical political manifestation in an attack on individual property and a call for federal power, were becoming marketable commodities. Ideologies contending that the problem was not individual corruption but systemic oppression were becoming more acceptable, but they still needed the right press packaging.

Chapter 9

Of Muckrakers and Presidents

The first developer of better press packaging for the rising *oppression story* was Joseph Pulitzer, a native of Hungary whose own rag-to-riches tale began when he tried to join the Austrian army in 1864 and was rejected due to "weak eyes" and an "unpromising physique." In America, however, a Union Army decimated by 3 years of warfare was desperate for soldiers and wary of relying on a draft that was provoking riots in northern cities. The north sent recruiters to comb Europe and sign up anyone who could hold a bayonet, weak eyes or not. Pulitzer enlisted, ended up spending a year in the cavalry cleaning up after mules, and came out at war's end never having fought Confederates but ready to turn the tables on those who had taken advantage of his poor knowledge of English to make him the frequent butt of practical jokes.[1]

For Pulitzer, journalism became a weapon to avenge himself on his oppressors. In the late 1860s he became a superb reporter in St. Louis, working 18 hours a day and learning to hit the bullseye with dart-like English sentences. He also saved his money, studied the financial aspects of newspapers, and during the 1870s was able to buy first a small, German-language newspaper, the *Westliche Post,* and then (using his profits) a virtually bankrupt English-language newspaper. When he merged that cheap newspaper with another in similar distress, he suddenly had a publication with an Associated Press franchise and a name that would become mighty in journalism, the *St. Louis Post-Dispatch.*

The *Post-Dispatch* built circulation, and profits for Pulitzer, by slamming into individuals who found it hard to hit back; Pulitzer found a market for gossip and salacious stories.[2] The *Post-Dispatch* particularly liked going after ministers—

not just ministers engaged in scandalous conduct, but any who inadvertently provided opportunities for assault. When one sick reverend, on doctor's orders taking medicine with an alcoholic base, inadvertently breathed into the face of a woman who sat down next to him on a streetcar, she moved to another seat. The incident would have been forgotten immediately, except that a Pulitzer reporter who happened to be at the scene wrote a story that appeared under the following decked headline:

ROCK AND RYE. Rev. Dr. Geo. A. Lofton Goes Upon a Saintly Spree/ He is Said to Have Been Intoxicated and Grossly Insulted a Lady/ A Terrible Clerical Scandal Involving the Pastor of the Third Baptist Church.[3]

This story proved typical of local coverage that often came under attack but was enormously successful at building circulation.

In coverage of national politics, Pulitzer was a liberal Democrat who learned the usefulness of character assassination by studying the Radical Republican press of the 1860s and 1870s. For example, the *Post-Dispatch* used headlines such as "GRABBER GARFIELD" to attack in 1880 Republican presidential nominee James Garfield. The murkier the charges were, the more the *Post-Dispatch* shouted that they were "so clear, so well founded . . . so thoroughly convincing, that there is nothing left but to believe them."[4] Even one of Pulitzer's sympathetic biographers has noted that "a strain of irresponsibility was evident in Pulitzer's developing style of journalism."[5] Increasingly, the *Post-Dispatch* showed little concern for accuracy. Once, when it misidentified a young man who supposedly had urged adultery upon a chorus girl, the *Post-Dispatch* corrected itself but at the same time made fun of the man who was irate because he had been defamed.[6]

Pulitzer used his St. Louis profits to buy the *New York World* in 1883. He bullseyed the new immigrant market (one he understood well from personal experience) by combining easy-to-read, gripping stories (good for learning English) with economic envy.[7] Pulitzer's first edition of the *World*, on May 11, 1883, hit the pavement running with its front-page stories about a Wall Street plunger, a Pittsburgh hanging, a riot in Haiti, and a wronged servant girl. Typical *World* headlines were like a dragon's fire: "DEATH RIDES THE BLAST," "SCREAMING FOR MERCY," "BAPTIZED IN BLOOD," "A MOTHER'S AWFUL CRIME," "A BRIDE BUT NOT A WIFE," and "VICTIMS OF HIS PASSION." Readers who paid a penny in response to such appeals would encounter, on inside pages, Pulitzer's political agenda: tax large incomes, tax corporations, tax inheritances, redistribute income.

In the early 1890s, Pulitzer stopped short of calling for outright socialism, Bellamy-style; yet, the *World's* constant juxtaposition of current horror with future social salvation transmitted the message of hope through science and material progress, evenly distributed by benign government agents. Features such as "Experimenting with an Electric Needle and an Ape's Brain" showed that scientific transformation of man's thought patterns was just around the corner, and stories such as "Science Can Wash Your Heart" suggested that immortality was possible. In the meantime, however, monstrous crime and terrible scandal rode mankind. In one sense Pulitzer was merely imitating the methodology of the Puritan press two centuries before: emphasize bad news so that the need for the good news becomes even greater. But the message was totally changed: Instead of pointing readers toward man's corruption and God's grace, the *World* portrayed itself as the battler against systemic oppression, and proposed running over anyone (including business owners in American, Spaniards in Cuba, and Boers in South Africa) who stood in the way of "progress."[8]

The *World's* circulation soared to 60,000 in 1884, 250,000 in 1886, and 1 million during the Spanish–American War of 1898. For journalists yearning to transform society and have fun and profit, the *World* became the New York workplace of choice, much as the *Tribune* was a generation before. The *World's* full-time force numbered 1,300 in the mid-1890s, and the growing arrogance of what had become a major institution soon was apparent: Pulitzer argued that "The World should be more powerful than the President," because the President came from partisan politics and was elected to a 4-year term, while the World "goes on year after year and is absolutely free to tell the truth."[9] By 1900, Pulitzer was spending most of his time on his yacht, with 75 employees trained to cater to his whims. As one biographer put it, "The yacht represented the logical end toward which the eccentric despot, so concerned with democracy, had been working for decades. It gave him *complete control*. It was an absolute monarchy."[10]

Pulitzer began the process of framing the *oppression story* for twentieth century popular consumption, but it was William Randolph Hearst who took Pulitzer's insights, spread them across the nation, and in doing so enabled proponents of the rising macrostory to go on the attack once more. As one reporter described his excitement upon going to work for Hearst,

> At last I was to be the kind of journalist I had dreamed of being. I was to enlighten and uplift humanity. Unequaled newspaper enterprise, combined with a far-reaching philanthropy, was to reform . . . the whole United States. The printing press, too often used for selfish ends, had become a mighty engine for good in the world, and I was to be a part of the directing force. Proudly I was to march under the banner of William R. Hearst, helping to guide civilization's forward strides. The banner was a yellow one, to be sure, but yellow probably only the better to attract that part of humanity which otherwise might remain indifferent to Mr. Hearst's principles. Glaring headlines of various hues, and an occasional scandal would easily be excused, I thought, if they hastened the millennium.[11]

Hearst's union of rhetorical violence and centralizing vision was in turn picked up by a group of early 20th-century magazine writers who became known as "muckrakers" and heavily influenced practice for decades to come.

Hearst, unlike Greeley or Pulitzer, was born—in 1863—with a silver spoon in his mouth and bars of silver to stack; George Hearst was owner of rich mines and a California seat in the U.S. senate. George Hearst paid for young Willie to meander through Harvard, work for a short time on Pulitzer's *World,* and decide that the pleasure of journalistic power was greater than anything life as a playboy could offer. George Hearst had won a failing newspaper, the *San Francisco Examiner,* in a poker game; when Willie begged for it, his father handed it over.

Young Hearst loved newspapering. He would examine newspaper proofs by standing above them and turning pages with his toes while manifesting curious emotional reactions. One young editor, James Coleman, recorded his first experience with this curious procedure:

> My eyes strained wide and I tried vainly to keep from swallowing my bubble gum when Hearst suddenly spread the proofs on the floor, and began a sort of tap dance around and between them. . . . The cadence of it speeded up with his reactions of disturbance and slowed down to a strolling rhythm when he approved. Between dances, he scribbled illegible corrections on the margins and finally gave the proofs back to me.[12]

Hearst made the *Examiner* profitable by adopting Pulitzer's combination of sensationalism and exposure of oppression. In 1895 he purchased the *New York Journal* and soon became famous for sending dozens of reporters to the scenes of crimes on bicycles or in carriages pulled by fire and cavalry horses; Hearst himself could be seen "leaping wild-eyed and long-legged into a carriage, to be whisked like a field marshall to the scene of battle."[13]

Hearst ordered his editors to "make a great and continuous noise to attract readers; denounce crooked wealth and promise better conditions for the poor to keep readers. INCREASE CIRCULATION." As one historian has noted, the "yellow journalism" pioneered by Pulitzer and Hearst was characterized not only by big headlines and exciting stories, but by "ostentatious sympathy with the underdog. . . .' "[14] Hearst's capital-S Sympathy was his first step toward making readers think he cared about them; calls for socialism came next. Hearst wrote in one signed editorial that socialistic management was the key to advancement, for

> Combination and organization are necessary steps in industrial progress. We are advancing toward a complete organization in which the government will stand at the head and be the trust of trusts. It is ridiculous to attempt to stop this development.[15]

By 1904 Hearst was explicitly arguing that "the greatest need of this republic today is an aggressive and well organized radical party."[16] Liberal Herbert Croly compared Hearst to Robespierre, writing that Hearst's ambition was to bring about a "socialistic millennium."[17] Hearst evidently believed that the press had the power to "so exert the forces of publicity that public opinion" would compel such an outcome.[18] His editorial writers worked hard to press issues into a class struggle mold; one of the *Journal's* classic editorials portrayed

> the horse after a hard day's work grazing in a swampy meadow. He has done his duty and is getting what he can in return. On the Horse's flank you see a leech sucking blood. The leech is the trust. The horse is the labor union.[19]

The *New York Journal* ran big cartoons showing Mark Hanna, McKinley's campaign manager, as a fat bully dressed in clothes filled with dollar signs, with McKinley a puppet on his lap. Hearst's viciousness seemed unlimited; as one observer noted, Hanna was depicted as "an amalgam of all sins. He was foulness compact . . . He sent poor sailors, forced on his ships by bestial labor masters, out to sea on the wintry lakes cold and starving, unpaid and mutinous."[20] Hearst's discretionary coverage screamed that he favored the poor; such posturing was worth millions of dollars to him. Hearst sold enough newspapers to make Louis Wiley, business manager of the *Times*, cry out that crusading should be considered "a commercial trade."[21]

Day after day, Hearst's newspapers in San Francisco, New York, and then across the country, provided an artful combination of sensation and hope. On the one hand, the present was tragedy, with headlines such as "He murdered his friends" or "He ran amuck with a hatchet."[22] A woman already in jail for beating a man senseless with a beer bottle, stabbed her jailer with a hat-pin; a maidservant poisoned her mistress' soup.[23] In New York, a boy shot and killed his father, who was beating his mother; another woman told "How She Horsewhipped Husband," and an 11-year-old drank a bottle of acid because she did "not want to live."[24] On the other hand, the future would be much better. Someday, wealth now used for "barbaric" displays of wealth could be used to fight "distress and misery."[25] Science (actually, pseudo-science) would help: the *San Francisco Examiner* reported that one professor had produced "solidified air" and another had found out that what a woman eats determines the gender of her baby.[26]

Hearst made an idol out of circulation, but he also tried making one out of himself. He began instructing his reporters and editors to praise him at every possibility. He posed as a benefactor of the poor, sending pale children on jaunts to the beach. A reporter sent to cover one expedition, however, later wrote that she was given only one container of ice cream to be dealt out on a Coney Island trip:

> When at last I placed a dab on each saucer, a little fellow in ragged knickerbockers got up and declared that the Journal was a fake and I thought there was going to be a riot. I took away the ice-cream from a deaf and dumb kid who couldn't holler and gave it to the malcontent. Then I had to write my story beginning: "Thousands of children, pale-faced but happy, danced merrily down Coney Island's beaches

yesterday and were soon sporting in the sun-lit waves shouting, 'God bless Mr. Hearst.' "[27]

Once, when Hearst ordered all his reporters to mention his newspapers' "comic supplements" in their stories whenever possible, one reporter filed this report from a disaster scene,

> I was the first to reach the injured and dying. "God bless Mr. Hearst," a little child cried as I stooped to lave her brow. Then she smiled and died. I spread one of our comic supplements over the pale, still face.[28]

Some Hearstian efforts were serious, not ludicrous. When Governor Goebel of Kentucky was assassinated early in 1901, the *Journal* printed a quatrain by reporter Ambrose Bierce: "The bullet that pierced Goebel's breast/ Can not be found in all the West;/ Good reason, it is speeding here/ To stretch McKinley on his bier."[29] Soon afterward the *Journal* editorialized that "if bad institutions and bad men can be got rid of only by killing, then the killing must be done." When the anarchist Czolgosz assassinated President McKinley later that year, the killer was said to have been arrested with a copy of the *Journal* in his coat pocket.[30] Hearst was hanged in effigy, circulation for a time dropped, and President Theodore Roosevelt said that Czolgosz had probably been led to his crime by "reckless utterances of those who, on the stump and in the public press, appeal to dark and evil spirits."[31] But Hearst bounced back, changing the name of his New York morning edition to the *American*.

Hearst showed through such conduct that he was the prototypical solipsistic journalist of the 20th century, moving around real individuals as if they were make-believe characters.[32] Some opposed him: Congressman John A. Sullivan called Hearst the Nero of American politics for his attempts to incite class conflict, and others labeled Hearst a socialist and hung his picture with red flags underneath it.[33] For a time, Hearst was able to convince some voters to accept their role in his dreams. He used his newspaper clout to win election to Congress by a big margin, and wrote after the landslide:

> We have won a splendid victory. We are allying ourselves with the workingman, the real Americans. This is just the beginning of our political actions. Our social aspirations have a greater chance than ever to be realized.[34]

Hearst was on his way. But the movement he represented was, with its newspaper base, a big city phenomenon. The key question was whether his emphasis on oppression would spread around the country. As it turned out, it did, at least in part through the influence of national magazines such as *Munsey's, McClure's, Cosmopolitan, Everybody's,* and *The Arena,* which provided an outlet for freelancing radicals, particularly in the years 1903 through 1906. *Munsey's* for a time was the most popular, with popular fiction and reportage covering ownership of popular utilities and similar subjects attracting a circulation of 700,000 monthly.[35] *The Arena* was less popular but more consistent in promoting socialist ideas, as it pushed its 100,000 readers to "agitate, educate, organize, and move forward, casting aside timidity and insisting that the Republic shall no longer lag behind in the march of progress."[36]

The hopes of the radicals, although diverse in some aspects, tended often to parallel those of Horace Greeley two generations before. For example, Upton Sinclair, at first a believer in communalism, invested profits from his book *The Jungle* in a New Jersey commune, "Home Colony"; it failed, but Sinclair thought it a good try, an "industrial Republic in the making."[37] After seeing what went into some cans of meat Sinclair espoused another of Greeley's favorite causes, vegetarianism, and also argued that meat eating had no place in an agricultural system managed on principles of efficiency and nutrition.[38] Sinclair for a time had new causes every year, but eventually, like Greeley, became an apologist for terrorism—in this case, that of Lenin rather than John Brown.[39] Like Greeley, Sinclair also confused holiness and hatred, eventually declaring that Jesus had been an anarchist and agitator whose vision of violent upheaval was covered up by church institutions.[40]

Sinclair was one of the first major journalists to explicitly adopt socialism; others moved in that direction more slowly as they abandoned youthful Christian allegiances and sought a new faith. Ray Stannard Baker, after reading Bellamy's *Looking Backward* and Henry George's *Progress and Poverty,* was among those who became annoyed at the idea that God, not journalists, brought salvation; as Baker wrote in his memoirs, "I was temperamentally impatient. I wanted explanations promptly. I wanted to know what *I* should do to help save the world."[41] When Baker's father suggested other ways to save the world, Baker responded, "I'm on my way up. If my strength and grit hold out I'm going to make my influence felt before I get through with it."[42] In 1899, after 2 years of New York journalism, Baker wrote to his father that "The longer I am in my present work, the greater seem the responsibilities and opportunities of high grade journalism."[43] Five years later, he was still writing that he had "a mission to perform," and felt successful: "I think we have struck the right Grail."[44]

The most famous of the radicals, Lincoln Steffens, wrote that he began his quest as a student at the University of California during the 1880s, where professors "could not agree upon what was knowledge, nor upon what was good and what evil, nor why."[45] To find out about good and evil, Steffens wrote that he had to become a journalist. He certainly saw evil—"graft and corruption" were everywhere—but he did not see them as coming from within. Once, discussing the Biblical fall within the garden of Eden, he said the culprit was not Adam, or Eve, or even the snake: "It was, it is, the apple." Good people were corrupted by a bad environment—and the goal of journalists, Steffens believed, was to change the environment by working to eliminate capitalism, which he saw as the 20th-century equivalent of the apple.

Steffens and other leading muckrakers generally shared two biographical elements. First, most came from elite colleges: Burton Hendrick came from Yale, Baker from the University of Michigan, Will Irwin from Stanford, David Graham Phillips from DePauw and Princeton, George Kibbee Turner from Williams College, Lincoln Steffens from the University of California at Berkeley, Ida Tarbell from The Sorbonne.[46] Second, many had experience with the newspapers of Pulitzer, Hearst, or both. Charles Edward Russell, for example, served as city editor of Pulitzer's *New York World,* managing editor of Hearst's *New York Journal,* and publisher of Hearst's Chicago entry, the *American;* he left those posts to freelance and become a Socialist Party politician. Lincoln Steffens, David Graham Phillips, and others had Pulitzer/Hearst reporting experience.[47]

Such apprenticeships often were vital in the development of writing styles that could both appeal to magazine readers and proselytize them for causes of the left. The sense of mission also tended to grow during years of training; many Pulitzer and Hearst alumni felt that their mission was

> to set forth some new and wonderful truth of world-wide importance, in a manner to make the nations of the earth sit up and take notice—to cause the heart of humanity to throb and thrill, from Greenland to the Ganges—a message in words that would enthuse and enthrall, gleam and glitter, dazzle and delight.[48]

Liveliness often tended to slide into viciousness, however, as it had in coverage of Andrew Johnson. Apparently, when journalists believe or argue that poverty and war can be ended if only certain steps are taken, those who refuse to step lively are commonly depicted as villains; as French revolutionary writers showed during the Reign of Terror, the furor is doubled when the journalists have keen personal ambition.

In America's 20th century, William Randolph Hearst was the first journalistic leader to assault regularly those who stood in his path. When Hearst could not get the Democratic presidential nomination in 1904, he called Judge Alton Parker, the party's nominee, a "living, breathing cockroach from under the sink," and labeled the party's chairman "a plague spot in the community spreading vileness."[49] At one time, Hearst's New York newspaper had 2,000 names on its S-List (persons to be mentioned only with scorn), and a reporter had to be assigned to read copy just to make sure mistakes of honesty were not made. Through all this, Hearst retained the support of leading journalists of the left; Charles Russell praised him, and Upton Sinclair declared in his book *The Industrial Republic* that a bright socialist future would not be far off if Hearst became president.[50] Steffens wrote a sympathetic profile of Hearst and explained that the publisher "was driving toward his unannounced purpose to establish some measure of democracy, with patient but ruthless—force."[51]

Members of the media elite who learned from Pulitzer or Hearst also tended to follow them in their virulence. For example, when the U.S. Senate in 1906 debated the Pure Food and Drug Act, Senator Joseph W. Bailey of Texas spoke in opposition, saying:

> I believe that the man who would sell to the women and children of this country articles of food calculated to impair their health is a public enemy, and ought to be sent to prison. No senator here is more earnestly in favor of legislation against adulterated food and drink as I am. . . . But I insist that such legislation belongs to the states and not to the general government. When something happens not exactly in accord with public sentiment, the people rush to Congress until it will happen after a while that Congress will have so much to do that it will do nothing well.[52]

But David Graham Phillips ridiculed that statement, saying that Bailey opposed good food and was participating in the "treason of the Senate." Within Phillips' understanding, anyone opposing federal legislation in a good cause was corrupt and uncaring.

The term *muckraking,* which came to describe journalistic behavior during this century's first decade, grew out of President Theodore Roosevelt's response to the early articles in Phillips' series. Before the series Roosevelt already was a media critic: After meeting Steffens and publisher S. S. McClure in October 1905, Roosevelt told McClure

> It is an unfortunate thing to encourage people to believe that all crimes are connected with business, and that the crime of graft is the only crime. I wish very much that you could have articles showing up the hideous iniquity of which mobs are guilty, the wrongs of violence by the poor as well as the wrongs of corruption by the rich . . . [showing] that you stand as much against anarchic violence and crimes of brutality as against corruption and crimes of greed. . . .[53]

When the series began Theodore Roosevelt in 1906 could have let the attacks on certain senators slide by; he had been personally friendly to several of the magazine writers and needed their help in passing his own reform package. But Roosevelt was a fighter, and he had long been critical of Hearst on both ethical and ideological grounds. (Hearst, for his part, had called Roosevelt one who "has sold himself to the devil and will live up to the bargain."[54]) Roosevelt complained that

> the man who in a yellow newspaper or in a yellow magazine makes a ferocious attack on good men or even attacks on bad men with exaggeration or for things they

have not done, is a potent enemy of those of us who are really striving in good faith to expose bad men and drive them from power.[55]

In 1906, the president felt, it was time to oppose those magazine writers who peddled Hearst's politics and defamatory tendencies on slick pages rather than newsprint.

Roosevelt let fly in a speech full of such memorable critiques of journalistic practice that it deserves quoting at length. He said:

> In Bunyan's *Pilgrim's Progress* you may recall the description of the Man with the Muck-rake, the man who could look no way but downward, with the muck-rake in his hand; who was offered a celestial crown for his muck-rake, but who would neither look up nor regard the crown he was offered, but continued to rake to himself the filth of the floor.

> In *Pilgrim's Progress* the Man with the Muck-rake is set forth as the example of him whose vision is fixed on carnal instead of on spiritual things. Yet he also typifies the man who in this life consistently refuses to see aught that is lofty, and fixes his eyes with solemn intentness only on that which is vile and debasing. Now, it is very necessary that we should not flinch from seeing what is vile and debasing. There is filth on the floor, and it must be scraped up with the muck-rake; and there are times and places where this service is the most needed of all the services that can be performed. But the man who never does anything else, who never thinks or speaks or writes, save of his feats with the muck-rake, speedily becomes, not a help to society, not an incitement to good, but one of the most potent forces for evil.

Roosevelt argued, much as Marchamont Nedham and other Puritans had, that exposure of wrongdoing was vital, but that writers must remember

> that the attack is of use only if it is absolutely truthful. The liar is no whit better than the thief, and if his mendacity takes the form of slander, he may be worse than most thieves. It puts a premium upon knavery untruthfully to attack an honest man, or even with hysterical exaggeration to assail a bad man with untruth. An epidemic of indiscriminate assault upon character does not good, but very great harm. The soul of every scoundrel is gladdened whenever an honest man is assailed, or even when a scoundrel is untruthfully assailed.

Roosevelt concluded that:

> The effort to make financial or political profit out of the destruction of character can only result in public calamity. Gross and reckless assaults on character, whether on the stump or in newspaper, magazine, or book, create a morbid and vicious public sentiment, and at the same time act as a profound deterrent to able men of normal sensitiveness and tend to prevent them from entering the public service at any price.

Hundreds of favorable responses to Roosevelt's speech indicate that his concern about press bullying was widely shared. Protests about the media elite's ideological agenda were common:

> Socialism—that's where these leaders of the magazines and newspapers are headed for. The Sentimentalist who looks to find there the Kingdom of Brotherly Love upon Earth, the honest man, hysterical with anger at the crimes of high finance, the brave fool spoiling for a fight, the good citizen who says to himself, 'that the evil is so great the whole must be swept away—' all alike are following the lead of the statesmen of the yellow press towards the ruinous experiment of straight-out socialism.[56]

Such complaints, although addressed to a modern ideological development, had an old-fashioned ring to them. After all, Andrew Bradford, editor in Philadelphia of the *American Weekly Mercury* two centuries before, had opposed "that unwarrantable License which some People of much fire, but little judgment have taken of endeavouring to subvert the Fundamental Points of Religion or Morality."[57]

A downward curve for the political prospects of William Randolph Hearst may be dated from the time of Roosevelt's speech, although other factors contributed to the failure of the publisher's ambitions.[58] For a while, Hearst retained the support of journalists on the left, but as he lost elections and the sensationalism of his newspapers seemed a bit embarrassing, radicals edged away from him. Hearst in turn lost his patience with them, and by the 1920s and 1930s was stoutly opposing governmental control of the economy. (Perhaps because of Hearst's "treason" to the left after 1920, he is often regarded by journalism historians as a bad guy, and Pulitzer—who left money to found a journalism school at Columbia and to hand out prizes—is given a white hat.[59])

Although the muckrakers abandoned their one-time standard bearer, they did not drop their flag. The media elite's opposition to Roosevelt was particularly intense in that the president was himself at times a writer-reformer; it is especially hard for those who see themselves as altruists to be depicted as malefactors by one of their own. A few lesser known reporters wrote confessional statements backing up Roosevelt's charges; one Hearst veteran acknowledged himself to be "a veritable Hessian of the press, even a hired assassin of character, striking from the dark, or from behind the mask of journalistic zeal for public welfare . . ."[60] But the leaders soldiered on, unrepentant.

Upton Sinclair claimed to speak for those journalistic leaders—"I know, more or less intimately, nearly every man who at present is raking muck in America"— in issuing a strong reply to Roosevelt's accusations.[61] Sinclair wrote of how all the leading muckrakers shared a belief:

> that the history of humanity up to the present time represents a series of failures. Races emerge from barbarism. They are joyous and proud and strong; they struggle

and conquer, they toil and achieve. . . . But all the time there is a worm within the bud, which gnaws at it; and just when the flower seems most perfect, its petals fall, and it is scattered and trampled into the dust.[62]

The worm for Sinclair was private property, and he wrote of how he and the other leading muckrakers had realized that to kill it, they needed to lead "a revolt against capitalism."[63] The problem, however, was that people were forgetful, so it was up to journalists to be no less than "the faculty of recollection in the growing social mind." The muckraker, Sinclair wrote, "represents the effort of the race to profit by experience, and to do otherwise than repeat infinitely the blunders which have proved fatal in the past." The muckraker "as forerunner of a revolution," Sinclair concluded, "will be recognized in the future as a benefactor of his race."[64]

Those reporters who had little thought of being benefactors—they had a job to do and a paycheck to get—might scowl at such notions. And yet, with all the cynicism that journalists love to show, the streak of pride would grudgingly show itself: one reporter reminisced of how, for a time, he had been

battling for the people, and making tyrants quail, in a truly heroic journalistic style. I was forging shafts of ripping, tearing words that would demolish the fort of the robber chiefs who were taking unlawful tribute from the public. I called the gas company 'the Gorgon-headed monopoly,' 'the banded infamy,' and 'a greeder gorger from the public purse.' I felt myself as heroic as those who had led the crusades of old. I was a lieutenant of a modern Godfrey or a Richard the Lionhearted in a holy war. Pen and typewriter, mightier than sword and cannon, were my weapons. In the press was concentrated the strength of an army, and this I directed.[65]

Top college students who enjoyed writing began gravitating more and more toward journalism; Walter Lippmann, for example, went from Harvard to an internship with Lincoln Steffens, and also became a protege of Charles Edward Russell.

Steffens and Russell, in turn, set the standard for "the right stuff" in leading-edge journalism much as had Horace Greeley two generations before; they trained a generation of young journalists to see not only poverty and corruption as the responsibility of capitalism, but all war as the result of capitalist desires to find "a dumping ground abroad for a surplus domestic product . . . for all times, and in all places, and under all conditions, Capitalism is War."[66] When the young journalists came to editorial power during the 1930s, some would argue as did their elders that the solution to all problems was socialism, which could be achieved only through raising inter-class hostility. (And, because the oppression was go great and the final victory so crucial, smearing some individuals along the way would not matter.)

Few journalists early in the century matched Steffens and Russell in clarity of political theology. Some, such as Ray Stannard Baker, merely found themselves attracted to the Socialist Party's "high & unselfish ideals," with its "community spirit of service" that offered "brotherhood nearer than anything I know to the real church . . . I must join something."[67] Still, the trend was clear, and many of the media elite were ready to adopt a Marxist perspective as long as it was given a spiritual gloss. For example, David Graham Phillips, whose attacks on the Senate justified Roosevelt's famous response, also wrote novels in which heroines compared Karl Marx to Jesus Christ, not unfavorably:

> They were both labor leaders—labor agitators. The first proclaimed the brotherhood of man. But he regarded this world as hopeless and called on the weary and heavy-laden masses to look to the next world for the righting of their wrongs. Then—eighteen centuries after—came the second Jew—and he said 'No! not in the hereafter, but in the here. Here and now, my brothers. Let us make this world a heaven. Let us redeem ourselves and destroy this devil of ignorance who is holding us in this hell!'[68]

The passage concluded, "It was three hundred years before the first Jew began to triumph. It won't be so long before there are monuments to Marx in clean and beautiful and free cities all over the earth."[69]

Most elite journalists in the years before World War I were content to locate social problems in the environment rather than in man himself. Will Irwin, for example, wrote of his desire to change "an American habit of mind"; he was upset because when Americans "find any institution going wrong, we think first of individual dishonesty." Irwin's goal was to teach readers "to attribute the unfair working of social forces to faults in the system of things."[70] Even "moderates" such as William Allen White argued that capitalism was a product of "diabolical self-interest" and that journalists should be "preparing the ground for a nationalization of industries that may pass from control to ownership—from industrial bonds to government bonds and then to the breaking up of great fortunes holding the government bonds by inheritance & income taxes."[71]

Although Roosevelt's attack in 1906 had an effect, muckraking remained a major journalistic genre through 1917; then, as Americans went to fight overseas, war reporting became dominant for a time. The year 1917 also marks the end of an era because the tragedy of trench warfare in France was compounded by the Soviet seizure of power in Moscow, the fall-out from which would coat much of the 20th century. After the Bolshevik Revolution a few muckrakers, including John Spargo, distanced themselves from the blood that flowed and the red flag that signified the willingness to spill more. Others took a harder line; a contemporary remembered Lincoln Steffens "talking revolution and blood—and sucking the guts out of a chocolate eclair impaled on an upright fork."[72]

Four hundred years earlier, modern journalism had begun with the sound of
Luther hammering on the cathedral door. In 1917 a new dispensation appeared to
be underway; Steffens baptized the Russian Revolution, writing of how Petrograd
mobs made him "think of the mobs that followed Jesus about." (Later he found
the Exodus story a better vehicle and wrote *Moses in Red,* which attempted to
prove that "not Lenin, but Nature required the excesses of the Russian revolution;
or, if you please, God."[73]) For centuries much of American journalism had
emphasized *restraint,* but Steffens would praise Soviet leaders—as Benjamin
Bache had lauded the French revolutionaries—for their willingness to "lay out
consciously and carry through ruthlessly" a program "to arrange the conditions
of social living . . . to adjust the forces of economic life."[74]

Steffens' most famous (and often misquoted) remark was, upon returning
from the Soviet Union, "I have gone over into the future, and it works."[75]
From 1917 on, leading American writers would look to the Soviet Union—
and later to China, Cuba, North Vietnam, or Nicaragua, as each revolution
was successively discredited—for hints on how to change the world.[76] Steffens
set the standard for those who wanted to make sure the future would work;
when other radicals still thought Steffens soft, a playful child of the despised
bourgeoisie "wandering among the social battlefields," he proved himself by
engaging in "slander and character assassination" against anyone who stood
in the way of "progress."[77]

Earlier journalists had pointed readers toward the Bible and, later, the
Constitution; but after 1917, leading editors such as Oswald Garrison Villard
argued that "There are plain masses seeking a journalistic Moses to clarify
their minds, to give them a program of reconstruction."[78] Leading newspapers
and magazines of the next seven decades would display the words of those
who saw man as possessing unlimited potential that a strong and benevolent
state could help to liberate, if only journalistic influence were brought to bear
on the side of perceived righteousness. A journalism that emphasized the
oppression story could once again achieve the muckraking heights as "Argus-
eyed guardian of the people's rights, the omnipotent champion of the oppressed,
the scourge of the oppressor, the light of the land, the greatest uplifting force
in civilization."[79]

The story of those next seven decades could fill another book. But, briefly,
what became most ironic during this period was the tendency of many journalists
to apologize for and promote new forms of oppression, while claiming that they
were fighting for liberty. In doing so, they often neglected the lessons in liberty
provided by their courageous predecessors, and genuflected before a future that
claimed to work but was in many ways a curious merger of the official and
oppression stories. *Corruption story* journalists had viewed centralized government as part of the problem; *oppression story* journalists would see it as the center
of the solution, the weapon that could force social changes and coerce America
into utopia. American journalism, which had developed as an antiestablishment

force, had become part of a new establishment that did not have the self-understanding to recognize itself as one.

A key question for the press, as the last decade of the 20th century began, was whether the best and brightest journalists would have the grace to look at themselves and say, with Edmund in *King Lear,* "The wheel is come full circle; I am here."

Appendix A: 16th-, 17th-, and 18th-Century Moral Tales

Before newspapers were an everyday occurrence in England, many news ballads sensationally covered current events while communicating biblical morality. The "ballads"—quickly composed, event-oriented songs printed on single sheets of paper and sold in the streets—apparently were everywhere. In the words of one historian:

> Ballads were not written for poetry. They were, in the main, the equivalent of modern newspapers, and it cannot well be denied that customarily they performed their function as creditably in verse as the average newspaper does in prose. Journalistic ballads outnumbered all other types. . . . In them are clearly reflected the lives and thoughts, the hopes and fears, the beliefs and amusements, of sixteenth and seventeenth century Englishmen.[1]

The ballads were on vastly different subjects, but they often had a common theological thrust. To cite a very early example, one report of a strange animal birth in 1562 first provided a description of the piglet whose head was shaped like that of a dolphin, and then gave "An Admonition unto the Reader":

> Let us knowe by these ugly sights,/ And eke consider well,/ That our God is the Lord of mights,/ Who rules both heaven and hell./ By whose strong hand these monsters here/ Were formed as ye see,/ That it mighte to the world appere,/ Almightie him to bee/ Who might also us men have formde/ After a straunge device.[2]

124

The emphasis on God's sovereignty in that stanza was followed by the corollary story of man's sinfulness in the next:

And loke what great deformitie/ In bodies ye beholde;/ Much more is in our mindes truly,/ An hundred thousand folde./ So that we have great cause in deede,/ Our sinnes for to confesse,/ And eke to call to God with speede,/ The same for to redresse.

An account by another writer of that same incident drew a similar moral: "These straunge and monstrous thinges Almighty God sendeth amongest us, that we shuld not be forgetfull of his almighty power, nor unthankeful for his great mercies so plentifully poured upon us."[3]

Ballads frequently cited earthquakes as tokens of God's power. Within several days of an April 6, 1580 earthquake, five pamphlets or ballads about it were for sale on the streets. The titles tell the message: "A godly newe ballat moving us to repent by ye example of ye erthquake."[4] "Alarm for London and Londoners settinge forthe the thunderinge peales of Gods mercye." "A true and terrible example of Gods wrathe shewed by ye generall earthquake." (One title sounds as if it has rock 'n roll potential—"Quake, quake, it is tyme to quake. When towers and townes and all Doo shake.")

Fire reporting, then as now, was dramatic. In 1586 one report of a fire in the town of Beckles observed:

The flame whereof increasing still/ The blustering windes did blowe,/ And into divers buildings by/ Disperst it to and fro;/ So kindling in most grievous fort,/ It waxed huge and hie;/ The river then was frozen, so/ No water they could come by.[5]

The balladeer-reporter went on to write that the fire was part of God's providence. That did not imply that the fire was necessarily punishment for the townsfolks' sins. It did suggest that the fire was a warning, and that residents should "Seeke not your neighbors lasting spoyle/ By greedy sute in lawe;/ Live not in discord and debate,/ Which doth destruction draw." Beckle was "a mirrour to all such/ That doth in pleasure stay." God's judgment could come at any time, and Englishmen should have their spiritual affairs in order.

During this period, for the first time in English-language publications, "news" began to be organized. Networks of reporters and publishers emerged, and timeliness became significant: Many ballads and pamphlets were published 2 days after the events took place, and reports of some executions were prepared largely in advance, like obituaries today, with only last-minute (literally) details added. The emphasis on telling a moral tale continued, however. A typical account of spousal murder concerned an innkeeper's wife becoming friendly with "a Person of ill fame and very dissolute liver . . . in a more familiar manner, than was convenient," and then conspiring with him to murder her husband"; the murderess eventually was executed.[6]

Publications were not afraid to be sensational. In 1624 a newsbook entitled *The crying Murther: Contayning the cruell and most horrible Butcher of Mr. Trat*, told of how four murderers,

> with their hands already smoking in his blood, did cut up his carcass, unbowel and quarter it; then did they burn his head and privy members, parboil his flesh and salt it up, that so the sudden stink and putrefaction being hindered, the murderers might the longer be free from [discovery].[7]

But the body was found "all saving the head and members, disposed in this manner and form following. His arms, legs, thighs, and bowels were powdered up into two earthen steens or pots in a lower room of the house . . ., the bulk of his carcass was placed in a vat or tub." The murderers were hanged, and "died obstinate and unrepenting sinners." The pamphlet's author was careful to say that his story was based on "intelligence which I have received from credible persons, engaged in their trial."

Writers saw an important purpose in such coverage. John Reynolds in 1622 had provided one of the fullest rationales for stories of crime and disaster when he wrote of his desire to help readers understand the dangers of "the bewitching World, the alluring Flesh, and the inticing Devill."[8] He listed items that should be viewed critically:

> Wealth, Riches, Dignities, Honours, Preferments, Sumptuous houses, perfumed Beds, Vessels of gold and silver, pompous Apparell, Delicious fare . . . Perfuming, Powdering, Crisping, Painting, Amorous kisses, Sweet smiles, Sugared speeches, Wanton embracings, and Lascivious dalliance. . . .

Reynolds argued that Satan would take advantage of whatever tendencies his careless readers might possess:

> Are we inclined to wantonnesse, and Lasciviousnesse, he will fit us with meanes and opportunity to accomplish our carnall desires: or are wee addicted to covetousness and honours, hee will either cause us to breake our hearts, or our necks, to obtaine it: for it is indifferent to him, either how or in what manner we inlarge and fill up the empty roomes of his vast and infernall kingdome. . . .[9]

Reynolds wrote of two ways to avoid citizenship in that infernal kingdom: Worshiping and praying to God, and learning from the errors of others. Journalism could play a crucial role in the latter task. Reynolds wrote that his accounts of evil thought leading to evil action were for our detestation, not for our imitation: Since it is a poynt of (true and happy) wisdome in all men to beware by other mens harmes; Reade it then with a full intent to profit thy selfe thereby, and so thou mayest boldly, and safely rest assured, that the sight of their sinnes and punishments, will prove the reformation of thine owne.[10]

Reynolds, like other journalists of his time, stressed a condemnation of sin and a proclamation of the need for repentance and future avoidance. His writing was democratic in coverage and style but not at all in theology; early journalists proposed not that each man should be an oracle unto himself, but that sin was real, that all were ensnared in it, and some captured by it. He wanted readers to avoid entangling alliances of the kind depicted in a ballad, *Murder upon Murder,* in which "a man of honest parentage" married "a filthy whore," who "sotted" his mind so that they lived a "vile loose life" and were "bent to cruelty."[11]

Other ballads presented what their writers perceived as the general mood of early 17th-century England. One composition by John Barker—"A Balade declaryng how neybourhed, love, and trew dealyng is gone"—lugubriously stated:

Now straunge it is to men of age,
The which they se before their face,
This world to be in such outrage,
It was never sene in so bad case.
Neibourhed nor love is none,
Trew dealyng now is fled and gone

Where shall one fynde a man to trust,
Alwaye to stande in tyme of neede?
The most parte now they are unjust,
Fayre in wordes, but false indeede.
Neybourhed nor love is none,
True dealyng now is fled and gone[12]

The ballad went on that way for 19 verses, but in the 20th gave the hope:

Graunt, oh God, for thy mercyes sake,
That neighbourhed and dealyng trewe
May once agayne our spirites awake,
That we our lyves may chaunge a-new;
Then neybourhed and love alone
May come agayne to every one.

Later in the century, the corruption story was carried on through ballads of domestic tragedy combined with pleas for repentance. For example, in 1661 the ballad "Misery to be lamented" reported that a man had been buried alive and was unable to get out of his coffin, but cried out so loud that people who heard his shouts dug up the coffin and opened it: "His Coffin opened was, wherein/ a dolefull sight they then beheld:/ With strugling he had bruis'd his skin,/ his head and eyes were sadly sweld." The conclusion was,

> Now let us all with one consent/ turn to the Lord with heart and mind:/ And of our grievous sins repent,/ that so we may God's mercy find,/ And to conclude to God let's call,/ from such a death Lord keep us all.[13]

By the last third of the 17th century, specific genres of sensational reporting were emerging. For example, "The Bloody Butcher," a ballad broadside of 1667, began with an exclamation about "What horrid execrable Crimes/ Possess us in these latter Times;/Not Pestilence, nor Sword, nor Fire,/ Will make us from our Sins retyre."[14] The report told of a husband and pregnant wife arguing about his adultery, and then:

> With a strong long sharp-poynted knife,/ Into the back he stabs his wife:/ Flesh of his flesh, bone of his bone,/ With one dead-doing blow is gone.

> She faltred, fainted, fell down dead,/ Upon the ground her bloud was shed;/ The little infant in the womb/ Received there both Life and Toomb.

> Then was he Apprehended, by/ Some Neighbours that did hear her cry/ Out Murther, murther, and for this,/ He judg'd and Executed is.

> Let this a warning be to those,/ Whose Passions are their greatest Foes . . ./ Return to God, reform your Lives,/ Men be not bitter to your wives.

The consistency of themes during this period is indicated by a similar story 30 years later, "The Murtherer Justly Condemned," that also spotlighted an adulterer who killed his wife:

> He had long been absent which made her suspect,/ Both her and his business he did much neglect,/ Which put her in passion, that streightway she went,/ To know by this usage what to her he meant.

> In Leaden-Hall Market she found him, and there/ The cause of her grief she did freely declare./ Though justly reproved, yet so Angry he grew,/ That at her with violence his Knife he then threw.[15]

The story continued with the man tried, found guilty, and awaiting hanging:

> His Drunken Debauchries now swarm in his mind,/ And how he to her and himself was unkind,/ By spending his money so idley on those,/ That Lewdly had brought him to trouble and woes,/ And though for Repentance it is not too late,/ Yet death now looks terrible on life's short date.

Finally, the practical application was rammed home:

> Thus let all Rash men well consider his fall,/ How innocence loudly for Vengeance
> do's call,/ And govern their passions that bring them to shame,/ For which when
> too late they themselves do much blame.
>
> Consider how Rashness brings troubles and fears,/ Shame, Ruin, and death, it oft
> for them prepares,/ Then let all be warn'd how they rashly proceed,/ Least trouble
> and anguish for them be decreed.

Hundreds of similar crime ballads were sold in the streets during this period.
They typically showed a strong faith in biblical right and wrong and a stress on
God's sovereignty, while at the same time claiming accuracy of reporting. "Sad
News from Salisbury," for example, presented tragedies "incredible to believe,
but that some who were in the same Storm are alive to justify the truth thereof."[16]
That stress on eyewitnesses was important because the purpose of the tale was
not mere amusement, but testimony to be taken as important only if true; the
story was to be a "warning to all,/ Least greater Judgments on this land befall."
The specific detail, rather than emphasizing the plight of nobles or gentlefolk,
was thoroughly democratic:

> Collins the Taunton Carryer, people say,/ Upon the Douns did strangly loose his
> way,/ Two of his Passengers were starv'd with cold,/ A fearful Spectacle for to
> behold. . . .
>
> And this for truth report us plainly tells,/ The Carryer that belong'd to Bath and
> Wells,' His own dear Son was frozen unto death;/ And on the Downs did loose his
> dearest breath. . . .
>
> And thirty more in Sometshire were lost/ In this unusual Snow and cruel Frost,/
> Who littel thought when they went out of door,/ Their wives & children they should
> see no more. . . .

Then came the crucial journalistic question, then as now—not just who, what,
when, where, and how, but *why:*

> This judgment came from god's almighty hand/ For sins committed in our native
> land,/ Lord grant that it to us a warning be/ And teach us how to shun iniquitie.
>
> Our sins for vengeance do to Heaven cry,/ Yet we like sinners live in vanity,/ O
> grant that we our sinful lives may mend,/ That we may live with thee when life
> doth end.
>
> From storms & tempests Lord preserve us still,/ Teach us they holy laws for to
> fulfill,/ So shall we gainers be by loosing breath,/ And ride triumphant o're the
> second death.

Fires often provided the fuel for disaster stories, including a typical one entitled "A Sad and True Relation of a great fire."[17] The story began, "Give thanks, reyoyce all, you that are secure,/ No man doth know how long life may indure/ Regard dear hearts, at the truth the authour aims,/ Concerning those that suffer in fiery flames." The author, with superior artistry, then switched to point-of-view from a neighboring woman who, while nursing at night a sick child, saw the fire: "In the Merchants lower Rooms she espied,/ The Violent flames and then aloud she cryed/ Fire, Fire . . ." Other stanzas vividly described what was found in the wreckage, and then returned to the great story:

four lumps of flesh was after found./ About the bigness of a man's hand were they,/ As black as a Coal, and a skul or two there lay;/ O little did they think over night being merry,/ That before morn in fiery flames to fry. . . .

All you that are Masters of a family,/ Govern well your house and fear the God on high,/ For when to sleep that we do close our eyes,/ The Lord doth know whither ever we shall rise.

The emphasis on God's sovereignty was accompanied by a stress on his mercy. That was a theme especially of prisoner stories, which were often told in the first person. "Luke Hutton's Lamentation" included details of the crime (a woodcut showed one man with a knife at the other's stomach) and the prisoner's hanging at York, and ended with a prayer: "Lord Jesus forgive me, with mercy relieve me,/ Receive O sweet Saviour, my spirit unto thee."[18] Those dying of natural causes also had first-person accounts written about them. The title of one long one gave the essential detail: "The Godly Maid of Leicester. Being a true Relation of Elizabeth Streeton, who lying on her Death-bed, was wonderfully delivered from the Temptations of Satan, worth the noting of all that would live and die in the fear of God."[19] Her deathbed statement (assuming poetic license) was that

Christ doth ne'r forsake his Flock,/ who evermore on him depend,/ He was my Fortress and my Rock/ and brought my troubles to an end. . . ./ For I have fought a happy Flight,/ and overcome, by God's good Grace,/ The Divel in his power and might,/ and run with Comfort now my Race.

Suicides, however, were treated very differently. The title/lead of one ballad was,

The Devil's cruelty to Mankind, BEING A true Relation of the Life and Death of George Gibbs, a Sawyer by his Trade, who being many times tempted by the Divill to destroy himselfe, did on Fryday being the 7 of March 1663. Most cruelly Ripp up his own Belly, and pull'd out his Bowells and Guts, and cut them in pieces: to the Amazement of all the Beholders, the sorrow of his Friends, and the great grief of his Wife, being not long married: and both young People.[20]

The gruesome epic told how Gibbs lingered for 8 hours, and how neighbors realized the lesson: "Trust not too much to your own strength/ to God continual pray/Resist the Divil elce at length,/ hee'l lead you his Broad way."

Other genres, including "advice ballads," also emerged.[21] They too proceeded from a Christian worldview that acknowledged the ravages of sin and prescribed virtuous personal conduct, made possible by God's grace, as a way of overcoming evil.

The ballads performed a similar function in England's American colonies for a time; as in England, they often emphasized sensational events and tried to combine reporting and teaching. One note immediately under a headline said of the story that followed, "Very proper to be read by all Persons, but especially young People."[22] Crime coverage typically discussed the criminal's downfall: "No timely Warnings would he hear,/ From kind Reproofs he turn'd his Ear,/ Provoked God for to depart,/ And leave him to an harden'd Heart."[23] Warnings sometimes were explicit: "Oh! may the Fate of this young Man/ scarce turn'd of Twenty Three,/ A Warning prove to all our Youth,/ of high and low Degree."[24]

In the sense of carrying a message, these ballads were akin to sermons, and their conclusions often emphasized God's mercy: "So here we leave his pitious Case,/ In tender Arms of Sov'reign Grace,/ Altho' his Crimes are great and sore;/ Grace can abound and pardon more."[25] At the same time, the ballads insisted that they offered not parable but news account, and prided themselves on attribution and eyewitness testimony; for example, the end of one account of a fight with Indians has the reporter noting,

> Thus I have summed up this tragick scene,/ As from their mouths it told to me has been;/ No alteration but in some expressions/ Us'd other words; then pardon such digressions,/ Since I us'd such only for sake of verse,/ Which might not less nor more than truth rehearse.[26]

By the 1720s in England, the old-style ballad/moral tale was beginning to receive sarcastic treatment. Daniel Defoe in 1722 noted in his preface to *Moll Flanders,*

> there is not a wicked action in any part of it, but is first and last rendered unhappy and unfortunate; there is not a superlative villain brought upon the stage, but either he is brought to an unhappy end, or brought to be a penitent; there is not an ill thing mentioned but it is condemned, even in the relation. . . .[27]

But in the colonies, the excitement of the Great Awakening—that reinvigoration of the colonial church led by evangelist George Whitefield and theologian Jonathan Edwards during the 1730s—gave new impetus to biblical sensationalism. Benjamin Franklin wrote, "It seemed as if all the world was growing religious, so that one could not walk through the town in an evening without hearing psalms sung in different families of every street."[28]

Earthquakes, for example, received attention as—in the title of one ballad following a June, 1744, quake—*Tokens of God's Power and Wrath*. Through earthquakes, the ballad proposed, God showed power and then mercy: "Justly may we now stand amaz'd/ At GOD's abundant Grace,/ To think so base and vile a World/ Is not all on a Blaze."[29] When another earthquake struck in 1755, the *Boston News-Letter* reported 2 days after the quake that "the Inhabitants of the Town were, in general, put into great Consternation, fearing, every Moment, least they should be buried under their Houses; but, thro' the Divine Favour, no life was lost."[30] A ballad called the earthquake "A Solemn Warning to the World" and reported how "In Depth of Sleep, or Scenes of Guilt,/ Sinners securely lay;/ When sudden shook the tott'ring Ground,/ And threatned to give Way.[31]

Fire coverage also was reinvigorated. One fire that destroyed over 300 buildings was covered as "the Rebuke of God's Hand." The reporter gave the basic news and then explicitly tried to deal with the "why," observing that God's

> Judgments oftentimes he does retard,/ While we run on in Sin and don't regard;/ And when he sends them then we think He's hard:/ But pray examine, think on what's the Cause,/ Isn't it Contempt of his most righteous Laws?/ Then can we clear ourselves, aren't we to blame/ Who sin without Remorse, and cast off Shame/ And pay no Rev'rence to his holy Name?—/ This is the Cause He sent this Judgment down,/ This awful Desolation on the Town. . . ."[32]

Coverage of a crime story in 1756 and 1757 showed a tendency toward division of labor, with the newspapers increasingly providing short bits of news and the ballads presented more detail. The *Boston News-Letter* in 1756 succinctly reported that

> a sorrowful Affair happened at Watertown, one John Herrington and Paul Learned, scuffling together, the former struck a long Knife in the other's Back, which gave him a mortal wound, and died within two Hours after. Herrington we hear surrendered himself up to Justice.

Ballads that covered the same crime and eventual execution of Herrington made it a pointed story of God's mercy, with the convicted man first wondering whether his guilt is so great that God will not hear his prayers. Soon, however, he was shown to be praying, with the particular request that his life not pass in vain, but that he might become a symbol of God's grace: "Dispell the Mists that cloud my Mind,/ And all my Pangs abate;/ Give this Example to Mankind,/ Of Love and Grace compleat." The final verse of that ballad showed the victory, just prior to Harrington's execution: "Then shall this Truth be ever known,/ While God sustains this Frame;/ In me his boundless Mercy shone,/ And Goodness is his Name."[33]

Right up to the American revolution, ballads continued to emphasize both God's anger with sin and his mercy toward repentant sinners. One man about to be executed was depicted as praying to Christ, "Thou who did'st suffer Death and Shame,/ Such Rebels to restore:/ O! for they great and glorious Name,/ Accept one Rebel more."[34]

Appendix B:

Journalism Historians

and Religion

As the research behind this book suggests, all interpretive journalism has a religious or philosophical component. Any story that goes beyond "who/what/when/where/how" into "why" stirs up questions of meaning and causality. Those questions are essentially religious (or "world view," if we are scrupulous about restricting the term *religion* to beliefs pertaining to a deity). Therefore, historians *should* examine how presuppositions have influenced action, both in earlier times and in our own century as well; few, however, have. This appendix provides a brief overview of the oversights.

19TH-CENTURY INTERPRETATIONS

The tendency among journalism historians to stand apart from independent journalism's biblical base began early. American journalism's first two major historians, Isaiah Thomas and Frederic Hudson, were not Christian believers, and they tended to be embarrassed by the origins of American journalistic practice. Nevertheless, they did pay some attention to a historical record that in those days was too recent to forget.

Isaiah Thomas, author in 1810 of the massive *History of Printing in America,*

134

worshipped liberty and economic progress. He saw America as the leading manifestation of both. He showed his commitment through courageous action as a leading Patriot printer and editor during the American Revolution. Thomas never showed much interest in the Bible; he had been apprenticed to a printer who cared little about Christianity and knew less.[1] (The apprentice may also have been understandably hostile to the Puritan heritage because his great grandfather was hanged as a witch.) Bored with catechisms, Thomas was in a rush to go on to things more exciting, in his case deism and an Enlightenment sense of having progressed "beyond" the Bible.[2]

Yet, Thomas' bias did not keep him from conscientiously recording specific detail concerning the religious connections of early printer/journalists. His listing of what was printed is valuable in itself. Titles such as "Speedy Repentance Urged," a news report/sermon about a murderer, "With certain Memorable Providences relating to some other murders," show practical applications of a Christian world view.[3] But Thomas went beyond the bare essentials to comment about the religious underpinnings of journalistic pioneers such as Samuel Kneeland,[4] Richard Draper,[5] and others. Thomas sympathetically portrayed men such as Bartholomew Green, first printer and second owner of the Boston *News-Letter,* and "a very humble and exemplary Christian" with a "tender sympathy to the poor and afflicted."[6]

Thomas' history was standard for many decades. At mid-century, Joseph T. Buckingham and James Parton wrote about some journalistic personalities,[7] but the second general history, Frederic Hudson's *Journalism in the United States from 1690 to 1872,* did not emerge until the Gilded Age.[8] Hudson, like Thomas, tended to identify journalistic progress with religious regress, but his book was also like Thomas' in that concern for accurate detail and recording of crucial documents often seemed to overcome bias. For example, Hudson reprinted the entire first (and only) issue of *Publick Occurrences,* allowing attentive readers to see the way editor Benjamin Harris' stress on God's sovereignty affected his coverage of news items. Hudson also reprinted Andrew Hamilton's masterful speech at the 1735 Zenger trial, allowing readers to see the biblical basis of the Zenger defense.[9] Hudson even provided an autobiographical sketch of editor Nathaniel Willis[10] and briefly gave the history of some of New York's Christian newspapers.[11]

The third general history written in the 19th century, S. N. D. North's *History and Present Condition of the Newspaper and Periodical Press of the United States,*[12] was far below those by Thomas and Hudson in that it had a purely materialist emphasis. The first two historians both spotlighted the role of individual editors and their choices, but North—who had been commissioned by the U.S. Census Bureau to study newspapers for the 1880 census—saw the growth of newspapers almost purely in terms of industrialization and new technology. With statistical tables replacing discussion of ideas at North's inn, there was no room for discussion of religion's impact.

EARLY 20TH-CENTURY WORKS

The first general history of journalism published in the 20th century, James Melvin Lee's *History of American Journalism* (1917), also reflected a developmental emphasis that ignored theological considerations.[13] It was methodologically similar to Thomas' century-old work in its tracing of printing's progress colony-by-colony (and territory-by-territory, and state-by-state, and so on, and so on). However, it lacked the patriot printer's fervor and pride. Lee apparently believed that "neutral" reporting was the highest journalistic calling. He was unable to appreciate journalists of an earlier age who saw world view context as vital. For example, Lee labeled the early 19th century—a time of great ideological debate in the press, with Christian-based publications dominant and editorial passion evident—as "the darkest period in the history of American journalism."[14]

George Henry Payne's *History of Journalism in the United States,*[15] published only 3 years after Lee's, showed appreciation of the courage of some early Christian journalists. For example, Payne quoted Benjamin Harris' declaration on being sentenced to prison in England for publishing a work openly critical of the King—"I hope God will give me patience to go through with it"—and wrote that, "There is something of the best of American journalism in that simple declaration."[16] Yet, although Payne praised "the democratic tendency that came with Christianity,"[17] he was conventional in his criticism of Puritanism,[18] and evidently viewed religion as a vestigial organ of the body politic.

The next author of a general journalism history, Willard Bleyer, wanted that organ surgically removed. In his *Main Currents of American Journalism* (1927), Bleyer equated "Church" with "restrictions on freedom of discussion,"[19] and ignored differences among church traditions. Bleyer, essentially a developmental historian, had the elite Progressive belief that the "unthinking masses" were ruled by emotion and primitive faith.[20] The goal of journalists, as members of the enlightened class, was to point the way to social reform. Bleyer wanted to make sure that future developments in journalism would reflect the high points of the progressive past: In the 1930s he argued for professional licensing of journalists and for legal requirements that newspapers be run in what was defined as the public interest.[21]

Some popular critics and historians of the 1920s and 1930s also fostered hostility to the idea of Christian influence in journalism history. Oswald Garrison Villard, in *Some Newspapers and Newspaper-Men,* attacked Christian belief and twisted Bible passages to promote an early version of liberation theology. Villard wrote that "There are plain masses seeking a journalistic Moses to clarify their minds, to give them a program of reconstruction, a moral issue through which to rebuild a broken-down society."[22] George Seldes similarly examined recent newspaper history and saw press, church, and "big business" embracing each other adulterously.[23]

Both academic and popular progressive historians more and more seemed to consider Christianity a conservative ally of the upper class, and therefore a reactionary foe of the masses' drive for equality. A new publication during the inter-war period, *Journalism Quarterly,* showed some of the same tendencies and (probably reflecting the lack of interest among journalism professors) ignored the Reformation origins of American journalism. However, one article did go on at great length about an early deistic editor.[24]

MID-CENTURY DEVELOPMENTAL INFLUENCES

Frank Luther Mott, the leading journalism historian of the 1940s and 1950s, expressed scorn for George Seldes' acceptance of inaccuracy. He wrote of one Seldes book that "the way to read our author is to forget about facts and concentrate on the gyrations of flashing mind and a violent set of emotions."[25] Mott showed, in his large, general text *American Journalism,*[26] that he never met a fact about journalism history he didn't like—and, therefore, the Christian heritage did receive some mention. Mott noted that from 1801 to 1833 "a phenomenon of the times was the 'religious newspaper,' a weekly journal which printed some secular news [and] often competed successfully with the secular papers. . . . Many of these papers were conducted with great vigor and ability."[27]

Mott, however, refused to see religious influences as in any way significant for the larger development of journalism, and thus left many important stories incomplete. For example, Mott wrote that in the *Courant* inoculation debate Episcopalians were lining up on one side and Calvinists such as the Mathers on the other—but Mott did not see, or did not explain, how journalistic visions grew out of theological distinctives.[28] He did not explain the role of religion in the Harris or Zenger episodes, or in many other controversies as well. In short, Mott deserves great credit for his perseverance in scholarship, but his developmental perspective led him to believe that as newspapers became more "professional" they would leave world views behind. Thus, his discussion of more recent decades ignored religion entirely, except to note the existence of some ghettoized churchly publications. The tendency was still to equate the dominant American religious heritage with suppression of thought and opposition to press freedom.

PROGRESSIVE/DEVELOPMENTAL SYNTHESIS

It is no wonder, given Mott's scholarship but density, that a new, simpler textbook of the 1950s, Edwin Emery's *The Press and America,* now in its sixth edition, was able to sweep the field.[29] *The Press and America* was widely accepted not only for its ease of presentation, but because the text's liberalism, materialism, and emphasis on class struggle fit perfectly with academic orthodoxy of recent decades. Power, the book informed students, is "grasped by one class at the expense of another."[30] Politics is a battle of "the rights of property versus the rights of the individual."[31] The American Revolution began because journalists and others saw "the need for a realignment of class power."[32] In one astounding paragraph about the Revolution. *The Press and America* five times brought in "class struggle . . . class conflict . . . class struggle . . . class leaders . . . a class insisting upon a greater share of control."[33] This struggle continued into the early twentieth century, when "crusaders for social justice" fought against "unrestricted economic individualism."[34]

The book's historical materialism included a treatment of religion as superstructure and material as base. *The Press and America* termed Puritan theology "religious double talk" and equated it with the antebellum slavery debate as "the basket in which all the differences of peoples, regions, and ideologies could be carried."[35] The few mentions of religion showed the authors accepting stereotypes that historians who took theology seriously long had discredited. For example, *The Press and America* equated Calvinism with a gospel of prosperity, in which money is the sign of "having passed through the eye of the needle into the circle of the elect."[36] (In reality, Calvinists frequently warned about the snares of wealth: "Riches are no part of your felicity," Richard Baxter wrote; "riches are nothing but plentiful provision for tempting corruptible flesh."[37])

The Press and America, influential because it was so widely used as a textbook, was one of many works that emphasized the relation of media and society. Books by Sidney Kobre also tried to take into account cultural forces, but in practice Christian influence received only minor attention in his books, and the attention it received was as negative as that in Emery. For example, Kobre wrote of the problems faced by those "who dared defy the wrath of the Puritan clergy and the royal governor," as if those were one force.[38]

The few *Journalism Quarterly* articles that touched on religious/historical aspects during the 1950s and 1960s often mixed progressivism with theological know-nothingism. This approach probably reflected the general ignorance of, or antipathy toward, Christianity among many professional historians.[39] For example, Howard H. Fogel in 1960 was amazed that Cotton Mather campaigned for a colonial charter following the downfall of royal governor Sir Edmund Andros: "His agreement and acceptance of the Charter and his subsequent fighting for it seems remarkable considering how limited the role of the clergy in the government's affairs would be."[40] That was not at all remarkable, because Reformation political theory required a limited role for the clergy in government, but Fogel was echoing the prejudice that a free press must have emerged in a battle against "theocracy."[41]

A few other articles published during the 1950s and 1960s also looked at journalism history and religion. Henry S. Stroupe, in "The Beginning of Religious Journalism in North Carolina, 1823–1865," related the Christian press to religious reawakening.[42] Elizabeth Barnes described religion's role in an early 19th-century magazine, the *Panoplist*.[43] John M. Havas gave background on *The Journal of Commerce*.[44] Robert Lee assessed the relationship of Yale College president Timothy Dwight and an early Christian publication, the Boston *Palladium*.[45] Donald F. Brod in 1965 examined press coverage of the Scopes trial four decades before, but missed major issues.[46] A book by Stroupe profiled 159 antebellum religious publications of the South Atlantic states.[47]

In addition, a few dissertations and monographs produced during the late 1960s and 1970s provided useful information about some specialized Protestant publications. William Jesse Stone, Jr., in "A Historical Survey of Leading Texas Denominational Newspapers: 1846–1861," noted that in many Texas antebellum issues "the 'news hole' content was often as much secular as sacred."[48] Alfred Roger Gobbel, in "The Christian Century: Its Editorial Policies and Positions, 1908–1966," examined that magazine's attempt to merge Christianity and liberalism.[49] Claude W. Summerlin, in "A History of Southern Baptist State Newspapers," narrated developments from 1802 through 1967.[50] Wesley Norton's published history of early 19th-century Midwest newspapers showed how they helped to shape public thought on a host of moral issues.[51] Robert W. Ross' *So It Was True: The American Protestant Press and the Nazi Persecution of the Jews,* showed that Protestant denominations publications reported news of Nazi atrocities, but could not quite grasp the full extent of depravity.[52]

Also worth noting are publications specializing in the Jewish and Catholic journalistic heritages in America. Two articles by Sidney Kobre on Mordecai Noah, and a biography of Noah published in 1936, were milestones before 1980.[53] In 1981, Jonathan D. Sarna produced a book-length examination of Noah's attempt to harmonize minority identity, national allegiance, and political editing.[54] Then came an intriguing article by Kathryn T. Theus on mid-19th-century Reform Jewish newspapers.[55] Other recent works deserving mention include Mary Lonan Reilly's examination of the history of the Catholic Press Association,[56] and M. R. Real's overview of specialized Catholic publications.[57] Robert Peel showed how the *Christian Science Monitor* was founded in response to sensational attacks on Mary Baker Eddy by *McClure's* and by Joseph Pulitzer's *World*.[58] In 1980, Harold H. Osmer's *U.S. Religious Journalism and the Korean War* examined the reaction of specialized religious publications to communism and containment.[59] A reference work, *Religious Periodicals in the United States,* profiled various publications.[60] Quentin J. Schultze has done fine work on Christian broadcasting; his recent article, "Evangelical Radio and the Rise of the Electronic Church, 1921–1948," showed how evangelical Christians, despite restrictive network and regulatory policies, built audiences through creative programming.[61]

These points of light were very welcome, but they still tended to examine what could be called *marginalized religion*. It was good to have information about publications *of* and *about* various groups, but only a few historians have been writing articles examining the impact of world views on the journalistic mainstream; their work is footnoted in various parts of this book. I do hope that my overview, as a whole, will encourage more detailed work on mainstream beliefs.

Journalism history textbooks, it should be noted, are not alone in having dropped down the memory hole Christianity's central role in American history. In 1986, a National Institute of Education study of 60 representative pre-college social studies textbooks found Christianity virtually excluded.[62] In books for Grades 1 through 4 that introduced children to an understanding of American society, researcher Paul Vitz and his associates found not a single word about Christianity. Fifth-grade history texts made it appear that religious life ceased to exist in America about a century ago. Fundamentalists were described as people who followed an ancient agricultural way of life. Pilgrims were defined as "people who took long trips." Some journalism history textbooks are more sophisticated but not different in kind. Should we laugh? Should we cry? No, we should get to work.

Appendix C:
Methodological Notes

This book has narrated the history of three macrostories in American journalism from its European beginnings in the 16th and 17th century through 1917, when the impact of the Russian Revolution began to open up a new phase in journalistic perceptions. The coming together of the *official story* and the *oppression story* during recent decades is a phenomenon that needs more examination by both liberals and conservatives. But it is especially important that conservatives understand the historical significance of the *corruption story,* for there is danger that the right, in its battle against the capture of leading media by the left, will come to oppose investigation and exposure generally.

One of my goals in writing this book, therefore, has been to honor those who fought to establish the corruption story as journalistically valid; my hope is that in removing dirty bathwater and screaming babies we do not throw out the bathtub that some heroes of early journalism built. One of the most famous historical chapters of the New Testament—chapter 11 of Hebrews—describes the travails of "heroes of faith." We are told that "Some faced jeers and flogging, while still others were chained and put in prison. They were stoned, they were sawed in two, they were put to death by the sword." Those lines come near the end of a chapter that summarizes the stories of Abel, Noah, Abraham, Moses, and others whose names have come down to us, and concludes with praise for many unknown soldiers as well. The first line of chapter 12 then gives the practical application of the long account: "Therefore, since we are surrounded by such a great cloud of witnesses, let us throw off everything that hinders and the sin that so easily entangles, and let us run with perseverance the race marked out for us."

The early history of English and American journalism has its own great cloud of witnesses. Some were martyred in the belief that they should speak and write the truth revealed in the Bible, and in the faith that this truth would make them free. The names of some in the great cloud, and the means of their deaths, are included in the index. Other names in the index testify to the power of other world views; the index includes several references to technological developments, such as the "Hoe cylinder press," but the emphasis is on people, and the ideas that animated their lives.

This emphasis is deliberate. The traditional method of teaching history has involved storytelling about giants of the past whose lives provide lessons (of emulation or avoidance) for those in the classroom who will be the leaders of the future. There are dangers in the "great man" (or "great person") approach, but there are greater dangers when history is depersonalized. If we keep in mind the efforts of the past, we are more likely to realize our deep responsibility not only to those who come after us but to those who came before us. Furthermore, some of the difficulties of personal history can be overcome if we see journalists not as autonomous saints or sinners, but as proponents of macrostories that affected the way millions of readers and listeners viewed the world.

A narrative history of macrostory change intrinsically raises many methodological questions. After all, some researchers trained largely in quantitative methodology smell a rat unless there are numbers involved in a study. A quick way to deal with such objections is to counter them with the need to look for rats whether or not the numbers are present; just as seeing is not believing in an age of video wizards, so counting should not be believing at a time when statistical manipulation is rampant. But the question of numbers deserves something better than a flip reply; the introductions to two books published in 1988 presented deeper responses to potential critiques from those who demand numbers.

The first introduction, that of Charles Murray to his fine book *In Pursuit,* noted the old joke about a drunkard who drops his keys in one place but then looks for them under a streetlamp because "the light's better." As Murray then pointed out concerning analysis of social policy questions,

> We have looked where the light is, and for modern policy analysis the light consists of quantitative analysis. I do not say this altogether critically. Give a policy analyst variables that can be expressed in numbers, and he has at hand a powerful array of analytic tools to probe their meaning. The limitation—and it has become more and more confining over the years—is that so few of the interesting variables in the social sciences can be expressed in numbers. The more complicated the constructs one wants to examine, the less likely that they can be crammed within the quantitative paradigms.[1]

At a time when many communications researchers have fallen in love with quantitative analysis, Murray's point needs strong emphasis: The important questions in journalism cannot be dealt with satisfactorily through techniques of quantitative content analysis or survey research.

The other introductory note I like is a model defense of the qualitative approach. It was offered by Joshua Muravchik at the beginning of his monograph, *News Coverage of the Sandinista Revolution:*

> A more formal or quantitative method is often regarded as lending objectivity to a study, but in this case I think it would have had the opposite effect. . . . Any quantitative analysis would entail assigning news stories to categories that could be counted, categories like 'pro-Sandinista' and 'anti-Sandinista,' or more complex or sophisticated ones. But whatever the categories, the reader without access to my files would have no independent means of evaluating whether I had assigned stories fairly. In contrast with the common-sense discursive approach that I have employed, any skeptical reader can easily check to see whether I have quoted accurately and fairly or whether any of my generalizations are too broad.[2]

Similarly, I propose to anyone interested in further analysis of the macrostories: Crank the microfilm and see for yourself. It is good that, given justified concern about the potential plasticity of historical narrative, storytellers can only gain reader confidence the old-fashioned way: By earning it. It is good to treat even historians with a reputation for accuracy to the slogan of recent disarmament talks: "Trust, but verify." It is important to demand from writers considerable quotation and other specific detail to back up arguments, along with full footnoting so that fancy footwork can be examined, if necessary.

But those are not the only checks on subjectivity run amuck. The concept of "macrostory," which is based on the integration of existing ideas concerning "narrative framework" and "world view," provides a structure of analysis that allows us to see and keep records of the ways that world views interact with journalistic coverage.

Narrative framework (known to language patricians as "archetypal framework" and to plebians as "story formula") is something that every reporter learns on the job, if not before. Almost every thoughtful journalist has stories of how the lesson is taught; a good one was told by Robert Darnton, a reporter who later became a history professor. When he was a police beat novice on the *Newark Star Ledger* in 1959, Darnton wrote a straightforward story about a boy whose bicycle had been stolen in the park. When he showed the story to an older reporter, the veteran told him, "You can't write that sort of story straight," and proceeded (making up detail when useful) to show Darnton how a pro would handle the theft:

> Every week Billy put his twenty-five-cents allowance in his piggy bank. He wanted to buy a bike. Finally, the big day came. He chose a shiny red Schwinn, and took it out for a spin in the park. Every day for a week he rode proudly around the same

route. But yesterday three toughs jumped him in the middle of the park. They knocked him from the bike and ran off with it. Battered and bleeding, Billy trudged home to his father, George F. Wagner of 43 Elm Street. "Never mind, son," his dad said. "I'll buy you a new bike, and you can use it on a paper route to earn money to pay me back.[3]

Darnton, after finding facts to fit that formula, had his first byline, a front-page story. Soon the commissioner of parks announced that the park would have additional security, and neighbors were collecting money to buy Billy a new bike. As Darnton recounted, "I had struck several chords by manipulating stock sentiments and figures: the boy and his bike, piggy-bank savings, heartless bullies, the comforting father."[4]

The implications of "narrative framework" for concepts of journalistic objectivity were discussed intelligently by NYU professor Mitchell Stephens in his book published in 1988, *A History of News*. Stephens wrote that "journalists' supposed objectivity" is:

compromised by the narrative frameworks they impose on their stories—their decision, for example, on which combination of formulas a particular crime might be made to fit: woeful victim ("his life savings"), noble victim ("a former Boy Scout"), tearful relatives ("their only child"), twist of fate ("had his car not been in the shop"), awful irony ("scoffed at fear of crime"), despicable criminal ("despite the victim's pleas"), psychologically scarred criminal ("abandoned by his parents"), shocked acquaintances ("seemed such a quiet boy"), the wages of poverty ("unemployed for seven months"), the scourge of drugs ("to support his habit"), or the breakdown of societal values ("the fourth such crime in this month"). Most events provide sufficient facts to support a multiplicity of possible formulas; journalists choose among them.[5]

Stephens' point was good, but he did not follow through on the question of why journalists choose one narrative framework and not another. To go deeper, we need to understand the nature of "world view"; essentially, world views are clusters of convictions and values not verifiable by the means of natural science. Every person, whether religious or atheistic, has a world view. When astronomer Carl Sagan says there is only the cosmos and nothing beyond it, we need to ask him how he learned that. We will find that he did not discover that by peering through a telescope, but by certain assumptions or presuppositions that he brought *to* his telescope. Similarly when psychologist B. F. Skinner says that human beings are made solely of matter, and that we think with our bodies because bodies are all we are, we need to ask how he learned that. The answer he gives will have nothing at all to do with science; it is as much a matter of faith as anything Jerry Falwell says. The scientists who hold to these beliefs hold them sincerely, no doubt, and they often believe that those who do not agree with them are primitive or foolish or blinded by religious dogma—but they still hold them as matters of faith.

If this is true of "hard science," it is even more evident in that "social science" known as policy analysis. As Charles Murray has noted:

> Policy analysis is decisively affected by the analyst's conception of human nature. One may consider a government policy to be practical or impractical, safe or hazardous, only according to one's conception of what is good for humans, and that in turn has to be based on one's conclusions about the potentials and limitations of humans acting as social creatures.[6]

Journalistic coverage is similarly affected; to show that, we might look at several modes of coverage.

First, say a journalist is writing about foreign policy issues that include questions of disarmament treaties, defense spending, and so on. Journalists who believe that leaders across the world naturally want to avoid war but are forced into it through mistrust or institutional problems will emphasize attempts to change the institutional framework through restraining arms production, eliminating military alliances, deemphasizing nationalism, having more negotiations, and the like. This has been the predominant current framework within American journalism for many "in-depth" stories on such issues.

A journalist proceeding from a different view of human nature, however, might ask other questions: What if war is very natural, given man's greed for power? What if some leaders see war as a permissible way to gain more power, in the belief that they can achieve victory without overwhelming losses? Of course, history is full of mistaken calculations of that sort—dictators have a tendency to overrate their own power—but they may still plunge ahead unless restrained by the obvious power of their adversaries. Journalists who do not assume a benign human nature concerning warfare would emphasize inquiry into whether steps were being taken to raise the cost of war to potential aggressors, and whether those dictators might be overthrown by popular upheaval. For these journalists, the most important news would involve plans for military preparedness and alliances, specific evidence concerning the evil of dictators and the possibilities of overthrowing them, attempts to arouse the public, and so on.

Stories concerning domestic crime also are tied to world views. A journalist who believes that man is naturally good but is corrupted by societal pressures will also believe that criminals are often driven to their crimes by some external cause, often an institutional failure. Criminals are victims. They have been treated badly and have thus deviated from their true natures. They deserve sympathy, not punishment. Murder is due to circumstance; executions are thus unfair. Journalists with such beliefs will want to stress the socioeconomic "reasons" for crime. They will produce stories about reducing crime by spending more money on early childhood education so that potential criminals get off to a better start. We are seeing many such stories now.

On the other hand, those who see the committing of crimes as part of human nature, unless people are restrained by man's force or God's grace, will see the individual as responsible. They will emphasize the need to take hard steps to cut down on crime, and to pray for spiritual change. They will argue that crime must always lead to punishment, both because criminals deserve such a reward and because punishment is a powerful force in keeping people from doing what they want to do.

We might also look briefly—and all these glances are brief and simplifying— at stories concerning economic inequality. Some say that when there is inequality, government should try to end it; journalists who believe this will construct stories, in which people call for action of some sort; any inequalities are instances of wrong doing that should be exposed and challenged. On the other hand, those who see equality of process (e.g., a ban on discrimination by race) as essential, but do not demand equality of result, are likely to produce stories that emphasize individual entrepreneurship rather than societal "oppression."

World views are influential not only in coverage of political matters but in those soft features known as "lifestyle" stories. The *Austin American-Statesman*, for example, has regularly praised thinkers and writers who argue that life is best when we follow our natural instincts and are not "repressed"; the goal, as one article advised, should be to "follow your bliss." An alternate view suggests that we learn not to be ourselves, but to be better than ourselves; such a view, which pokes fun at our belief that whatever we want to do is right, does not receive much favorable press. Larry McMurtry noted even in the 1970s that:

> One seldom, nowadays, hears anyone described as 'a person of character.' The concept goes with an ideal of maturity, discipline and integration that strongly implies repression: people of character, after all, cannot do just anything, and an ability to do just about anything with just about anyone—in the name, perhaps, of Human Potential—is certainly one of the most *moderne* abilities.[7]

What is "character" to some is seen as "hang-up" by others.

These views of human nature tend to be consistent across the boundaries of particular issues: A journalist who sees aggression as something natural (and to be guarded against) in international relations is not likely to assume that crime arises merely from poverty. Nor is such a journalist likely to believe that it is generally best for desires to be met and restraints abolished. Such a journalist will not write from the assumption that people are naturally good but are oppressed by the institutions and other pressures around them.

The concept of *macrostory*, in short, cuts against recent ideas of journalistic objectivity by noting that reporters put news stories in narrative frameworks chosen in relation to world views.[8] However, the concept does not argue that there is no objective truth, nor does it argue that subjectivity reigns totally in modern journalism. It is important to distinguish between *obligatory* and *discretionary* coverage and writing. Obligatory stories are the occurrences that readers, within a particular media community and cultural framework, expect to see covered. Earthquakes, coach or car accidents, major fires and other local disasters, the death of kings and presidents, the doings of the rich and famous— all are grist for a local publication's mill, almost regardless of its editors' and reporters' world views.[9] But journalists can and do deviate from obligatory coverage in three ways. They cover obligatory stories but delve deeper, particularly by asking "why." They choose to cover stories that do not demand coverage but that support their world view concerns. Or they do both by covering discretionary stories in depth.

Any story that goes beyond obligatory coverage becomes highly dependent on journalistic world views. As John Corry of the *New York Times* has noted, "There are fewer rules of pure journalism here than journalists pretend, even to themselves. Journalists, especially big-time journalists, deal in attitudes and ideas as much as events."[10] That has been true throughout journalism history.

Appendix D:

Defending the

Corruption Story

Journalists who embraced the corruption macrostory sometimes had to defend themselves against arguments that exposure of wrong-doing would increase its incidence or corrupt general discourse. In August 1834, the Reverend J. R. McDowell, editor of a hard-hitting New York monthly appropriately titled *McDowell's Journal*—his motto was, "The world is our field, prevention is our aim"—printed a spirited justification of the biblical sensationalism he practiced. McDowell's discussion, more thorough than any others I have seen, provides valuable insights into the logic of some early crusading journalists, but to my knowledge it has never been reprinted. A few excerpts follow; for easier modern reading I have re-paragraphed some of McDowell's material and deleted some italics and other overly used attention-getting devices of the time.

SHALL LICENTIOUSNESS BE CONCEALED, OR EXPOSED?

This I apprehend is one great question before the community; and the final decision of it will doubtless constitute an interesting and important era in the history of this vice. It is assumed that the Bible is our only rule of Faith and Practice, and is a competent arbiter of the question.

First.—I propose for decision the general question: *Shall Vice and Sin be concealed, or exposed?* In deciding this question, I inquire, What does the Bible TEACH? and What does the Bible PRACTICE?

1. *What does the Bible TEACH?*

(1.) Cry aloud and *spare not;* lift up thy voice like a trumpet, and SHOW MY PEOPLE THEIR TRANSGRESSIONS, AND THE HOUSE OF JACOB THEIR SINS. (Isaiah 58:1) *Show my people their transgressions.*—He must tell them how very bad they really were . . . He must deal faithfully and plainly with them . . . God sees sin in his people, in the house of Jacob, and is displeased with it. They are often unapt and unwilling to see their own sins, and need to have them showed them, and to be told, *Thus and thus thou hast done.*

He must be vehement and in good earnest herein, must cry *aloud, and not spare;* not spare them, nor touch them with his reproofs, as if he were afraid of hurting them, but search the wound to the bottom, lay it bare to the bone; not spare himself or his own pains, but cry as loud as he can; though he spend his strength, and waste his spirits, though he get their ill will by it, and get himself into an ill name; yet he must not spare . . .

(2.) Son of Man, CAUSE JERUSALEM TO KNOW HER ABOMINATIONS. (Ezekiel 16:2) God not only commands Ezekiel to expose abominations, but details minutely the abominations to be made known. It will be recollected that we are now investigating the *general* precept of the Bible in regard to concealing, or exposing vice and sin. . . .

(5.) The Lord said moreover unto me, son of many, wilt though judge [plead for] Aholah and Aholibah? Yea, DECLARE UNTO THEM THEIR ABOMINATIONS. (Ezekiel 23:36) Please examine the whole chapter. In the 33d Chapter of Ezekiel is pointed out the duty of watchmen to blow the trumpet and warn the people of approaching danger. But it is in vain for a watchman to shout "Danger!" unless the people are distinctly told what the danger is. Certainly that was the uniform practice of the ancient prophets. And doubtless St. Paul approved of the same practice, for he says: Therefore watch, and remember that by the space of three years I *ceased not to warn every one night and day with tears.* (Acts 20:31)

And he also . . . commanded Titus to do so likewise (Titus 1:13) saying: "This witness is true; wherefore *rebuke them sharply,* that they may be sound in the faith". . . . Here then we have authority not only to *warn,* but to *rebuke,* and to rebuke *sharply.*" [Whether] we are to expose them (even were it possible thus to rebuke them and still conceal their vices) will appear more clearly under the second head.

(6.) If thy brother, the son of thy mother, or thy son or thy daughter, or the wife of thy bosom, or thy friend, which is as thine own soul, entice thee secretly, saying Let us go and serve other gods . . . neither shalt thou spare, neither shalt thou CONCEAL him . . . And all Israel shall hear, and *fear* and shall do no more any such wickedness as this is among you (Deuteronomy 13: 6-11). Hence it appears such idolators were to be made *public examples,* for the good of all.

(7.) *And have no fellowship with the unfruitful works of darkness, but rather reprove them.* (Ephesians 5:11) . . . Endeavor to expose their wickedness, and make the perpetrators *ashamed* of them . . . If it should be said that the perceptive duties that have been cited to expose vice and sin, have special or sole reference to the sins of the *church,* and not to those of the world, than I reply both the church and the world are under the same moral government of God—both are amenable to the same laws—both will stand at the same final Tribunal—and both will be either condemned or acquitted by the same general principles.

Moreover, St. Paul, particularly in the first chapter of the Romans, and the other apostles did expose and denounce the sins and vices of the *gentiles* as well as those of the *church*. And finally, it would be hard indeed to charge upon the church all the sins, and vices, and abominations that are exposed and condemned in the Bible. The precept therefore, has as much respect to the abominations of the *world,* as to those of the *church*. And as there is nothing in the Scriptures of an opposite spirit and import to the general scope of the passages quoted, we are forced to the conclusion that the BIBLE PRECEPT is, to DETECT, EXPOSE, and PUNISH VICE and SIN.

2. *What does the Bible PRACTICE?*

(1.) When Adam and Eve had eaten of the forbidden fruit and thus transgressed the commands of God, *they hid themselves, as vice and sin are wont to do.* Then what did God do? He went into the garden and sought for them saying "Adam where art thou?" And *detected, exposed,* and punished them.

(2.) When Cain committed fratricide, the Lord suffered him not to escape, but detected him, saying unto Cain, "Where is Abel thy brother?" "What hast thou done?" And thus did the Lord expose and severely punish Cain. Genesis 4: 8-14.

(3.) In like manner, was the wickedness done by Jacob's sons to their brother Joseph in selling him into Egypt, and then in lying to their father about his death—*detected and exposed.*

(4.) Another interesting illustration of the Bible practice is found in the case of Achan, whose theft so seriously troubled the armies of Israel. Showing very clearly God's utter abhorrence of concealed vice and sin, and his determination to have it detected, exposed, and punished . . .

(20.) In the book of Esther is a very interesting narrative of Haman's wicked devices against the Jews, and of his detection, exposure and punishment. "And when Haman saw that Mordecai bowed not, nor did him reverence, then was Haman full of wrath. And he thought scorn to lay hands on Mordecai alone; for they had showed him the people of Mordecai: wherefore Haman sought to destroy all the Jews that were throughout the whole kingdom of Ahasuerus, even the people of Mordecai." (Esther 3:5,6) But when the plot had advanced so far that the destruction of the people of Mordecai seemed inevitable, then the Lord saw fit to detect and expose the machinations of Haman. And cold indeed must be the heart that can read this story and not rejoice at the developments of the 7th chapter. And colder and harder still must be the heart that would advocate the concealment and protection of vice and crime, and sin. . . .

(27.) The 16th of Ezekiel is not the only chapter that exposes vice and sin. Among other chapters of the *same character,* we may mention—The fifty-ninth of Isaiah, the fourth of Hosea—see also the 1st, 2d and 3d.), the twenty-second of Ezekiel, and the Prophets generally, the twenty-third of Matthew, the first of Romans.

Of the twenty-third chapter of Ezekiel, Dr. Clark remarks, In this chapter there are many of what we would call indelicate expressions, [if the term "indelicate," is a form of *reproach,* query, if it is right in the sight of God for us thus to stigmatize his Holy Word!] because a parallel is run between *idolatry* and *prostitution,* and the circumstances of the latter illustrate the peculiarities of the former. Ezekiel was among the Jews, what *Juvenal* was among the Romans; a ROUGH REPROVER OF THE MOST ABOMINABLE VICES. THEY BOTH SPOKE OF THINGS AS THEY FOUND THEM; STRIPPED VICE NAKED, AND SCOURGED IT PUBLICLY. THE ORIGINAL IS STILL MORE ROUGH THAN THE TRANS-LATION.

(29.) See how God speaks of Licentiousness.—Will you denounce God as indecent? As collateral evidence and illustration of the Bible method of dealing with vice and sin, especially of *speaking* upon the subject of Licentiousness, let us examine some of the laws which God gave to Israel . . . "Moreover thou shalt not lie carnally with thy neighbor's wife to defile thyself with her. And thou shalt not let any of thy seed pass through the fire to Molech, neither shalt thou profane the name of thy God: I am the LORD. Thou shalt not lie with mankind, as with womankind; it is abomination. Neither shalt thou lie with any beast to defile thyself therewith . . ."

At this time when so many honest Christians are anxiously inquiring and seeking for light, and truth, and correct principles, and for the proper mode of speaking and conversing upon the subject of licentiousness, it is peculiarly interesting and important to know how God spake upon this subject: for true Christians will never hesitate to follow an example set by their Father in heaven. God's mode and style of speaking upon the subject I have exhibited in the selections indiscriminately made from all the sacred writings . . . It will be well for us not to become "wise above what is written." Shall we be "wiser than God?" "Shall any teach God knowledge?" (Job 21:22)

TAKE NOTICE: Not only did the allwise Jehovah speak in this style, and give these laws and statutes on the subject of Licentiousness, but he gave commandment, saying "thou shalt teach them diligently unto thy children, and shalt talk of them when thou sittest in thy house, and when thou walkest by the way, and when thou liest down, and when thou risest up." (Deuteronomy 6:6-9) . . .

And thou shalt teach them diligently unto thy children. Under all the Divine dispensations from the beginning, no duty is set higher, or more insisted on, than that of instructing children in the knowledge of religion. [And what is "the knowledge of religion," but the knowledge of vice and virtue, of sin and holiness, of evil and good, of wrong, and right?] . . . Christian parents are most expressly enjoined to "bring up their children in the nurture and admonition of the Lord;" and to the praise of young Timothy, as well as of those relations, who had been his instructors, it is said, "that from a child he had known the Holy Scriptures, able to make him wise unto salvation, through faith which is in Jesus Christ."

Now is it to be supposed that "young Timothy" was taught to omit, in his reading of the Scriptures, all those chapters that relate to licentiousness? Must "young Timothy" be kept in profound ignorance of this vice against which the Bible thunders so loudly? Is only a part of the Bible "profitable for doctrine, for reproof and for instruction in righteousness?" . . .

No concealment of vice at the final Judgment . . . O, the developments and disclosures of that awful day! "When God shall judge the SECRETS of men." (Romans 2:16) When every disgusting abomination shall be stripped naked, and vice in all its horrid deformity and odiousness shall be exposed to the assembled universe! Ah! whither will fastidiousness then flee—and how shall squeamishness veil her face? Will the rocks and the mountains afford a hiding place?

Let us think, speak, and act with sole reference to our final account. We are to give account of ourselves to God, and not to man. If duty requires the detection, exposure, and punishment of vice, we are not to inquire or regard what the world will say; our only concern is to know what God thinks, and what he will say. Hear the Lord Jesus—"What I tell you in darkness, that speak ye in light: and what ye hear in the ear, that preach ye upon the housetops. And fear not them that kill the body, but are not able to kill the soul; but rather fear him that is able to destroy both soul and body in hell." (Matthew 10:27,28)

Conclusion of the argument

Having adopted the Bible as our only Rule of Faith and Practice, and having ascertained, that it is both the Doctrine and the Practice of the Bible to expose vice and sin, and having also ascertained that licentiousness, which is one of the most flagrant and abominable of all vices, is not recognized by the Bible as an exception to the general rule of exposing vice and sin—It necessarily follows, THAT IT IS OUR DUTY TO EXPOSE LICENTIOUSNESS.

The code of criminal law proscribed by every civilized and christian government, requires the most diligent and energetic efforts to *detect, expose, and punish vice.* Look at the combination of wisdoms and power in the Legislative, the Judicial and the Executive departments of all our governments, both superior and subordinate, to effect these objects. It is only upon the detection and punishment of vice, that the peace and safety of society depend. Banish from the community the vigilance of a Police by day, and of a Watch by night—Deprive the constable of his staff, and the sheriff of his power—Demolish Bridewell and Jail, Penitentiary and Prison— Paralyze the strong arm of the law—Close every court of Judicature—in short, abolish the whole system of means and measures, or powers and functions, organized for the *detection, exposure, and punishment of vice*—And then shall you see commence the Reign of Terror and the Misrule of Anarchy. Then shall the assassin plunge the dirk and the dagger at noon-day, and blood shall deluge the land. . . .

Burglary and Burning, Riot and Rain, Pillage and Plunder, Death and Destruction shall become the watchwords of an infuriated mob. The domestic fireside, that sacred retreat of innocence and virtue, shall be invaded by *Lust and Rape,* and the dwelling place of a mother's purity and of a daughter's chastity, shall be converted into the Brothel and the House of Death. Order, Temperance, and Sobriety, shall be ingulfed in the whirlpool and confusion of bachanalian revelry, and midnight debauchery. The Sabbath shall no longer be sanctified by the church-going bell, by the prayers, and praises, and precepts of God's Holy Sanctuary, by the quiet devotions of the social circle, or the aspirations of calm retirement: but the Lord's Day shall become the grand Jubilee of Tumult and Banqueting, of Horse-racing and Gambling, of the Parade of Military and the Pageantry of Pride and Folly, of the Desolation of Error and the Havoc of Infidelity.

And yet all these horrors are but the inauspicious beginning of that Reign of Terror, and the Misrule of Anarchy, consequent upon the abolition of Penal Law, and the Concealment and protection of vice. Those therefore who oppose the detection and exposure of vice, must see that they are acting in opposition to the best interests of society, and to the collective wisdom and experience of legislators in every age of the world. *But this is not all:* Such opposers must find themselves acting in fearful opposition to the Precept and Practice of the Bible, and of the Bible's God.

Notes

INTRODUCTION

1. Roy Basler, ed., *The Collected Works of Abraham Lincoln* (Rutgers, 1953), vol. II, p. 385.

2. William Camden, *Annales* (London, 1625), book 3, p. 16. Stubbes' offending pamphlet is also available in some rare book libraries: See *The Discourie of a Gaping Gulf Whereinto England is like to be swallowed by another French marriage; if the Lord forbid not the banes, by letting her Majestie see the sin and punishment thereof* (London, 1579).

3. Ibid.

CHAPTER 1
UNNATURAL ACTS

1. Quoted often; the best brief, readily available summary of the conditions of Luther's time and his battle against indulgences is found in Roland Bainton, *Here I Stand* (New York, 1956).

2. Ibid, p. 61.

3. Margaret Aston, *The Fifteenth Century: The Prospect for Europe* (London, 1968), p. 76: "Printing was recognized as a new power and publicity came into its own."

4. This response came at the Diet of Worms when Archbishop of Trier Eck asked how opponents of Christianity would "exult to hear Christians discussing whether they have been wrong all these years. Martin . . . would you put your judgment above that of

so many famous men . . .? For a time the protection offered by Frederick was the only material force preserving Luther from many enemies who wished to kill him—yet Luther continued to criticize Frederick's prized relics collection. (Frederick, nevertheless, protected him, and in 1523 finally agreed not to exhibit his relic collection, but to place most of it in storage.)

5. Elizabeth Eisenstein, *The Printing Press as an Agent of Change* (Cambridge, England, 1980), vol. I, p. 426.

6. Ibid., p. 330.

7. Bainton, p. 63.

8. Luther advocated civil disobedience in some instances but was opposed to anarchistic revolution. If each person were to take justice into his own hands, he wrote, there would be "neither authority, nor government, nor order nor land, but only murder and bloodshed."

9. Bainton, p. 120.

10. Eisenstein, p. 304.

11. Quoted in Frederick Siebert, *Freedom of the Press in England, 1476–1776* (Urbana, Illinois, 1952), p. 45.

12. Henry VIII broke from Rome not on grounds of principle, as did Luther and Calvin, but in order to make himself the principal arbiter of theology, especially when it came to his own divorce of first wife Katharine of Aragon. Benjamin Hart suggested correctly that "to place the king at the head of the church was a far more oppressive and corrupting influence on Christianity than the pope in far-off Italy. The bishops, formerly responsible to the Roman authority, often served as an effective check on royal power. Now they were little more than a political arm of the state, used to stamp out religious dissent, which was seen as a threat to social order." (Benjamin Hart, *Faith and Freedom* (Dallas, 1988), p. 61)

13. Siebert, p. 49.

14. 34 and 35 Henry VIII, c. 1. The 1542–1543 law stated, "There shall be no annotations or preambles in Bibles or New Testaments in English. The Bible shall not be read in English in any church. No women or artificers, prentices, journeymen, servingmen of the degree of yeomen or under, husbandmen, nor labourers, shall read the New Testament in English. Nothing shall be taught or maintained contrary to the King's instructions. And if any spiritual person preach, teach, or maintain anything contrary to the King's instructions or determinations, made or to be made, and shall be thereof convict, he shall for his first offence recant, for his second abjure and bear a fagot, and for his third shall be adjudged an heretick, and be burned."

15. The Bible had to be carefully followed, and the interpretations of those who had studied it at length were not to be negligently disregarded. But in the end, neither individual consciences nor church leaders were to be in charge: The Bible was viewed as clear enough so that ordinary individuals could read it themselves and see its truths for themselves.

16. When Henry died in 1547 and his son Edward VI briefly took over, restrictions were eased, but when Mary assumed the throne upon Edward's death in 1553 and attempted to reassert Catholic dominance, freedom fled.

17. For more details see M. A. Shaaber, *Some Forerunners of the Newspaper in England* (New York, 1966), p. 76.

18. Ibid., p. 71.

19. See, for instance, *The complaynt of Veritie, made by John Bradford,* and *The*

wordes of Maister Hooper at his death were published in 1559, and *A briefe Treatise concerning the burnynge of Bucer and Phagius at Cambrydge* came out in 1562. These and others are cited in Shaaber, p. 77.

20. John Foxe, *Actes and monuments of matters most speciall and memorable, happenying in the church, with an universall history of the same,* 6th edition (London, 1610), pp. 586, 606, 609, 612, 946, 1033, 1423, 1527, 1547, 1738, etc. A much more readily accessible paperback edition, but without the woodcuts, is published as *Foxe's Book of Martyrs* (Springdale, PA, 1981).

21. Foxe was following the biblical tradition of the apostle Luke, who wrote at the beginning of his gospel that "I myself have carefully investigated everything from the beginning" in order to "write an orderly account" dependent not on speculation but on eyewitnesses.

22. *Foxe's Book of Martyrs,* op. cit., pp. 212–213.

23. Ibid, p. 213.

24. Ibid., pp. 309.

25. Ibid., pp. 351–387.

26. Ibid., loc. cit.

27. Ibid., pp. 201–202.

28. Miles Coverdale, ed., *Certain most godly, fruitful, and comfortable letters of such true saintes and holy martyrs of God, as in the late bloodye persecution here with in this realme, gave their lyues for the defence of Christes holy gospel: written in the tyme of theyr . . . imprysonment . . .* (London: John Day, 1564), p. ii.

29. The Stationers Company, a group of government-certified printers granted a publishing monopoly, sent out spies to determine each printer's number of orders, number of employees, and wages paid them. That information, along with identification of customers and works currently being published, allowed officials to make sure presses were not used for "seditious" purposes.

30. Siebert, pp. 91–92.

31. G. W. Prothero, *Select Statutes and other Constitutional Documents illustrative of the reigns of Elizabeth and James I* (Oxford, 1894), p. 400.

32. Ibid., pp. 427–428.

33. Leland Ryken, *Worldly Saints: The Puritans As They Really Were* (Grand Rapids, 1986), p. 124.

34. Patrick Collinson, *The Elizabethan Puritan Movement* (Berkeley, 1967), p. 380. The last word of that quotation, "simpletons," shows how the Puritan emphasis on Bible reading by everyone was folly to those who scorned democracy.

35. Jack Bartlett Rogers, *Scripture in the Westminster Confession* (Grand Rapids, 1967), p. 383.

36. Quoted in Ryken, p. 384.

37. Everett Emerson, ed., *English Puritanism from John Hooper to John Milton* (Durham, NC, 1968), p. 153.

38. Ryken, p. 105. The Puritans did at times fall into repetitive prolixity to make sure that their meaning was clear; sometimes their motto seemed to be "clarity, clarity, clarity," as a fuller quotation from Perkins indicates: "Preaching must be plain, perspicuous, and evident . . . It is a by-word among us: *It was a very plain sermon:* And I say again, *the plainer, the better.*"

39. Ibid., pp. 105, 106.

CHAPTER 2
PERILS OF THE PURITAN PRESS

1. A Cologne publication, *Mercurius Gallobelgicus,* commenced publication in 1594 and continued semi-annually for four decades, but its summaries of diplomatic and military events and other news were in Latin, and the publication thus made no claim to popular appeal.

2. See Joseph Frank, *The Beginnings of the English Newspaper 1620–1660* (Cambridge, MA, 1961), p. 13.

3. *Boston Gazette,* June 2, 1755; cited in Jeffery A. Smith, *Printers and Press Freedom: The Ideology of Early American Journalism* (New York, 1988), p. 21.

4. Frank, p. 41.

5. Ibid., p. 80.

6. Ibid., p. 91.

7. There were errors, of course, and Puritan editors learned from hard experience that sources were not always reliable. Frank describes how the editor of one newspaper, *The True Informer* (1643–1646), observed that "Truth is the daughter of Time. Relations of Battels, fights, skirmishes, and other passages and proceedings of concernment are not alwaies to be taken or credited at the first hand, for that many times they are uncertaine, and the truth doth not so conspicuously appeare till a second or third relation" (p. 55). But the *goal* of truth-telling led to vigorous attempts to uncover the reality of events; in the words of Richard Sibbes, "Truth feareth nothing so much as concealment, and desireth nothing so much as clearly to be laid open to the view of all: when it is most naked, it is most lovely and powerful."

8. Hyder Rollin, *Cavalier and Puritan* (New York: University Press, 1923), p. 44. Average newspaper circulation was only 500, but copies were passed from hand to hand; most London males, and many females, were literate, and most read all or part of one of the weekly newspapers. In addition, one page ballads, customarily selling for a cent, also continued their practice of covering news events.

9. In 1642 Parliament decreed that "no person or persons shall Print, publish, or utter, any Booke or Pamphlet, false or scandalous, to the proceedings of the Houses of Parliament," but the emphasis was on falsehood, not embarrassment, and enforcement was largely absent. For additional perspective, see Frederick Siebert, *Freedom of the Press in England, 1476–1776* (Urbana, IL, 1952), p. 182.

10. Samuel Hartlib, *A description of the Famous Kingdom of Macaria* (London, 1641); quoted in Siebert, p. 192.

11. William Walwyn, *The Compassionate Samaritane* (London, 1644), p. A5.

12. Henry Robinson, *Liberty of Conscience* (London, 1644), p. 17.

13. John Milton, *Aeropagetica,* in many editions; here, in Douglas Bush, ed., *The Portable Milton* (New York, 1949), p. 199.

14. Ibid., loc. cit.

15. Quoted in Joseph Frank, *Cromwell's Press Agent: A Critical Biography of Marchamont Nedham, 1620–1678* (Latham, Md., 1980), p. 186.

16. *Mercurius Britanicus,* June 10–17, 1644.

17. Ibid., August 12–19, 1644.

18. Ibid., June 24–July 1, 1644.

19. Ibid., June 10–17, 1644.

20. Ibid., July 1–8, 1644.

21. Ibid., August 12–19, 1644.

22. Ibid.

23. Ibid.

24. Ibid., October 21–28, 1644.

25. Ibid., May 20–27, 1644.

26. Ibid., May 25–June 2, 1645.

27. Parliament, trying at that time to work out a compromise with King Charles, was not pleased when Nedham described the monarch as "a wilfull King . . . with a guilty Conscience, bloody Hands, a Heart full of broken Vowes and Protestations."

28. Quoted in Frank, *Nedham*, p. 100.

29. Francis Wortley, *Characters and Elegies* (London, 1646), p. 26.

30. Marchamont Nedham, *Independencie No Schism* (London, 1646), p. 40.

31. Rollin, p. 45.

32. See John Adair, *Founding Fathers* (Grand Rapids, MI 1986), p. 218.

33. *Mercurius Pragmaticus,* October 19–26, 1647.

34. Ibid., October 12–20, 1647.

35. Ibid., November 21–28, 1648.

36. Frank, *Nedham,* p. 45.

37. *Mercurius Pragmaticus,* October 5–12, 1647.

38. Marchamont Nedham, *Ding Dong* (London, 1648), pp. 1–2.

39. Marchamont Nedham, *A Short History of the English Rebellion* (London, 1661), p. 4.

40. Ibid., p. 7.

41. Ibid., pp. 11, 14.

42. Ibid., p. 31.

43. William Waller, *Vindication,* quoted in Adair, p. 220.

44. Frank, *The Beginnings of the English Newspaper,* p. 194.

45. Ibid., p. 185.

46. *Mercurius Pragmaticus,* p. 34.

47. Ibid., p. 37.

48. Marchamont Nedham, *The Great Feast at the Sheep-shearing of the City and Citizens, on the 7th of June last,* p. 6.

49. Marchamount Needham, *The Case of the Commonwealth of England, Stated, or The Equity, Utility, and Necessity, of a Submission to the present Government* (London, 1650).

50. Ibid., p. 40.

51. Ibid., p. 30.

52. Ibid., loc. cit.

53. Holles quoted in Adair, p. 220.

54. Nedham edited the *Mercurius Politicus* through the demise of the Cromwellian regime in 1660. From 1655 to 1660 he also edited *The Publick Intelligencer;* it appeared on Monday and *Politicus* on Thursday, with some pages duplicated.

55. Frank, *Nedham,* p. 207.

56. See, for example, *Publick Intelligencer,* July 5–12, 1658, execution of Edmond Stacy.

57. Marchamont Nedham, *The Excellencie of a Free State* (London: 1656), p. 45.

58. *Mercurius Politicus,* March, 1657.

59. Adair, p. 228.

60. Ibid., loc. cit.

61. Marchamont Nedham, *Interest will not Lie* (London, 1659).

62. Marchamont Nedham, *Newes From Brussels* (London, 1660).

63. *A Rope for Pol* (London, 1660).

64. Quoted in Frank, *Nedham,* p. 127.

65. Charles II executed many of those who had signed the death warrant for his father, and even hanged (by what was left of their necks) the semi-decayed corpses of Cromwell and two other leaders. But Nedham in 1647 and 1648 had opposed the execution and given aid and comfort to Charles I, and that twist evidently was remembered by Charles II.

66. Preamble of 13 & 14 Charles II, c. 33.

67. In 1664 the First Conventicle Act made it illegal for five or more people not of the same household to meet together for worship except in accordance with the Anglican liturgy. In 1665 the Five Mile Act forbade ejected ministers to come within 5 miles of any place where they had ministered, unless they would swear never to attempt "any alteration of government either in Church or State." In 1670 the Second Conventicle Act imposed heavier penalties on preachers or others who defied the law. Seizure and sale of Dissenters' goods was authorized, with one third of the revenue gained paid to informers.

68. 15 Charles II 1663, in *Howell's State Trials,* p. 513.

CHAPTER 3
PLANTING OF CORRUPTION STORY

1. Quoted in Leonard Levy, *Emergence of a Free Press* (New York, 1985), p. 18.

2. Ibid., pp. 19–20.

3. Charles M. Andrews, ed., *Narratives of the Insurrections, 1675–1690* (New York, 1915), p. 309.

4. Ibid.

5. During this period, walking the tightrope of reformation without revolution was akin to walking the plank. For example, in 1698 Philip Clark, although a member of the Maryland assembly, was sentenced to 6 months in jail for criticizing Governor Francis Nicholson. According to the governor's Council, Clark's criticism was incitement to rebellion not because he actually suggested such an activity, but because his critique would reduce the esteem in which the governor was held—and that was seen as the first step toward rebellion.

6. John Harvard's gift of books for a new college was important, but Harvard's founders had to overcome political as well as material obstacles: They were challenging royal authority. In England, the universities at Oxford and Cambridge were arms of the government, which had a monopoly on the granting of college diplomas; Harvard, however, awarded its first diplomas in 1642, without royal authorization. The timing, it turned out, was good: In 1642 a king besieged and eventually to be beheaded was in no position to assert his authority.

7. Quoted in Benjamin Hart, *Faith and Freedom* (Dallas, TX, 1988), p. 121.

160 Notes

8. Clyde Duniway, *The Development of Freedom of the Press in Massachusetts* (Cambridge, MA, 1906), pp. 34–35.

9. Samuel Danforth, *The City of Sodom Enquired Into* (Cambridge, MA, 1674), cited in David Nord, "Teleology and News: The Religious Roots of American Journalism, 1630–1730, paper presented to the History Division, Association for Education in Journalism and Mass Communication (AEJMC), Portland, OR, July, 1988, p. 8.

10. Cited in Isaiah Thomas, *History of Printing in America* (Worcester, MA, two volumes, 1810), I, 83.

11. Harry S. Stout, *The New England Soul: Preaching and Religious Culture in Colonial New England* (New York, 1986), p. 3.

12. Ibid. As Stout noted, "Twice on Sunday and often once during the week, every minister in New England delivered sermons lasting between one and two hours in length. Collectively over the entire span of the colonial period, sermons totalled over five million separate messages in a society whose population never exceeded one-half million. . . . The average weekly churchgoer in New England (and there were far more churchgoers than church members) listened to something like seven thousand sermons in a lifetime, totaling somewhere around fifteen thousand hours of concentrated listening." (pp. 3–4)

13. See Alice M. Baldwin, *The New England Clergy and the American Revolution* (New York, 1928), p. 4.

14. Studies show that most publications in New England in the seventeenth century were event oriented. David Nord's review of the seventeenth century titles listed in Charles Evans' *American Bibliography* shows that 426 of 777 (55%) were linked clearly to events. (Nord, p. 10)

15. Quoted in Stout, p. 77.

16. Cited in Nord, p. 12. Nord, an exception to the lack of interest among leading journalism historians in the religious roots of American journalism, pointed out correctly that "Increase Mather's publication record in the last quarter of the seventeenth century represents the first major flowering [of] indigenous American journalism."

17. *Some Meditations Concerning our Honourable Gentlemen and Fellow-Souldiers* (Boston, 1675).

18. Increase Mather, *A Brief History . . .* (Boston, 1676), included in *So Dreadfull a Judgment: Puritan Responses to King Philip's War, 1676–1677,* Richard Slotkin and James K. Folsom, eds., (Middletown, Conn. 1978), pp. 113, 119.

19. Ibid., p. 109. On another occasion colonial soldiers pursued Philip's army into a swamp but withdrew just as Philip was about to surrender. "The desperate Distress which the Enemy was in was unknown to us," Mather reported; rather than bewailing a lost opportunity, however, he wrote how "God saw that we were not yet fit for Deliverance" (p. 90).

20. Ibid., p. 92.

21. Ibid., p. 130.

22. Ibid., p. 140.

23. Ibid., pp. 176–177.

24. Ibid., pp. 191, 193.

25. Increase Mather, *An Essay for the Recording of Illustrious Providences* (Boston, 1684), preface.

26. Ibid.

27. Ibid.

28. Ibid.

29. Mather, *A Brief History* . . ., p. 125. Nord, in noting the protest of Robert Middlekauff that Mather's procedure was "not genuinely empirical," pointed out that "it is empirical in its way. The empirical data are the statements of the sources. Mather's method is the empiricism of the news reporter, not the scientist."

30. Mather wrote about not only political events but storms, earthquakes, and fires. He stated, in *Burnings Bewailed* (Boston, 1711), that all such events were "ordered by the Providence of God . . . When a fire is kindled among a people, it is the Lord that hath kindled it."

31. Nord, p. 11.

32. Increase Mather, *A Brief History* . . ., in Slotkin and Folsom, p. 81.

33. Cotton Mather, *Magnalia Christi Americana* (London, 1702), vol. II, p. 341.

34. Quoted in Barrett Wendell, *Cotton Mather* (New York, 1891), p. 46.

35. Wise was ordered to pay a fine of 50 pounds (the equivalent of about $5,000) and to post a bond for 1,000 pounds ($100,000) to guarantee his good behavior.

36. Kenneth Silverman, *The Life and Time of Cotton Mather* (New York, 1984), p. 74.

37. Willian and Mary's ascension was called the "Glorious Revolution," because the coup was militarily unresisted and the bloodshed of the English civil war was not repeated.

38. Duniway, pp. 67–68.

39. *A Short but Just Account of the Tryal of Benjamin Harris* . . . (London, 1679), p. 8.

40. Benjamin Harris, *A Relation of the Fearful Estate of Francis Spira* (London, 1683), p. 4.

41. Some details of his life, although not his theology, are provided in J. G. Muddiman, "Benjamin Harris, the First American Journalist," *Notes and Queries* 163 (1932), pp. 129–133, 147–150, 166–170, 223, and 273–274 (Muddiman's article was spread over several issues).

42. Harris, *Spira,* p. 11.

43. Ibid., p. 13.

44. See Carolyn Cline (Southwest Texas State University), "The Puritan Revolutionary: The Role of Cotton Mather in the Founding of *Publick Occurrences,*' " paper presented to AEJMC, p. 4.

45. *Publick Occurrences Both Foreign and Domestick,* September 25, 1690.

46. Ibid.

47. Ibid.

48. Ibid.

49. Ibid.

50. See Cline, op. cit.

51. One of the stories he produced, entitled "The Irreligious Life, and Miserable Death of Mr. George Edwards, who committed suicide on January 4, 1704," indicates the type of coverage of news events that Harris evidently would have developed in America, if he had been given the opportunity. Harris first described how "Edwards threw himself upon a Belief, that All Things came by Nature, and that what Christians call the Providence of God, was purely Accident and Chance." Then, ideas had consequences: "These Notions thus imbid'd, led him to a voluptuous and sensual Life; and consequently devoted him to an Atheistical Conversation." For years Edwards "continued to run on in Infidelity,

Impenitence, and Drunkenness. In his drink he was Mad, and out of it, in a mellancholly despairing Condition. . . . Thus he hurry'd away his Precious Time, 'till his Estate became morgag'd, and his Affairs ran backwards; the thoughts of which, with the Horrors of Conscience for disowning his Maker, and living a prophane, debauch'd Life, threw him into extream Despair." Finally Edwards shot and killed himself: "Here was the dreadful End of his Atheism, and Infidelity, his Irreligion and Impiety. In this horrible manner did he cut off his Life and Hopes at one Blow, and, without any Fear of God, or Regard to the Good of his Soul, launch'd out into an unalterable Eternity." (included in sixth edition of Benjamin Harris, *A Relation of the Fearful Estate of Francis Spira* (London, 1718).

52. Chadwick Hansen, "Some of the Witches Were Guilty," in Marc Mappen, ed., *Witches and Historians* (Huntington, NY, 1980), p. 46.

53. See "Appendix: List of Known Witchcraft Cases in Seventeenth Century New England," in John Demos, *Entertaining Satan* (New York, 1982), pp. 401–409.

54. Quoted in Perry Miller, *The New England Mind: From Colony to Province* (Boston, 1953), p. 194. *The Return of Several Ministers,* a pamphlet of unknown authorship published in June 1692, made the same point.

55. Chadwick Hansen, *Witchcraft at Salem* (New York, 1969), argues that some of those executed probably did try to practice witchcraft, but others did not.

56. Mather made this offer in August 1692, while again stating that spectral evidence is fallacious.

57. Increase Mather's strong sense of God's sovereignty led him to state that it would be better for ten of the guilty to escape than for one innocent person to be put to death wrongly; he argued that if there is no convincing proof of a crime, God does not intend the perpetrator to be discovered.

58. Increase Mather, *Cases of Conscience* (Boston, 1692), p. 10.

59. Miller, p. 195.

60. "Command" was Mather's word for it.

61. Cotton Mather, *The Wonders of the Invisible World* (Boston, 1692), p. 1.

62. Miller, p. 191.

63. Quoted in Clyde Augustus Duniway, *The Development of Freedom of the Press in Massachusetts* (New York, 1905, reprinted 1969), p. 73.

64. The grounds for acquittal were technical, but the jury did pass up an opportunity to shut up a writer disliked by New England leaders.

65. Thomas Maule, *New-England Persecutors Mauled with their own Weapons* (New York, 1697).

66. *Boston News-Letter,* August 6, 1705.

67. Ibid., April 30, 1704.

68. *Ibid.,* July 24 and October 30, 1704.

69. Ibid., June 30, 1704.

70. Ibid., May 29, 1704; June 5, June 12, 19, 26, and July 3, 1704.

71. Mather, *The Voice of God in Stormy Winds* (Boston, 1704), quoted in Nord, p. 29.

72. Begun on December 21, 1719, by editor William Brooker, Campbell's successor as postmaster.

73. Perry Miller (p. 206) found excerpts in Mather's diaries of 1694 and 1696 that show him still churning about the "unheard of DELUSIONS" at Salem and the "Inextricable

Things we have met withal." Later, Mather continued to agonize about how "divers were condemned, against whom the chief evidence was found in the spectral exhibitions."

74. *Boston News-Letter*, July 24, 1721.

75. John B. Blake, "The Inoculation Controversy in Boston: 1721–1722," *New England Quarterly* 35 (December, 1952), p. 493.

76. Historians have given the *Courant* an anti-establishment reputation, because it opposed Cotton Mather, but that is an error; the "establishment," although united in religious belief, had become politically pluralistic.

77. Ironically, it was the bravery of Mather that resurrected tales of his former cravenness. As Perry Miller noted concerning the witchcraft trials, they were quickly forgotten at the time, and seen as just one more problem that temporarily overtook New England: "For twenty-eight years this cataclysm hardly appears on the record—until summoned from the deep by opponents of inoculation as a stick to beat the clergy for yet another 'delusion.' Only in 1721 does it begin to be that blot on New England's fame which has been enlarged, as much by friends as by foes, into its greatest disgrace." (Miller, p. 191).

CHAPTER 4
ESTABLISHMENT OF AMERICAN PRESS LIBERTY

1. *Boston News-Letter*, January 21, 1723.

2. Massachusetts had fewer political shocks during the second quarter of the 18th century, but "remarkable judgments" such as earthquakes still could cause excitement. In October 1727, a "horrid rumbling" and "weighty shaking" was felt throughout New England. Thomas Paine of Weymouth, Massachusetts, using good specific detail, reported that "the motion of the Earth was very great, like the waves of the sea. . . . The strongest Houses shook prodigiously and the tops of some Chimnees were thrown down." Aftershocks over the next 9 days, in Paine's words, "mightily kept up the Terror of it in the People, and drove them to all possible needs of Reformation." (Thomas Paine, *The Doctrine of Earthquakes* (Boston, 1728).) Seventeen news sermons about the earthquake were published.

3. *Boston New-Letter*, January 4, 1733.

4. Mark A. Noll, *Christians in the American Revolution* (Washington, 1977), noted that during this period the theological composition of the colonial population began to change, as Anglican state churches of the middle and southern colonies lost their hold on the populace. By the American Revolution, 75% of all colonists would be identified with denominations—Congregationalist, Presbyterian, Baptist, and German or Dutch Reformed—that had arisen from the Reformed and Puritan wing of European Protestantism (p. 30).

5. *American Weekly Mercury*, February 26, 1722.

6. *New York Weekly Journal*, November 12, 1733.

7. Ibid.

8. Ibid., December 31, 1733, p. 2; see also January 13, 1735, p. 3.

9. Ibid.

10. *Journal*, March 11, 1734, p. 2.

11. Jonathan Dickinson, *The Vanity of Human Institutions in the Worship of God* (New York, 1736), p. 11, and quoted in David Nord, "The Authority of Truth: Religion and the John Peter Zenger Case," *Journalism Quarterly*, Summer, 1985, p. 234.

12. Ibid., p. 31. Dickinson added, "If they without conviction submit to our opinions, they subject their consciences to human, and not to divine authority; and our requiring this of any is demanding a subjection to us, and not to Christ." In publishing such material, Zenger was spreading around ideas long current in New England; as minister Ebenezer Pemberton had argued in 1710, "kings and royal governors must govern themselves by unalterable Principles, and fixed Rules, and not by unaccountable humours, or arbitrary will . . . they take care that Righteous Laws be Enacted, none but such, and all such, as are necessary for the Safety of the Religion & Liberties of a People . . . [rulers] that are not skilful, thoughtful, vigilant and active to promote the Publick Safety and Happiness are not Gods but dead Idols."

13. James Alexander, *A Brief Narrative of the Case and Trial of John Peter Zenger*, Katz edition, p. 95.

14. The story of the trial is told in James Alexander, *A Brief Narrative of the Case and Trial of John Peter Zenger*, first published in 1736 and reprinted in several books including Livingston Rutherford, *John Peter Zenger, His Press, His Trial and a Bibliography of Zenger Imprints* (New York, 1904).

15. *The Press and America*, pp. 38, 44.

16. Alexander, op. cit.

17. *New York Journal*, December 31, 1733, p. 2; see also January 13, 1735, p. 3.

18. Alexander, op. cit. Hamilton's biblical references were frequent; he argued that, "If a libel is understood in the large and unlimited sense urged by Mr. Attorney, there is scarce a writing I know that may not be called a libel, or scarce any person safe from being called to account as a libeller: for Moses, meek as he was, libelled Cain; and who is it that has not libelled the devil?"

19. As David Nord (op. cit.) concluded in his excellent article, "Like the revival converts who asserted their right to interpret the law of God, the Zenger jury asserted the right of ordinary people to interpret the law of man. In both cases, the operative principle was not freedom, but truth. Andrew Hamilton, like a revival preacher, told the jurors that authority lay, not in them, but in truth. He did not ask them to condone individualism or to approve individual diversity of expression—only truth . . ."

20. *Maryland Gazette*, January 17, 1745.

21. *The Essential Rights and Liberties of Protestants* was signed "Philalethes," but Baldwin (p. 65) credited Williams and discussed possible attribution to other writers. This essay was following along George Whitefield's allowance for civil disobedience when he argued that laws "are good and obligatory when conformable to the laws of Christ and agreeable to the liberties of a free people; but when invented and compiled by men of little hearts and bigotted principles. . . . and when made use of only as ends to bind up the hands of a zealous few, they may be very legally broken." News sermon/pamphlets published during the years following the Zenger trial repeatedly distinguished between arbitrary and legal government. Restraint among all parties was vital, as Jared Elliot told Connecticut residents in 1738: "Arbitrary Despotick Government, is, When this Sovereign Power is directed by the Passions, Ignorance & Lust of them that Rule, And a Legal

Government is, When this Arbitrary & Sovereign Power puts itself under Restraints, and lays itself under Limitations."

Emphasis on literacy led to the idea that allegiance was not to persons but to written documents—the Bible, and laws based on the Bible (in England, those laws as a group made up the nation's constitutional framework).

22. Alice Baldwin, *The New England Clergy and the American Revolution* (New York, 1958), pp. 67–68.

23. Included in Williams Wells, ed., *The Life and Public Services of Samuel Adams* (New York, 1865–68), three vols, I, 22–23. Adams began his examination of questions concerning disobedience to government shortly after the Zenger case. The title of his master's thesis at Harvard in 1743, when Adams was 21, was "Whether it be lawful to resist the Supreme Magistrate, if the Commonwealth cannot be otherwise preserved." He maintained the affirmative, but no record of the thesis remains.

24. Ibid.

25. Donald Barr Chidsey, *The World of Samuel Adams* (Nashville, 1974), p. 9.

26. Quoted in Stewart Beach, *Samuel Adams: The Fateful Years, 1764–1776* (New York: 1965), p. 13.

27. Quoted in Pauline Maier, *The Old Revolutionaries* (New York, 1980), p. 37.

28. Ibid. p. 4.

29. Harry Cushing, ed., *The Writings of Samuel Adams*, 4 vols. (New York, 1904), vol. I, p. 33, and vol. III, p. 220.

30. Maier, p. 47.

31. Ibid., p. 7.

32. William Tudor, *The Life of James Otis* (Boston, 1823), pp. 274–75.

33. *Writings*, III, 284. Adams' willingness to emphasize emotional, human interest stories has bothered some historians who associate such techniques with propaganda. For example, John C. Miller's *Sam Adams, Pioneer in Propaganda* (Boston, 1936), is filled with hatred toward its protagonist.

34. *Boston Gazette*, January 21, 1771.

35. In 1988 politics, this might mean prison furloughs.

36. Ibid.

37. *Writings*, IV, 108.

38. *Boston Gazette*, January 21, 1771.

39. Ibid.

40. *Writings*, IV, 106–107. Adams realized extremely well the dangers of investigative journalism to the journalist; he noted that the writer who exposes does so "at the Risque of his own Reputation; for it is a thousand to one but those whose Craft he puts at Hazard, will give him the odious Epithets of suspicious dissatisfiable peevish quarrelsome &c."

41. Ibid., I, 10.

42. Ibid., I, 60.

43. Arthur M. Schlesinger, *Prelude to Independence* (New York, 1957), p. 22, tells this story.

44. *Boston Gazette*, April 4, 1768.

45. Ibid.

46. Ibid.

47. Ibid.

48. Ibid.

49. Adams, *Writings,* I, 27.

50. Ibid.

51. Ibid.

52. Ibid.

53. Ibid., I, 27–28.

54. See John W. Whitehead, *An American Dream* (Westchester, IL, 1987), p. 62.

55. John Lathrop, quoted in Baldwin, p. 181.

56. Ibid.

57. Stout, p. 7. As Stout noted, in prerevolutionary New England communications the terms "most often employed to justify resistance and to instill hope emanated from the Scriptures." John Locke was widely read, but his political ideas came out of the Bible and Reformation thought. (As Herbert Foster has noted, the citations in Locke's *Two Treatises of Government* "are almost entirely Calvinistic: Scripture seventy-nine times; seven Calvinists . . . one ex-Calvinist . . . and only one reference uninfected by Calvinism, the Scottish Catholic Barclay.")

58. *South-Carolina Gazette,* June 20, 1774.

59. *Pennsylvania Evening Post,* June 27, 1775.

60. *Virginia Gazette,* June 20, 1774.

61. *Norwich Packet,* November 6, 1775.

62. *Boston Evening Post,* November 4, 1765.

63. *Boston Gazette,* October 3, 1768.

64. *Boston Evening-Post,* June 16, 1770.

65. *Boston Gazette,* March 7, 1768.

66. *Massachusetts Spy,* October 8, 1772.

67. *Boston Gazette,* March 7, 1768, column signed "The True Patriot."

68. Stout, p. 6.

69. *The Melancholly Catastrophe* (Boston, 1774).

70. *Massachusetts Spy,* June 2, 1774. The reference is to David's lament concerning the death of King Saul.

71. Quoted in Hart, p. 262.

72. *Virginia Gazette,* December 8, 1775.

73. Maier, p. 3. Many historians have attacked Adams' beliefs and his methodology. John Eliot in 1807 called him "austere . . . rigid . . . opinionated." [*A Biographical Dictionary* (Salem, 1807), p. 7] James Hosmer in 1885 did not like the "sharp practice" that Adams as journalist sometimes used [Hosmer, *Samuel Adams* (Boston, 1885), pp. 68, 229, 368]. See Maier, pp. 11–16, for a discussion of 20th century historiographical trends.

74. Some historians have mistakenly assumed that references by Adams and his contemporaries to "Providence" meant a movement away from belief in a theistic God, when exactly the opposite is true: reference to God's Providence distinguished theists from deists who posited a clockwork universe, in which God created all but then went on vacation.

75. Samuel Adams, *An Oration Delivered at the State-House in Philadelphia, to a very Numerous Audience, on Thursday the 1st of August, 1776* (Philadelphia, 1776); reprinted in Wells, vol. III, p. 408.

76. Ibid.

77. Ibid.
78. Ibid.

CHAPTER 5
FIRST SURGE OF THE OPPRESSION STORY

1. Quoted in Schlesinger, p. 284.
2. Ibid., pp. 284–5.
3. *A brief account of the Execution of Elisha Thomas* (Portsmouth, N.H.: 1788).
4. *Connecticut Courant*, December 17, 1782.
5. Ibid.
6. *The Federalist* no. 10, available in many editions including Clinton Rossiter, ed., *The Federalist Papers* (New York, 1961), pp. 77–84.
7. Ibid., No. 6, pp. 53–60.
8. "Essays of Brutus" in Herbert J. Storing, ed., *The Anti-Federalist* (Chicago, 1985), pp. 112–113.
9. *The Federalist Papers,* op. cit., pp. 320–325.
10. Quoted in Leonard Levy, *Emergence of a Free Press* (New York, 1985), p. 200.
11. *Gazette,* January 14, 1790, quoted in Levy, p. 291.
12. Quoted in Louis Ingelhart, *Press Freedoms* (Westport, CT, 1987), p. 131.
13. Quoted in Levy, loc. cit.
14. James Billington, *Fire in the Minds of Men* (Princeton, 1980), p. 33: "Indeed, the emergence of dedicated, ideological revolutionaries in a traditional society (in Russia of the 1860s no less than in France of the 1790s) depended heavily on literate priests and seminarians becoming revolutionary journalists. . . . Journalism was the only income-producing profession practiced by Marx, Lenin, and many other leading revolutionaries during their long years of powerlessness and exile."
15. These and subsequent Rousseau quotations are from Paul Johnson, *Intellectuals* (London, 1988).
16. Billington, pp. 35, 62.
17. *The General Advertiser,* March 6, 1797.
18. *Aurora,* December 21 and 23, 1796.
19. Quoted in Walter Brasch and Dana Ulloth, *The Press and the State* (Lanham, Md., 1986), p. 104.
20. Hart, *Faith and Freedom,* pp. 307–308.
21. For an account sympathetic to Bache and his beliefs, see Bernard Fay, *The Two Franklins* (Boston, 1933), particularly pp. 264–361.
22. Quoted in Levy, p. 298.
23. Timothy Dwight, *The Nature, and Danger, of Infidel Philosophy* (Hartford, 1798), p. 9.
24. Thomas Paine became famous for his timely pamphlet *Common Sense* (1776), but by the 1790s Paine seemed a believer in his own infallibility; Paine's friend Etienne Dumont said of him, "He believed his book on the Rights of Man could take the place of all the books in the world and he said to me if it were in his power to demolish all the libraries in existence, he would do it so as to destroy all the errors of which they were the

depository—and with the Rights of Man begin a new chain of ideas and principles. He
knew by heart all his writings and knew nothing else."

25. Quoted in James M. Lee, *History of American Journalism* (Boston, 1917), p. 101.

26. Ibid., p. 102.

27. Franklin made a perhaps-jocular suggestions as to what specifically the offended
party should do: If a writer attacks your reputation, "break his head." If you cannot find
him immediately, "waylay him in the night, attack him from behind, and give him a
drubbing."

28. Ingelhart, p. 138.

29. Levy, p. 297.

30. See Aleine Austin, *Matthew Lyon* (University Park, Pa., 1981), pp. 108–109.

31. Lyon took his seat in the House on February 20, 1799. The Federalists obtained
a 49–45 vote for expulsion, but that fell far short of the necessary two-thirds majority.

32. Speech of July 10, 1798, quoted in Levy, pp. 301–302.

33. George Hay, *An Essay on the Liberty of the Press* (Philadelphia, 1799; reprinted
in Richmond, 1803), p. 25 (Richmond edition).

34. Harold Nelson, ed., *Freedom of the Press from Hamilton to the Warren Court*
(Indianapolis, 1967), p. 119.

35. Ibid.

36. Quoted in Hart, p. 309.

37. Quoted in Howard Kenberry, *The Rise of Religious Journalism in the United States*
(unpublished dissertation, University of Chicago, 1920), p. 20. Statistics are from the
American Almanac, 1835.

38. Roberta Moore, *Development of Protestant Journalism in the United States, 1743–
1850* (unpublished doctoral dissertation, Syracuse University, 1968), p. 237. There had
been 37 newspapers in the 13 colonies in 1775. According to the 1835 *American Almanac*,
the number of daily newspapers increased from 27 in 1810 to 90 in 1834.

39. Alexis de Tocqueville, *Democracy in America*, ed. J. P. Mayer, trans. George
Lawrence (New York, 1969), p. 69.

40. Sketch of Willis' life in the *Boston Recorder*, October 21, 1858, p. 167.

41. Ibid., loc. cit.

42. Ibid., January 3, 1816.

43. Ibid.

44. Ibid.

45. Ibid., March 29, 1822.

46. Ibid.

47. Ibid., December 23, 1817.

48. Ibid., August 18, 1826. In this the *Recorder* anticipated de Tocqueville's observa-
tion that "Americans of all ages, all conditions, and all dispositions constantly form
associations. . . . If it is proposed to inculcate some truth or to foster some feeling by the
encouragement of a great example, they form a society. . . . what political power could
ever [do what Americans voluntarily] perform every day with the assistance of the principle
of association" (book 2, chapter 5).

49. *Lexington Western Monitor*, August 3, 1814.

50. *New York American*, March 3, 1819.

51. *Christian Disciple and Theological Review*, February, 1814, pp. 61–62. This

quotation and others from the War of 1812 era are found in William Gribbin, *The Churches Militant* (New Haven, 1973).

52. Ibid., August 21, 1813.

53. Claudius Buchanan, *Christian Researchers in Asia: with notices of the translation of the Scriptures into the Oriental languages* (Boston, 1811), p. 34.

54. *New Hampshire Patriot*, March 2, 1813.

55. *Niles' Weekly Register*, January 30, 1813.

56. *Columbian Phoenix*, November 28, 1812.

57. *Baltimore Patriot*, April 28, 1813.

58. *Boston Yankee*, January 23, 1815.

59. *Niles' Weekly Register*, October 30, 1813.

60. Leggett's columns are most readily accessible in William Leggett, *Democratick Editorials* (Indianapolis, 1984); here, p. 3.

61. Ibid., loc. cit.

62. Ibid., p. 11.

63. Ibid., loc. cit.

64. Ibid., loc. cit.

65. Ibid., p. 13.

66. See, for example, pages of the *Boston Recorder* throughout the 1830s and 1840s.

CHAPTER 6
GREAT DEBATES OF JOURNALISM

1. Established publications then as now had a tendency to become dull, with long sentences and elliptical statements at a time when punchy paragraphs were demanded. The classic statement of stodginess and literary arrogance was offered by the editor of a Christian magazine, *Spirit of the Pilgrims:* He announced that "extended and labored articles" were the best kind, and that readers "uninterested in communications of this nature may as well give up their subscription and proceed no farther with us." *Spirit of the Pilgrims* soon went out of business.

2. New York *Sun,* April 4, 1835, and cited by James Stanford Bradshaw, "George H. Wisner and the New York *Sun,*" *Journalism History* 6:4, Winter 1979–80, p. 118.

3. Ibid., May 13, 1834.

4. Ibid., May 19, 1834.

5. Ibid., April 21, 1834.

6. Ibid., July 4, 1834.

7. Ibid., September 2, 1833.

8. Bradshaw, p. 120.

9. *New York Herald*, July 27, 1836.

10. Quoted in Isaac Pray, *Memoirs of James Gordon Bennett and His Times* (New York, 1855), p. 276.

11. See *New York Herald*, December 14, 1838, and July 2, 1845. For other views see Mott, p. 237, and Don Seitz, *The James Gordon Bennetts* (Indianapolis, 1928), p. 83.

12. Unitarianism, the belief Calvin considered most dangerous to orthodox trinitarian

Christianity, arose in the center of the Calvinistic commonwealth, Massachusetts. This was both ironic and logical, because Unitarianism was a reaction against the Reformed world view with its concept of man's fallenness, its untamed God, and its doctrine of salvation based on God's sovereignty. Harvard itself became the Unitarian Vatican, with publishing enterprises (the influential *Monthly Anthology and Boston Review*) and supporters such as William Emerson, minister at the First Unitarian Church and father of Ralph Waldo, and William Tudor (Harvard, 1798), future editor of the influential *North American Review*.

13. Albert Brisbane, *Association* (New York, 1843), p. 209.

14. Ibid., p. 207.

15. When William Henry Harrison was elected president in 1840, Horace Greeley expected a pay-off. He had edited *The Log Cabin,* a major Whig campaign organ, and thought that Governor Seward would ask that the position of postmaster of New York be given to him. He did not get it, nor was he able to get anything in what he called "the great scramble of the swell mob of coon-minstrels and cider-suckers at Washington." Greeley complained that "no one of the whole crowd . . . had done so much toward General Harrison's nomination and election as yours respectfully," yet he was "not counted in." (Letter of November 11, 1854, quoted in Frederick Hudson, *Journalism in the United States, From 1690 to 1872* (New York, 1873), pp. 549–550.)

16. Greeley letter to B. F. Ransom, March 15, 1841, in Horace Greeley, *Autobiography* (New York, 1872), pp. 68–74.

17. Greeley, *Hints Toward Reforms* (New York, 1854), p. 86.

18. Quoted in Jeter Allen Isely, *Horace Greeley and the Republican Party, 1853–1861* (Princeton, 1947), p. 15.

19. Brisbane, p. 205.

20. William Harlan Hale, *Horace Greeley: Voice of the People* (New York, 1950), p. 99.

21. Brook Farm, which attracted for a time some leading literary lights, became the best known of the communes; Nathaniel Hawthorne's *The Blithedale Romance* shows his sarcastic reaction to Brook Farm.

22. Ibid., p. 105.

23. E. L. Godkin quoted in Mott, p. 277.

24. Hale, p. 299.

25. Quoted in James Lee, p. 405.

26. Ibid.

27. Because the 1840s was a decade of utopian hopes that in some ways paralleled the 1960s, some readers also would be excited by commune coverage.

28. Quoted in Charles Sotheran, *Horace Greeley and Other Pioneers of American Socialism* (New York, 1892), p. 193.

29. Ibid., p. 195.

30. *New York Tribune,* November 20, 1846.

31. *New York Courier and Enquirer,* November 23, 1846 (hereafter noted as *Courier*).

32. *Tribune,* November 26, 1846.

33. *Courier,* November 30, 1846.

34. *Tribune,* December 1, 1846.

35. *Courier,* December 8, 1846.

36. *Tribune,* December 10, 1846.

37. *Courier,* December 14, 1846.

38. *Tribune,* December 16, 1846.

39. *Courier,* December 24, 1846.

40. Ibid.

41. *Courier,* December 24, and *Tribune,* December 28, 1846.

42. Ibid.

43. *Courier,* January 6, 1847.

44. Ibid. Raymond went on to state that Greeley's "blunder is exactly that of the man who should expect a water-wheel, by turning, to produce the water which is from the first to turn it;—who should look to the motion of a watch for the creation of the main-spring, which alone can give it motion. It is precisely the error which the would-be inventors of Perpetual Motion have constantly committed. Can anything be more palpably impossible? And is not this defect *fatal* to the whole system?"

45. Ibid.

46. *Tribune,* January 13, 1847.

47. Ibid.

48. Ibid.

49. Ibid.

50. *Courier,* January 20, 1847.

51. Ibid.

52. Ibid.

53. *Tribune,* January 29, 1847.

54. Ibid.

55. *Courier,* February 10, 1847.

56. Ibid.

57. *Tribune,* February 17, and *Courier,* March 5, 1847.

58. *Courier,* January 20, 1847.

59. Ibid., March 5, 1847.

60. Ibid.

61. *Tribune,* March 12, 1847.

62. *Courier,* March 19, 1847. Raymond also argued that few people in the communes would do any work, but Greeley insisted that production would not be a problem if well organized; he anticipated Bellamy's industrial army of the 1880s by arguing, curiously, "What Organization may do to render the repulsive attractive is seen in the case of War and Armies. Intrinsically the most revolting employment that can be suggested to a man is that of maiming and butchering his fellow-men by the wholesale, and taking his chance of being maimed or butchered in turn. And yet millions are found to rush into it, take delight in it, spend their lives in it, in preference to peaceful and better rewarded avocations. And why? Because (I speak of the regular soldier, who makes war his life-long profession) rulers have given to war an Organization, which satisfies two of the senses—that of Hearing by Music, that of Sight by glittering uniforms, precision of movement, and beauty of array. In a few, Ambition is also excited, while to the mass the assurance of an unfailing though meager subsistence is proffered. By these simple expedients the imagination is led captive, and millions constantly enlisted to shoot and be shot at for an average of not more than sixpence per day.

"O that the governments of the world were wise enough, good enough to bestow one-half the effort and expenses on the Organization of Labor that they have devoted to the Organization of Slaughter!"

63. *Tribune,* March 26, 1847.
64. *Courier,* April 16, 1847.
65. Ibid. Raymond wrote concerning Greeley's Associationism, "The Trinity in which it pretends to believe, is resolved into a trinity of the 'active, passive, and neutral principles of life and order.' It gravely declares that by the 'Kingdom of Heaven' is meant Association."
66. Ibid.
67. Ibid.
68. Ibid.
69. Ibid.
70. *Tribune,* April 28, 1847.
71. *Courier,* May 20, 1847.
72. Ibid.
73. Ibid., March 5, 1847.
74. Ibid.
75. Ibid., April 16, 1847.

CHAPTER 7
IRREPRESSIBLE CONFLICT IN THE PRESS

1. One of the phalanxes Greeley had joined, Red Bank in New Jersey, lasted the longest: 12 years, 1843 to 1855.
2. *On Association,* p. 213.
3. Ibid., p. 212.
4. *New York Tribune,* April 10, 1845.
5. See Horace Greeley, *Hints Toward Reforms.*
6. Greeley did, however, continue to give space to Brisbane; in 1858 the *Tribune* provided room for Brisbane to promote a massive, 100,000-acre commune. (*New York Daily Tribune,* July 12, 14, 23, August 18, 20, 27, 1858.)
7. Hale, pp. 135–136. Those Greeley worked closely with included George Henry Evans, an apostle of Tom Paine and editor of the *Working Man's Advocate,* and Lewis Masquerier, an early socialist.
8. Horace's wife Mary also had her ways. Once, when she had become a supporter of what today would be called the "animal rights" movement, she met writer Margaret Fuller on the street one day, touched Fuller's kid gloves and began to scream, "Skin of a beast, skin of a beast." Mary was wearing silk, and Margaret Fuller had the presence of mind to begin yelling, "Entrails of a worm, entrails of a worm."
9. *New York Evening Post,* September 7 and 9, 1835; included in *Democratick Editorials,* pp. 203, 206.
10. Ibid., *loc. cit.*
11. Ibid., September 9, 1835, and p. 209.

12. Ibid., August 8, 1835, and p. 197.

13. From biographical information distributed by the Greater Alton/Twin Rivers Convention & Visitors' Bureau.

14. Plaque on the Lovejoy monument, Alton, IL, visited by the author.

15. Clay archives, University of Kentucky Library, and quoted in H. Edward Richardson, *Cassius Marcellus Clay* (Lexington, KY, 1976), p. 34.

16. *True American* prospectus, February 19, 1845.

17. *True American,* August 16, 1845.

18. Quoted in Richardson, p. 46.

19. Ibid., p. 47.

20. Muhammed Ali, originally named Cassius Clay, showed a lack of historical sense (and a different theology) by changing monikers because he "didn't want a slave name." Freedom of choice, of course, but the original Cassius Clay freed his own slaves and risked his life many times to help free others.

21. Clay archives, University of Kentucky library.

22. Clay's later years were not particularly distinguished except by a variety of philosophical delusions and rapscallion activities.

23. *New York Daily Tribune,* October 17, 1851. See also April 12.

24. Ibid., May 2, 1854.

25. Ibid., July 12, 1860.

26. Ibid., August 22, 1860.

27. Ibid., March 10 and 26, 1856, and June 27, 1859.

28. Isely, p. 131.

29. *Daily Tribune* from August, 1855 to March, 1856.

30. Isely, op. cit.

31. This account is based on Otto Scott, *The Secret Six* (New York, 1979), pp. 5–9.

32. *New York Daily Tribune,* May 20, June 1, 3, 5, 6, 9, 14, 17, 1856.

33. Ibid., April 5, 8, 1856; October 28, 1859.

34. Isely, p. 177.

35. Lydia Maria Child, "The Kansas Emigrants," *New York Daily Tribune,* October 23 to November 4, 1856.

36. See Lloyd Chiasson, "A Newspaper Analysis of the John Brown Raid," *American Journalism,* Spring, 1985, p. 30.

37. *New York Daily Tribune,* November 9, 1859.

38. Ibid., November 17 and 19, 1859.

39. Quoted in Isely, p. 266.

40. Ibid., p. 266. Greeley wavered in his intellectual stand for violence as real, large-scale violence came nearer. In November 1860, he wrote concerning states wishing to secede that "we shall be in favor of letting them go in peace. Then who is to fight? And what for?" (*Daily Tribune,* November 2.) It is not clear now whether Greeley was playing a dangerous game of "chicken," or whether he truly believed the south would not leave and that, if it did, the north would not pursue. Once the southern states did secede, the *Tribune* abruptly changed its policy. This might indicate that Greeley was bluffing in his coverage, and that once his bluff was called, he advocated what he all along felt would be necessary. But consistency was not Greeley's strong point, and it may be unnecessary to look for it in this case; Greeley wrote what he wanted when he wanted.

41. *New York Herald,* March 7, 1850, p. 2. Cited in Gary Whitby, "Economic Elements of Opposition To Abolition and Support of South by Bennett in the New York *Herald," Journalism Quarterly,* Spring, 1988, p. 83.

42. Ibid.

43. *New York Herald,* October 20, December 10 and 22, 1859.

44. Ibid., November 26, 1860.

45. *New York World,* October 12, 1860.

46. Ibid., November 30, 1860.

47. Ibid.

48. Ibid.

49. Ibid.

50. Quoted in Llerena Friend, "Sam Houston," in H. Bailey Carroll et al, *Heroes of Texas* (Waco, 1966), p. 93.

51. Ibid., p. 92.

52. "Christian Patriotism" by Elbert S. Porter, in the *New York World,* December 1, 1860.

53. Ibid.

54. Ibid.

55. Even though some northern newspapers were more moderate, the *Tribune,* with its reach throughout the north and personification in Greeley, always seemed to be seen in the south as the embodiment of an aggressive northern spirit.

56. *Raleigh Register,* March 1, 1860.

57. See Howard C. Perkins, ed., *Northern Editorials on Secession,* I, pp. 88–92.

58. *Atlantic Monthly* CIII (May, 1909), p. 654.

59. George Talbot quoted in Isely, p. 54.

60. Ibid., p. 3.

61. *New York Daily Tribune,* April 7, 1858.

62. C. Vann Woodward, *The Burden of Southern History* (New York, 1961), pp. 63–68.

63. *New York World,* op. cit.

64. Charleston, Jacksonville, and Jackson newspapers, November 1860, quoted in Reynolds, p. 148.

65. *Richmond Dispatch,* January 6, 1860.

66. Ibid., January 26, 1861.

67. *Augusta Daily Constitutionalist,* December 7, 1860.

68. *Albany Patriot,* February 9, 1860.

69. Ibid., March 8, 1860.

70. May 19, 1860, letter, quoted in Donald E. Reynolds, *Editors Make War* (Nashville, 1966), p. 36.

71. Ibid., loc. cit.

72. *Hillsborough Recorder,* December 12, 1860.

73. *New York Herald,* January 29, 1861.

74. *New York Daily Tribune,* February 18 to 28, 1861.

75. Ibid., January 23 through 26, 1861.

76. Ibid., June 26 to July 4, 1861. One New York Greeley-watcher, James W. Nye, saw humor in the situation: "Imagine Greely [sic] booted & Spurred with Epaulets on his

Shoulders and with a whetted blade in his hands marching at the head of a column. . . . The idea of Greely turning warrior, is to ridiculus [sic] to be thought of."

77. Quoted by Thomas Keiser, " 'The Illinois Beast': One of Our Greatest Presidents," *Wall Street Journal*, February 11, 1988. Keiser's column was based on research by David Donald and Thomas Bailey.

78. Ibid.

79. James E. Pollard, *The Presidents and the Press* (New York, 1941), p. 352.

80. Quoted in George Fort Milton, *The Age of Hate: Andrew Johnson and the Radicals* (New York, 1930), p. 153. Milton also quotes other vengeful leaders, including Senator Benjamin Wade, who suggested that the north "hang ten or twelve of the worst of those fellows; perhaps, for full measure, I should make it thirteen, just a baker's dozen." (p. 56)

CHAPTER 8
OBSTACLES TO POWER

1. Frank Moore, *Life and Speeches of Andrew Johnson* (Boston, 1865), p. 471.

2. Ibid., p. 484.

3. Johnson quoted in Claude G. Bowers, *The Tragic Era* (New York, 1929), p. 41.

4. See William Harlan Hale, *Horace Greeley, Voice of the People* (New York, 1950), and Glynden Garlock Van Deusen, *Horace Greeley: Nineteenth Century Crusader* (Philadelphia, 1953).

5. C. Gregg Singer, *A Theological Interpretation of American History*, rev. ed. (Phillipsburgh, NJ, 1964), pp. 88–89.

6. Bowers, p. 109.

7. Ibid., loc. cit.

8. George Milton, *The Age of Hate* (New York, 1930), p. 357.

9. Ibid, p. 287.

10. Ibid., loc. cit.

11. *National Intelligencer*, February 23, 1866.

12. Gideon Welles, *Diary* (Boston, 1911), II, 432.

13. Ibid., loc. cit.

14. David Miller DeWitt, *The Impeachment and Trial of Andrew Johnson* (New York, 1903), p. 62.

15. Milton, p. 354.

16. Ibid., p. 359.

17. Ibid., loc. cit.

18. *New York Tribune*, February 26, 1866.

19. *New York Herald*, September 10, 1866.

20. Ibid., September 13, 1866.

21. David Ross Locke, *Swingin Round the Circle* (Boston, 1867), pp. 210–217.

22. *Cleveland Leader*, September 4, 1866.

23. Sarah Watts, *The Press and the Presidency* (New York, 1985), p. 211.

24. Ibid., loc. cit.

25. *New York Tribune,* September 6, 1866, and subsequent days.

26. *The Independent,* September 6, 1866.

27. Ibid.

28. Ibid., August 15, 1867.

29. *New York Tribune,* October 25, 1869.

30. Watts, p. 212.

31. Ibid., loc. cit.

32. *Congressional Globe,* January 3, 1867.

33. "The Public Situation," *The Independent,* September 19, 1867.

34. 1 Samuel 12:3.

35. *New York Tribune,* May 14, 18, 23, 1868.

36. *The Nation,* May 21, 1868.

37. Quoted in John F. Kennedy, *Profiles in Courage* (New York, 1963), p. 143.

38. Ibid., p. 148.

39. *New York Tribune,* May 14, 18, 23, 1868.

40. Ibid., September 2, 1868.

41. Albert Bigelow Paine, *Thomas Nast: His Period and His Pictures* (New York, 1904), p. 129.

42. Quoted in *New York World,* March 6, 1869.

43. Bowers, p. 284.

44. Ibid., loc. cit.

45. *New York Herald,* April 19, 1870.

46. Bowers, p. 355.

47. Ibid., loc. cit.

48. Quoted in *New York World,* February 8, 1873.

49. Paine, p. 270.

50. *New York Tribune,* December 5, 1872.

51. Hale, pp. 351–352.

52. November 13 statement quoted in Van Deusen, p. 423.

53. *New York Tribune,* April 7, 1877.

54. *The Nation,* April 5, 1877, p. 202.

55. Sumner said, "If we do not like the survival of the fittest, we have only one possible alternative, and that is the survival of the unfittest. The former is the law of civilization; the latter is the law of anti-civilization. We have our choice between the two, or we can go on, as in the past, vacillating between the two, but a third plan, the social desideratum—a plan for nourishing the unfittest and yet advancing civilization, no man will ever find." Christianity was that third plan, but Sumner found it wanting.

56. William Graham Sumner, *Folkways* (Boston, 1906), p. 65.

57. See Marvin Olasky, "Social Darwinism on the Editorial Page," *Journalism Quarterly,* Fall, 1988, pp. 420–424.

58. *Dallas Morning News,* November 15, 1887.

59. *Dallas Daily Times Herald,* January 29, 1891.

60. Ibid., January 17, 1891.

61. See *Proceedings of the Texas Press Association* from 1880 to 1900.

62. *Dallas Daily Times Herald,* January 30, 1891.

63. See Marvin Olasky, "Lenin, Grover Cleveland and Election Year Economics," *Countywide,* November 1, 1984.

64. Ibid.

65. Ibid.

66. Edmund Burke, *Reflections on the Revolution in France* (London, 1960), p. 44.

67. Icie F. Johnson, *William Rockhill Nelson and the Kansas City Star* (Kansas City, 1935), p. 81.

68. *Kansas City Star,* September 20, 1880.

69. Johnson, p. 61.

70. Ibid., p. 80.

71. "Where the Responsibility Rests," *Kansas City Star,* October 24, 1892.

72. Josephine Shaw Lowell, *Public Relief and Private Charity* (New York, 1884), p. 66.

73. Ibid., loc. cit.

74. Lowell's worldview also led her to emphasize effect on character: the problem with "outdoor relief," she wrote, is that "It fails to save the recipient of relief and community from moral harm, because human nature is so constituted that no man can receive as a gift what he should earn by his own labor without a moral deterioration . . ."

75. Many small newspapers came and went as the Greenback movement, along with political elements of the Granger and National Alliance farm movements, had their days in the sun. Most during the 1870–1900 period concentrated on useful ways to improve business and perhaps buy and sell in bulk to attain better prices; there may have been a thousand such newspapers, with circulation in the hundreds of thousands. Others appealed to envy and hatred.

76. Edward Bellamy, *Equality* (New York, 1897), p. 17.

77. Edward Bellamy, *Looking Backward* (Chicago, 1890), p. 276.

78. Ibid., loc. cit.

79. Richard Ely, *Social Aspects of Christianity* (New York, Thomas Crowell, 1895), pp. 24–25. This quotation is from Ely's second edition; the first edition was published in 1889.

80. Ibid., p. 92.

81. The book, published in a second edition in New York by Longmans, Green in 1895, was based on a series of eight lectures Fremantle delivered at Oxford in 1883. The lectures by Freeman, who was Canon of Canterbury and Fellow of Balliol College, Oxford, excited little attention either then or immediately upon their initial publication in 1885, but during the 1890s Ely's promotion of the book was extremely successful. By the middle of the decade, as Fremantle proudly noted, his work was "placed in the line of succession, reaching down from Aristotle's Politics . . ." (p. x)

82. Ibid, pp. 278–280.

83. Ibid., pp. 278–279.

84. Ibid., p. 281.

85. See Elizabeth Higgins, *Out of the West* (New York, 1902).

CHAPTER 9
OF MUCKRAKERS AND PRESIDENTS

1. One practical joke actually led Pulitzer into his career. Unsure about what to do upon his discharge from the cavalry, Pulitzer decided to move to where no one knew

German, so that he would be pushed into learning English to survive. He took the advice of a prankster who told him his best bet was St. Louis, but Pulitzer learned upon arrival that the city was a major German-language center, one "almost like the old country, there was so much German." He could not have moved forward so rapidly in journalism had he been in a community where German was not spoken, but in St. Louis Pulitzer was able to go to work on a St. Louis German-language newspaper, the *Westliche Post*.

2. See *St. Louis Post-Dispatch* front pages, e.g. August 18, 1882; September 8, 1882; June 25 to July 4, 1883.

3. Ibid., May 16, 1882.

4. Ibid., June 15 and July 24, 1880.

5. Julian Rammelkamp, *Pulitzer's Post-Dispatch, 1878–1888* (Princeton, 1967), p. 135.

6. *St. Louis Post-Dispatch,* June 29 and July 8, 1881.

7. Examples may be found in *New York World,* August 31 and September 8, 1883, and February 24 and September 2, 1884.

8. The *World* in 1898 seemed to have an "Enemy of the Month" club.

9. Robert Rutland, *The Newsmongers* (New York, 1973), p. 281. "Truth" for Pulitzer was not what it had been for John Peter Zenger, however; Zenger had called for individual responsibility before God, but Pulitzer demanded that all bow down to him. Wanting to be omnipresent, Pulitzer instructed his editors and reporters to spy on each other and send reports directly to him. He purposefully created overlapping authority so that he would have to be called in to break deadlocks. Pulitzer's system, according to one journalist, "produced in time a condition of suspicion, jealousy and hatred, a maelstrom of office politics that drove at least two editors to drink, one into suicide, a fourth into insanity."

10. Everyone told Pulitzer to be content, but he could not be. One reporter described how "when anything went wrong, and things seemed to go wrong with him very often, there would come from his office . . . a stream of profanity and filth." Pulitzer's friend and fellow newspaper editor Henry Watterson noted that "Absolute authority made Pulitzer a tyrant." Things became worse when Pulitzer gradually became blind during the 1890s. He called himself "the loneliest man in the world," but even his laudatory biographer noted that "the loneliness, although real, was instead the terrible isolation of the helpless megalomanic and egocentric . . ." Pulitzer was separated from his wife and children for most of his last 20 years because he wanted around him only "compliant attendants." His wife often wanted to join him, but Pulitzer raged at her, then complained that he had to eat dinner with "nobody at my table except paid employees."

11. William Salisbury, *The Career of a Journalist* (New York, 1908), pp. 146–147.

12. Allen Churchill, *Park Row,* p. 70.

13. Ibid., p. 87.

14. Frank Luther Mott, *American Journalism* (New York, 1941), p. 539.

15. Quoted in Ferdinand Lundberg, *Imperial Hearst* (New York, 1936).

16. Roy Everett Littlefield III, *William Randolph Hearst: His Role in American Progressivism* (Lanham, Md., 1980), p. 103.

17. Ibid., p. 153.

18. Ibid., p. xiii.

19. *Park Row,* p. 98.

20. Description by Thomas Beer quoted in Watts, p. 316.

21. Louis Wiley, "A Come-back from the *Times,*" *Collier's,* May 13, 1911, p. 28.

22. *New York Journal*, March 3, 26, 1901.

23. *San Francisco Examiner*, March 25, 26, 1901.

24. *New York American*, March 2, 4, 10, 1904.

25. *New York Journal*, February 2, 1898.

26. San Francisco *Examiner*, March 8, 31, 1901.

27. *Park Row*, p. 81.

28. Ibid. There is little evidence from Hearst's conduct of his newspaper that he actually cared about people at all. In the 1890s, when Hearst and Pulitzer had a bidding war for journalistic talent, Hearst hired many away and fired fast. When some new hires then demanded ironclad contracts, they received them, but those who did not do what Hearst wanted were forced into resignation through humiliation: Senior reporters were turned into copy boys or men's-room attendants until they gave up. But some fought back. One caused the drains to clog every few hours by stuffing them with copies of the Journal; the business office gave in. Another announced loudly at the saloon that the humiliation was making his brain crack, he felt a strong pressure to set the city room afire. He also was paid off.

29. *New York Journal*, February 4, 1901.

30. The stories were apparently inaccurate but nevertheless pointed.

31. Mott, p. 541.

32. Even circulation stunts showed a lack of concern about consequences: Once, to boost sales, Hearst advertised a feature on "faithless husbands" by sending to wives throughout the city postcards suggesting they buy the *Journal* and learn the truth about their husbands; each postcard was signed cryptically, "A Friend." Gore Vidal, in his novel *Empire* (New York, 1987), gets at Hearst's conception of press power when he has one character see "herself creating a world that would be all hers, since she, like Hearst, would have reinvented all the players, giving them their dialogue, moving them in and out of wars: 'Remember the Maine' . . . She too could use a newspaper to change the world. She felt giddy with potentiality" (p. 100).

33. *New York Times*, February 14 and November 1, 1905.

34. Littlefield, p. 123.

35. See *Munsey's*, January 1900, for an example of the magazine's treatment of public utilities.

36. Quoted in C. C. Regier, *The Era of the Muckrakers* (Chapel Hill, 1932), p. 19.

37. Upton Sinclair, *The Industrial Republic* (New York, 1907), pp. 280–283.

38. Sinclair's *The Jungle* did not lead to changes in working conditions, but led to inspections and a temporary reduction of demand for American meat. Sinclair complained that his investigative journalism had merely "taken a few millions away from the packers and given them to the Junkers of East Prussia and to Paris bankers who were backing meat-packing enterprises in the Argentine." (Fuller, p. 168.)

39. See Floyd Dell, *Upton Sinclair* (New York, 1927).

40. See especially Sinclair's novel of the 1920s, *They Call Me Carpenter*.

41. Ray Stannard Baker, *American Chronicle: The Autobiography of Ray Stannard Baker* (New York, 1945), p. 33.

42. Ibid., p. 47.

43. Quoted in Robert C. Bannister, Jr., *Ray Stannard Baker: The Mind and Thought of a Progressive* (New York, 1966), p. 105.

44. Ibid., loc. cit.

45. Not much has changed in Berkeley during the past century.

46. The radical journalists were a media elite, as David M. Chalmers has noted in *The Social and Political Ideas of the Muckrakers* (New York, 1964). Chalmers noted that "In the decade between 1903 and 1912, nearly two thousand articles of a muckraking variety appeared in the popular magazines, complemented by editorials, cartoons, and serials. . . . But of this vast outpouring, close to a third were written by a small group of twelve men and one woman who concentrated on and professionalized this kind of journalism."

47. The leading muckrakers were not united in every way politically, but they tended to see themselves as a fraternity, with frequent meetings in the backroom of Considine's Saloon on Broadway near 42nd St., luncheon discussions every Wednesday at Luchow's restaurant, and membership in the Liberal Club (President Lincoln Steffens, Vice President Charles Russell) on East 19th St. Many worked together at *McClure's* and, later, the *American Magazine.*

48. Salisbury, p. 150.

49. See Oliver Carlson and Ernest Sutherland Bates, *Hearst* (New York, 1936), p. 111.

50. Chalmers, p. 97.

51. Steffens' article appeared in *American Magazine,* November, 1906; this assessment of Hearst is from *The Autobiography of Lincoln Steffens* (New York, 1931), p. 543.

52. Quoted in *Cosmopolitan,* October, 1936.

53. Theodore Roosevelt to McClure, October 4, 1905, Baker Papers, quoted in Harold S. Wilson, *McClure's Magazine and the Muckrakers* (Princeton, 1970), p. 179.

54. Swanberg, *Citizen Hearst,* p. 242.

55. Roosevelt to Ray Stannard Baker, April 9, 1906, Baker Papers, quoted in Wilson, p. 181.

56. *American Magazine,* May, 1906, p. 111.

57. "Sentiments on the Liberty of the Press," *American Weekly Mercury,* April 25, 1734.

58. Among these might have been a general public weariness with the muckraking proposals of Hearst and other journalistic "reformers." As H. L. Mencken noted, "Reform does not last. The reformer quickly loses his public. . . . This is what has happened over and over again in every large American city—Chicago, New York, St. Louis, Cincinnati, Pittsburgh, New Orleans, Baltimore, San Francisco, St. Paul, Kansas City. Every one of these places has had its melodramatic reform campaigns and its inevitable reactions. The people have leaped to the overthrow of bosses, and then wearied of the ensuing tedium." ("Newspaper Morals," *The Atlantic Monthly,* March, 1914, p. 293)

59. Only one historian on the left, to my knowledge, has given Hearst the praise he deserves—from that ideological perspective—for stirring up class hatred. Louis Fuller, *Crusaders for American Liberalism,* p. 132: "Hearst, more than any other man, was the absolute expression of all the blind need and ignorance and resentment which troubled the worker and farmer. He dived to the bottom of the reader's mind and stirred up the filth and despair that had lain so quiet before. . . . Hearst was steeped in mire. His long campaign against McKinley was virulent to the degree of insanity. But did McKinley really deserve much better treatment? It would have been splendid if another, more upright, more principled man than Hearst had been present to carry on the quasi-Socialist battle. But no such man existed."

60. Salisbury, p. 522.

61. Upton Sinclair, "The Muckrake Man," *The Independent,* September 3, 1908, pp. 517–519.

62. Ibid., loc. cit.

63. Ibid., loc. cit.

64. Ibid., loc. cit.

65. Salisbury, pp. 196–197.

66. Charles Russell, *Doing Us Good and Plenty* (New York, 1914), p. 156.

67. Baker's manuscript Notebook I, pp. 111–112, and J, pp. 107–128, quoted in Chalmers, pp. 69–70. Baker eventually decided not to join the Socialist Party; he continued to hug a liberal social gospel.

68. David Graham Phillips, *The Conflict* (New York, 1912), p. 62. The novel was published shortly after Phillips' death in 1911.

69. See also John Spargo, *The Spiritual Significance of Socialism* (New York, 1908); Spargo argued that only socialism would allow honest examination of the spiritual problems of life, because only then would the masses be freed from those who taught superstitution and fearful dogma.

70. *Collier's,* March, 1911, pp. 18–20.

71. William Allen White to Baker, August 28, 1913, Baker Papers, quoted in Wilson, p. 270.

72. See Marvin Olasky, *Prodigal Press* (Westchester, IL, 1988), p. 55.

73. Steffens to Upton Sinclair, May 19, 1926, quoted in Wilson, p. 307.

74. See the later chapters of Steffens' *Autobiography* for the full panorama of his tribute to the left and his attack on those of the right or center.

75. His statement is usually reported as, "I have seen the future, and it works."

76. Books that have documented these tendencies include James Crowl, *Angels in Stalin's Paradise* (Lanham, Md., 1982); Joshua Muravchik, *News Coverage of the Sandanista Revolution* (Washington, DC, 1988); many others.

77. See Steffens' *Autobiography,* and Justin Kaplan, *Lincoln Steffens* (New York, 1974).

78. Villard, *Some Newspapers and Newspaper-men* (New York: Knopf, 1923), p. 314. Villard wrote that the crusading journalist should provide "moral and spiritual leadership" but did not offer specifics. Villard's moral relativism was evident in his statement that journalists should "recall Isaiah's saying: 'The voice said, Cry.' And he said, 'What shall I cry?' But if he is true to his ideals he will always know what to say." In the Bible, of course, Isaiah had been told to emphasize God's sovereignty, not his own conceptions: "All men are like grass,/and all their glory is like the flowers of the field./ The grass withers and the flowers fall,/ because the breath of the Lord blows on them."

79. Salisbury, p. 231.

APPENDIX A

1. Hyder E. Rollins, ed., *A Pepysian Garland: Black–Letter Broadside Ballads of the Years 1595–1693* (Cambridge: Cambridge University Press, 1922), p. xi.

2. *A Collection of Seventy Nine Black–Letter Ballads and Broadsides, Printed in the*

Reign of Queen Elizabeth, Between the Years 1559 and 1597 (London: Joseph Lilly, 1867), pp. 45–47.

3. Anon, *The description of a monstrous pig, the which was farrowed at Hamsted* (London: Garat Dewes, 1562).

4. This and other titles cited in M. A. Shaaber, *Some Forerunners of the Newspaper in England* (New York: Octagon, 1966), p. 164.

5. *A Collection of Black-Letter Ballads,* pp. 81–84.

6. J. A. Sharpe, "Domestic Homicide in Early Modern England," *Historical Journal* 24, 1 (1981), pp. 42–43; cited in Mitchell Stephens, *A History of News* (New York, 1988), p. 111. Sharpe's collection of 25 ballads of spousal murder—13 reporting the murder of husbands, 12 the murder of wives—shows that they were moral tales concerning the outcome of adultery.

7. Quoted in Stephens, p. 113.

8. John Reynolds, *The Triumphs of Gods Revenge Against the crying and Execrable Sinne of (Wilfull and Premeditated) Murther* (London: Edward Griffin/William Lee, 1640), 2nd ed., p. ii; first published in 1622.

9. Ibid., loc. cit.

10. Ibid., p. 211.

11. Quoted in Stephens, p. 115.

12. John Barker, "A Balade declaryng how neybourhed, loue, and trew dealyng is gone" in *A Collection of Seventy-Nine BlackLetter Ballads and Broadsides* (London, 1867), p. 134.

13. Hyder Rollins, ed, *The Pack of Autolycus, or, Strange and Terrible News of Ghosts, Apparitions, Monstrous Births, Showers of Wheat, Judgments of God, and other Prodigious and Fearful Happenings as told in Broadside Ballads of the Years 1624–1693* (Cambridge, MA, 1927), pp. 68–74.

14. *The Euing Collection of English Broadside Ballads* (Glasgow, 1971), pp. 26–27.

15. Ibid., p. 360. The murder took place May 5, 1697.

16. Ibid., pp. 251–252. The storm struck on December 23, 1684.

17. *The Pack of Autolycus,* pp. 103–106.

18. Euing, pp. 298–299.

19. Ibid., pp. 198–199.

20. *The Pack of Autolycus,* pp. 122–125.

21. One ballad, "The Trappand Virgin," had as its secondary headline, "Take my advice while you are free,/ and young-men do not trust,/ They promise fare as fare can be,/ but mean what is unjust." The ballad began, "Come mourn with me you Leadies all,/ whom Young men have betrayed,/ I was belov'd of great and small,/ and thought a virtuous Maid:/ At length a Young-Man to me came/ and he did me much wrong,/ For he betray'd a harmless Maid/ with his deludeing Tongue./ Such vows and Protestations he did to me often use,/ With sights, and Sobs that pittyed me,/ so that I could not chuse/ But condescend to his desire." Promises of marriage were not fulfilled, and the betrayed maid concluded, "Take warning by me Maidens fair . . . When they have got what they desire/ their passion's at an End." There was also a word for men: "False hearted men where e're you be/ think not for to Escape,/ For what you gain by Treachery/ is next kinn to a Rape." (Euing, p. 577).

22. *Advice from the Dead to the Living; Or, a Solemn Warning to the World. Occasioned by the untimely Death of poor Julian, Who was Executed on Boston Neck, on*

Thursday the 22d of March, 1733, for the Murder of Mr. John Rogers of Pembroke, the 12th of September, 1733 (Boston, 1733).

23. Ibid.

24. *A Mournful POEM on the Death of John Ormsby and Matthew Cushing, who were appointed to be executed on Boston Neck, the 17th of October, 1734* (Boston, 1734).

25. Ibid.

26. *Narrative, or Poem, Giving an Account of the Hostile Actions of some Pagan Indians,* in Ola Elizabeth Winslow, *American Broadside Verse* (New Haven, 1930), p. 115.

27. Daniel Defoe, *Moll Flanders* (New York, 1978 edition), p. 30.

28. Hart, p. 220.

29. *Tokens of God's Power and Wrath* (Boston, 1744).

30. *Boston News-Letter,* November 20, 1755.

31. Jonathan Newland, *Earthquakes Improved: Or Solemn Warning to the World; by the tremendous EARTHQUAKE which appeared on Tuesday Morning the 18th of November 1755, between four and five o'Clock* (Boston: 1755). The ballad continued vividly: "See! how poor Wretches from their Beds/ Affrightedly arise,/ And to their clatt'ring Windows run,/ With Horror in their Eyes!/ Around them crack their shatter'd Walls,/ The Beams and Timber creak;/ And the Inhabitants amaz'd/ With dismal Out-crys shreak./ Buildings leap up, the Joints give Way,/ The crumbling Chimney groans;/ The loos'ned Bricks tost from on high/ Come thund'ring on the Stones."

32. *A Poem On the Rebuke of God's Hand In the Awful Desolation made by FIRE in the Town of Boston, On the 20th Day of March, 1760.*

33. *The Agonies of a Soul departing out of Time into Eternity* (Boston, 1757).

34. *The Dying Groans of Levi Ames* (Boston, 1773).

APPENDIX B

1. Isaiah Thomas, *The History of Printing in America, with a Biography of Printers and an Account of Newspapers,* 2nd Ed. (Albany, NY, 1874), vol. 1, p. xxiv. Masters were supposed to instruct their apprentices in matters theological as well as occupational, and Thomas reports that his master gave him "a weekly lesson . . . by rote merely." The master asked "the question from the catechism 'What are the decrees of God;' I answered I could not tell, and then, boy-like, asked him what they were. He read the answer from the book. I was of the opinion he knew as little about the matter as myself."

2. Ibid.

3. Ibid., vol. II, p. 332.

4. Ibid., vol. I, p. 109.

5. Ibid., p. 147.

6. Quoted from the *Boston News-Letter,* January 4, 1733.

7. Neither Buckingham [*Specimens of Newspaper Literature: With Personal Memoirs, Anecdotes, and Reminiscences,* (1850)], nor Parton [*The Life and Times of Benjamin Franklin* (1864)], provided any systematic examination.

8. Frederick Hudson, *Journalism in the United States from 1690 to 1872* (New York, 1873).

9. Ibid., p. 89.

10. Ibid., pp. 289–293.

11. Ibid., pp. 296–305.

12. S. N. D. North, *History and Present Condition* . . . (Washington, DC, 1884).

13. James Melvin Lee, *History of American Journalism* (Garden City, NY, 1917).

14. Ibid., p. 143.

15. George Henry Payne, *History of Journalism in the United States* (New York, 1920).

16. Ibid., p. 21. Payne also described Harris reading the Bible while on the ship taking him to Boston. Payne himself showed a liberal deism in writing of how "humanity could be led to reverence the Deity through the simple processes of Eternal Law, unfolding and unraveling man's liberty, equality and happiness." (p. 11).

17. Ibid., p. 2.

18. Ibid., p. 11.

19. Willard G. Bleyer, *Main Currents in the History of American Journalism* (Cambridge, 1927), p. 2.

20. Ibid., p. 2.

21. See Bleyer, "Journalism in the United States: 1933," *Journalism Quarterly* 10 (1933), pp. 296–301, and "Freedom of the Press and the New Deal," *Journalism Quarterly* 11 (1934), pp. 22–35.

22. Villard, *Some Newspapers and Newspaper-men* (New York, 1923), p. 314.

23. See George Seldes, *Lords of the Press* (New York, 1945).

24. For example, see Chester E. Jorgenson, "A Brand Flung at Colonial Orthodoxy," *Journalism Quarterly* 12 (1935), pp. 272–277. Jorgenson looked at what he saw as the positive side of colonial printer Samuel Keimer: In Keimer's deism "superstition has given place to science," and "Calvin's wrathful and petulant God" was no more. Jorgenson applauded Keimer for "extolling reasonableness rather than saintliness, nature rather than scripture, humanitarian service rather than the spiritual ascent of the individual . . ." (In this Jorgenson differed from Benjamin Franklin, quoted in Thomas, I, 233; Franklin sympathized with Keimer's expressed theology but observed that Keimer "was a great knave at heart, that he possessed no particular religion, but a little of all upon occasion.")

25. Review of *The Facts Are* in *Journalism Quarterly* 20 (December, 1943), pp. 335–336.

26. Frank Luther Mott, *American Journalism* (New York: Macmillan, 1950).

27. Ibid., p. 206.

28. Ibid., pp. 16–17.

29. Henry Ladd Smith was co-author of the first edition; Michael Emery is now co-author.

30. Michael Emery and Edwin Emery, *The Press and America,* sixth edition (Englewood Cliffs, N.J., 1988), p. 13.

31. Ibid., p. 106.

32. Ibid., p. 58.

33. Ibid., p. 47.

34. Ibid., p. 245.

35. Ibid., p. 146.

36. Ibid., p. 20.

37. Richard Baxter, *Chapters from a Christian Directory,* ed. Jeannette Tawney (London, 1925), p. 50.

38. Sidney Kobre, *Development of American Journalism* (Dubuque, 1969), p. 3; see also pp. 5, 6, 24, 154. Kobre did write two articles on the remarkable Jewish editor of the early nineteenth century, Mordecai Noah; see Kobre, "The Editor Who Freed Hostages," *Media History Digest* 1, 2 (1981), pp. 55–57, 60.

39. My co-authored book *Turning Point,* with Herbert Schlossberg (Westchester, IL, 1987), notes some recent examples of academic bias.

40. Howard H. Fogel, "Colonial Theocracy and a Secular Press," *Journalism Quarterly* 37 (Autumn, 1960), pp. 525–532. Fogel wrote that "A theocracy, by definition closed and narrow, does not favor an inquisitive mind" (p. 527)—but doesn't that depend on the type of theocracy, and on whether it is clericocratic or bibliocratic?

41. Ibid.

42. *North Carolina Historical Review* 30 (January, 1953), pp. 1–22.

43. Elizabeth Barnes, "The *Panoplist:* 19th-Century Religious Magazine," *Journalism Quarterly* 36 (Summer, 1959), pp. 321–325.

44. John M. Havas, "Commerce and Calvinism: The Journal of Commerce, 1827–1865," *Journalism Quarterly* 38 (Winter, 1961), pp. 84–86.

45. Robert E. Lee, "Timothy Dwight and the Boston *Palladium,*" *New England Quarterly* 35 (1962), pp. 229–239.

46. Donald F. Brod, "The Scopes Trial: A Look at Press Coverage after Forty Years," *Journalism Quarterly* 42 (Spring, 1965), pp. 219–227. Brod's dissertation, "Church, State, and Press: Twentieth-Century Episodes in the United States" (University of Minnesota, 1969), was a more extensive examination of the Scopes trial and three other events concerning church-state relations. For a different view of the Scopes trial, see my article "When World Views Collide: Journalists and the Great Monkey Trial," *American Journalism* 4 (1987), pp. 133–146.

47. Henry Smith Stroupe, *The Religious Press in the South Atlantic States, 1802–1865. An Annotated Bibliography with Historical Introduction and Notes* (Durham, NC, 1956).

48. William Jesse Stone, Jr., "A Historical Survey of Leading Texas Denominational Newspapers: 1846–1861," PhD. dissertation, The University of Texas, 1974.

49. Alfred Roger Gobbel, "The Christian Century: Its Editorial Policies and Positions, 1908–1966," PhD. dissertation, University of Illinois, 1967.

50. Claude W. Summerlin, "A History of Southern Baptist State Newspapers," PhD. dissertation, University of Missouri, 1968.

51. Wesley Norton, *Religious Newspapers in the Old Northwest to 1861: A History, Bibliography, and Record of Opinion* (Athens, 1977).

52. Robert W. Ross, *So It Was True* (Minneapolis, 1980).

53. Isaac Goldberg, *Major Noah, American-Jewish Pioneer* (Philadelphia, 1936).

54. Jonathan D. Sarna *Jacksonian Jew: The Two Worlds of Mordecai Noah* (New York, 1981).

55. Kathryn T. Theus, "From Orthodoxy to Reform: Assimilation and the Jewish-English Press of Mid-Nineteenth Century America," *American Journalism* 1, 2 (1984), pp. 15–26.

56. Mary Lonan Reilly, "A History of the Catholic Press Association 1911–1968," PhD. dissertation, Notre Dame University, 1970.

57. M. R. Real, "Trends in Structure and Policy in the American Catholic Press," *Journalism Quarterly* 52 (Spring, 1975), pp. 265–271.

58. Robert Peel, *Mary Baker Eddy: The Years of Authority* (New York: Holt, Rinehart,

Winston, 1977). Earlier works on the *Monitor* include Erwin D. Canham, *Commitment to Freedom: The Story of the Christian Science Monitor* (Boston: Houghton Mifflin, 1958) and John A. Klempner, "A Newspaper in Dissonance: The *Christian Science Monitor* Election Coverage, 1928 and 1960," Ph.D. dissertation, Michigan State University, 1960.

59. Harold H. Osmer, *U.S. Religious Journalism and the Korean War* (Washington, 1980).

60. Charles H. Lippy, ed., *Religious Periodicals in the United States* (Westport, Connecticut, 1986).

61. *Journal of Broadcasting & Electronic Media* 32 (Summer, 1988).

62. Paul Vitz, *Religion and Traditional Values in Public School Textbooks* (Washington, DC, 1986).

APPENDIX C

1. Charles Murray, *In Pursuit* (New York, 1988), p. 16.

2. Joshua Muravchik, *News Coverage of the Sandinista Revolution* (Washington, DC:, 1988), pp. 5–6.

3. Robert Darnton, "Writing News and Telling Stories," *Daedalus* 104, 2 (1975), pp. 190–191.

4. Ibid., loc. cit.

5. Mitchell Stephens, *A History of News* (New York, 1988), p. 264.

6. Murray, op. cit.

7. *Washington Monthly,* May 14, 1975, p. 14.

8. As *New York Times* editor Lester Markel has noted, "The reporter, the most objective reporter, collects fifty facts. Out of the fifty facts he selects twelve to include in his story (there is such a thing as space limitation). Thus he discards thirty-eight. This is Judgment Number One. Then the reporter or editor decides which of the facts shall be the first paragraph of the story, thus emphasizing one fact above the other eleven. This is Judgment Number Two. Then the editor decides whether the story shall be placed on Page One or Page Twelve; on Page One it will command many times the attention it would on page twelve. This is Judgment Number Three. This so-called factual presentation is thus subjected to three judgments, all of them most humanly and most ungodly made." [Markel was quoted in William Rivers, *The Opinionmakers* (Boston, 1965), p. 43.

9. Some variation occurs, but the *Austin American-Statesman* ran basic, who/what/where/when articles about a girl killed crossing a highway, an airplane crash in Dallas, a hurricane closing in on Galveston, a major decision by the city council—and if there were other newspapers in Austin, they would have done the same.

10. John Corry, *TV News and the Dominant Culture* (Washington, 1986).

INDEX